# Code Name Lise

By George M James

Copyright 2015 George M James

D1445768

**License Notes**

Copyright, 2015, George M James

All rights reserved. No part of this publication may be reproduced, distributed, or transmitted in any form or by any means, including photocopying, recording, or other electronic or mechanical methods, without the prior written permission of the publisher, except in the case of brief quotations embodied in critical reviews and certain other non-commercial uses permitted by copyright law. For permission requests, write to the author at georgemjames48@gmail.com. Any person that does any unauthorised act in relation to this publication will be held liable to criminal prosecution and civil claims for damages.

First print: 2015

ISBN-13: 978-1517335519

ISBN-10: 1517335515

Published by GMJ Publishing

www.georgemjames.com

georgemjames48@gmail.com

# COVER DESIGN & EDITING

Cover design by Rebecca, the ONE, thank you.

The cover picture is of a Warsaw Pact ZU 23-2 23mm anti-aircraft cannon shooting, sometimes referred to in my books as the ZSU 23-2 (technically that is the self-propelled version but that is what we called the system). All GMJ Book covers have messages in them relating to something or some incident in the book. Where the cover has a black motive, or anything black on it, that is meant to signify death. That is a code to honour those that died for their country, as well as in honour of my wife, she too went home to our Lord before her time. GMJ

Editing by Alec Chapman nabolcat@gmail.com, thank you.

## Disclaimer

This book is a work of fiction. Names, characters, places, and incidents either are products of the author's imagination or are used fictitiously or adapted to suit the story. Any resemblance to actual persons, living or dead, events, or locales is entirely coincidental. The information contained in this book is for general information purposes only and while we endeavour to keep the information up to date and correct, we make no representations or warranties of any kind, express or implied, about the completeness, accuracy, reliability, suitability or availability with respect to this book or the information, products, services, or related graphics contained in this book for any purpose. Any reliance you place on such information is therefore strictly at your own risk. In no event will we be liable for any loss or damage including without limitation, indirect or consequential loss or damage, or any loss or damage whatsoever.

"US defense capabilities are and will remain second to none, and now because of the new defense budget of $700 billion our military will be far stronger than ever." White House spokeswoman Sarah Huckabee Sanders, 2 March 2018

"America has the best equipment anywhere in the world." Donald J Trump on 13 August 2018

"Chinese President Xi Jinping is also expected to make a pledge to change Beijing's economic, military, and political behaviour during his meeting with US President Donald Trump on the side-lines of the G20 summit in Buenos Aires on November 30. If Washington is not satisfied, there will be 'an all-out Cold War.' The US had no intention of ceding influence in Asia to China and will not back down if Beijing choses to continue its current policies. Then so be it. We are here to stay." Mike Pence, Vice President of the US, 13 November 2018

The Reality: "I'll never forgive Barack Obama for what he did to our United States military by not funding it properly. It was depleted. It was old and tired, and I came in and I had to fix it, and I'm in the process of spending tremendous amounts of money, so I'll never forgive him for what he did to our military. What he did made this country very unsafe..." Donald J Trump on 9 November 2018

"The United States has lost its military advantage to such a degree that it could potentially lose a future war with Russia or China. The US military could suffer unacceptably high casualties and loss of major capital assets in its next conflict. It might struggle to win, or perhaps lose, a war against China or Russia..." National Defence Strategy Commission to the US Congress, 14 November 2018

Your bluster is already called... "In the West you have the notion that if somebody hits you on the left cheek, you turn the other cheek. In our culture we punch back..." Chinese president Xi Jinping, he was talking on Donald J Trump's trade war with the world but he meant more than that. Later, on 29 October 2018, to his top military commanders... "Prepare for war." Do you know what Field Marshal Montgomery, 1st Viscount Montgomery of Alamein said? "Rule 1, on page 1 of the book of war, is: 'Do not march on Moscow'. Various people have tried it, Napoleon and Hitler, and it is no good. That is the first rule. I do not know whether your Lordships will know Rule 2 of war. It is: 'Do not go fighting with your land armies in China.' It is a vast country, with no clearly defined objectives.'

Sub-Sahara Africa - the new counter-terrorism battlefield: "We are decimating ISIS in the Middle East. What's happening is, they'll go to parts of Africa, they'll go to other places. When they get there, we meet them. It's a dangerous business. It's a tough war. We're beating ISIS very badly." Donald J Trump, 45th US President, October 2017

"Exactly what I was warning about since 2014 when the first book, Code Name VFO565, was published. The radicals are moving into Africa. The Israelis with Mossad are the kings in the Middle East, chasing them away. The South Africans with the South African Secret Service control sub-Saharan Africa. Within the above two spheres, you will find 80% of the radicals, the rest are hiding in Pakistan and Afghanistan. Wherever the War on Terror is being won, as Mr Trump noted, the threat moves away and mostly into Africa, the new battleground. But don't think for one moment that the fighting will be easy. Africa is like no other theatre in the world, nothing like what you have seen before. Regarding the QME, 'Qualitative Military Edge Doctrine,' it is a known myth and nothing more. As I write these books I wonder where the West is not lacking and yet, the idiotic bubble of "exceptionalism" continues unabatedly in the White House and everywhere else. It is not based on reality, my research shows you lacking in almost every important area from SRAAM, anti-tank missiles, artillery, armour, drones, AI, and electronic warfare. Bluntly stated, I don't see either the US or NATO winning a conventional war against Russia or China anytime soon unless major changes are made which is not throwing money at the Merchants of Death but demanding a positive return on investment. If a conventional war breaks out, I see you getting humiliated in the future. We can only hope I am wrong, in fact, I pray that I am wrong but I am not. What is even worse is that the Chinese are relentlessly making the strategic moves and today the USA is cut off already and yet this is not seen by those blinded by their arrogance. I reveal the above and much more in my books, especially 'American Military Might – Debunked' must be read with the much shorter Intelligence Briefing, it is important. And if you wish to know why the mightiest Protestant country ever, is abused, read Code Name Rebecca 65 where it is explained. This is not by chance." GMJ

"Special Forces Selection starts with God and ends with God's mercy in your favour. Have no doubt, without faith you will get nowhere. When a man is dying in combat, he cries for his mom or God, between the two, only God is always close by and able to help. Believe me, gentlemen, you will often cry for both of the above beings before we are done with you today. This program is not for everyone, 95% of you will not make it. Accept that and do your best, show me that you are worthy of Special Forces." Captain Geelslang Peter Ndebele at the first day of Selection to new recruits, his predictions were never wrong.

"When you hear a story, you remember, when you see the PowerPoint slides so beloved by Western Militaries, you forget within minutes and fall asleep. We don't do boring and we count success by results, not money wasted or tons of bombs dropped, we want to win at any cost payable by the enemy." Major Geoffrey Foxtrot on more than one occasion.

"Price is what you pay. Value is what you gain in knowledge." Major General Angelique Dawson-Foxtrot to GMJ years ago.

"She was spot on, as always. No one reads a GMJ Book without learning something or so I am told... but I paid dearly for the knowledge. When I walked out of operations, they asked me what will you do? I said I wanted to be normal. They said it is impossible, that I am not normal, I was chosen, born to be special, for the Great Game. No one walks out of operations. I said I wanted to be normal. And an older colleague stopped me, he shook hands, said, if you want to be normal, find love, find a good woman that will love you no matter what. You will slowly become what is in your DNA and not your training. I asked him, if you know this, why didn't you walk away years before? He said he could not find a woman to love him that much. He died a few weeks later in an operation in Burkina Faso." GMJ to Rebecca, the One, August 2018.

## BABA WETHU

Baba wethu osezulwini

Maliphathwe ngobungcwele igama lakho.

Umbuso wakho mawufike.

Intando yakho mayenziwe emhlabeni njengasezulwini.

Awusiphe namhla isinkwa sethu semihla ngemihla.

Usithethelele izono zethu

njengoba nathi sibathethelela abasonayo.

Ungasingenisi ekulingweni

kodwa usisindise kokubi.

Amen.

(The Lord's Prayer in Zulu, *Gloria in excelsis Deo*)

# DISCOVER OTHER BOOKS WRITTEN BY GEORGE M JAMES

1.      Code Name VFO565

2.      Code Name Pour Angelique

3.      Code Name Phoenix

4.      Code Name Lise

5.      Code Name Dawson

6.      Code Name Foxtrot

7.      Code Name Angel

8.      Code Name Odette

9.      Code Name Sanford

10.     Code Name Honey Bee

11.     Code Name Devorah

12.     Code Name Willow Bay

13.     Code Name Missa 72

14.     Code Name Cadillac

15.     Code Name Blue Tang

16.     Code Name OST-M

17.     Code Name Wrangler

18.     Code Name Casselberry

19.     Code Name Bella Dawn

20.     Code Name Green 41

21.     Code Name Celery 50

22.     Code Name Caribbean

23.     Code Name Butterfly

24.     Code Name Phantom

25. Code Name Mel's Choice

26. Code Name Halloween 38

27. Code Name Anika

28. Code Name Lucy

29. Code Name Moonlight

30. Code Name Oath 19

31. Code Name Ghost

32. Code Name Jen

33. Code Name Alphabet 32

34. Code Name One Alpha

35. American Military Might – Debunked (Non-fiction)

36. Code Name Ndebele 14

37. Code Name Dawn

38. Code Name VET 101

39. Code Name Angelique

40. Code Name GSSP-40

41. Code Name Mélisse

42. Code Name Wednesday 7

43. Code Name Unbutton

44. Code Name Rebecca 65

45. Code Name Swan 53

46. VOICES – War Crimes USA (Non-fiction)

47. GMJ Intelligence Briefing (Non-Fiction)

# TABLE OF CONTENTS

*"Let me tell you about the Afrikaners, Professor. I had the bad luck to have met a few through the years. They have not changed much since Kipling wrote his book. Let me quote for you since I was reading it just the other day: 'Take a community of Dutchmen of the type of those who defended themselves for fifty years against all the power of Spain at a time when Spain was the greatest power in the world. Intermix with them a strain of those inflexible French Huguenots who gave up home and fortune and left their country for ever at the time of the revocation of the Edict of Nantes. The product must obviously be one of the most rugged, virile, unconquerable races ever seen upon earth. Take this formidable people and train them for seven generations in constant warfare against savage men and ferocious beasts, in circumstances under which no weakling could survive, place them so that they acquire exceptional skill with weapons and in horsemanship, give them a country which is eminently suited to the tactics of the huntsman, the marksman, and the rider. Then, finally, put a finer temper upon their military qualities by a dour fatalistic Old Testament religion and an ardent and consuming patriotism. Combine all these qualities and all these impulses in one individual, and you have the modern Boer—the most formidable antagonist who ever crossed the path of Imperial Britain. Our military history has largely consisted in our conflicts with France, but Napoleon and all his veterans have never treated us so roughly as these hard-bitten farmers with their ancient theology and their inconveniently modern rifles.'"*

*In fact, it was Sir Arthur Conan Doyle, of Sherlock Holmes fame, who wrote the above in his book "The Great Boer War" back in 1902 and to explain how a supposedly backward nation could keep the entire British Empire busy for three years and cause twenty times more casualties than what they ever suffered in a colonial war. Since then the Afrikaner fought the*

14

*Germans, Italians, Japanese and his own insurgency without losing a fight. They were never defeated in battle in modern times.... (Taken from Code Name VFO565)*

## Author's Note

No GMJ Book is just written. The topic is carefully chosen to enlighten the reader to current dangers / events. In this book, we look at several subjects I wanted to highlight for you as I was shocked to read the other day that some of the most popular South African authors say that they have no messages to the readers in their books, they write for entertainment only. I am not like that and I am most certainly not part of the South African "author scene" and with no desire ever to be. To be honest, I find books without messages shallow and without purpose, written for sheep by sheep, an insult to readers. Because I started off as a non-fiction writer, I am different in writing style, I always have messages in my books and that is by design and not by chance. I want the knowledge inside my books distributed. I want people to think about what they just read and the books to be of practical value besides being good entertainment. Curiously, many times after a GMJ Book is published, that what is revealed is published in the media or hastily denied.

I am further told by many readers that the non-US based weapon systems I describe in my books are not readily known to them. That is understandable, most people will only know their own country's weapons. Thus, I added a page on my website (http://www.georgemjames.com/weapon-systems.html) to show you pictures of what I write about in the GMJ Books. Please hover your mouse over the picture, it will tell you what the picture represents and in which book, unless in many books, then only the name of the weapon system or place or person. Sometimes I forget that what is well known here may not be so well known there - I hope that you enjoy the page. Yet, that was not enough, the messages did not get through, and so, I wrote a lengthy book to debunk the American (NATO also) military myth called "QME" or the "Qualitative Military Edge Doctrine." The QME is something that every US General, Admiral, Congressman, Senator, President and Citizen holds as the holy grail of American Military Power and has been doing so for many years (also included here is NATO, Western Militaries, note, I don't mean the US alone, this is the last time I am saying so - the name is used because the US Military is NATO, not the other way around). It comes down to stating in simplified terms that the US Military has better technology and better training and because of this, they will have the edge against any numerically superior enemy, i.e. Russia, China, whoever, if a shooting war should break out. That is the myth and it is heard constantly in the mainstream media and everywhere else, seen as fact as much as the sun will rise in the east tomorrow. It is taken for granted that in any future military confrontation, the QME will ensure victory for the US and NATO. It is further believed that wild out of control spending is necessary: "US defense capabilities are and will remain second to none, and now because of the new defense budget of $700 billion our military will be far stronger than ever." White House spokeswoman Sarah Huckabee Sanders, 2 March 2018. Yep, rubbish in history, rubbish in real life, rubbish in general. The world outside the US smirked derisively, they know better. Patriotism and patriotic dismissals of bad news are dangerous when not based on facts. In "American Military Might – Debunked," I destroy the QME and show you how ridiculous it is to put your hopes on spending without positive returns, what are you getting for your money? You will see in that book and others how poorer countries are building better weapons for much less costs and you will wonder how on earth that is even possible. Facts do not care whether you prefer "Made in America" products or not, the question is:

16

"What is the best right now?" This is not a subjective opinion but objective, we look at facts and facts only. Bluntly put, if your aviators or pilots ever face the South African Denel V3E Agile Darter SRAAM in combat (see Code Name Blue Tang), they are dead. If they are in tanks and the Makopa anti-tank missile is launched at them (see Code Name Alphabet 32), they are dead. Yes, an African country with better military technology in crucial areas than the mighty US of A and NATO combined, it is shocking, absurd and yet true. And none of these weapons is exported to anyone that is an ally of the USA. Think about that.

In South Africa, after the 1994 changes when Mr Mandela took over, as I explained so many times in my books, Israel and the West instantly lost access to the latest (note I said latest, not all) South African Military technology. As is also explained in my books, the South African Secret Service has access to China's supercomputers to break ciphers and they do break them, I warned often enough on your ciphers being read by the enemy, see Code Name Odette, GMJ 8, and other books. Sub-Saharan Africa is the new battleground and yet the US is being replaced at a rate which is unbelievable. So far, my warning fell on deaf ears but we must persevere. As I write these books I wonder where the West is not lacking and yet, the idiotic bubble of "exceptionalism" continues unabatedly in the White House and everywhere else. It is not based on reality, my research shows you lacking in almost every important area from SRAAM, anti-tank missiles, artillery, armour, drones, AI, and electronic warfare. Bluntly stated, I don't see either the US or NATO winning a conventional war against Russia or China anytime soon unless major changes are made which is not throwing money at the Merchants of Death but demanding a positive return on investment. If a conventional war breaks out, I see you getting humiliated in the future. We can only hope I am wrong, in fact, I pray that I am wrong but I am not. What is even worse is that the Chinese are relentlessly making the strategic moves and today the USA is cut off already and yet this is not seen by those blinded by their arrogance. I reveal the above and much more in my books, American Military Might – Debunked should be read with the much shorter Intelligence Briefing.

GMJ Intelligence Briefing: Up until January 2019, I attached the often-mentioned Intelligence Briefing to every GMJ book at the request of many readers. It was a good idea. However, the briefing grew relentlessly in length to keep up with the latest Washington / London irrationalities / shenanigans designed to keep the US at perpetual war. The extra length added to the printing costs. It had to be updated once a month and all of the books reloaded on various websites. This placed an enormous burden on me, days of doing nothing else. The only logical solution was to create a separate book for the intelligence briefing combined with some of the expert political / military analysis to be found in the GMJ Series, i.e. on the MI6 / Ukrainian Skripal false flag operation, Jamal Khashoggi murder, the Niger Ambush and much more of interest to GMJ readers. And so, I created a lengthy book on its own. Since the intelligence contained is of a strategic nature and deliberately not tactical, it will be relevant in the foreseeable future. The warnings contained in this briefing are frightening for the US and NATO, logically set out, proven and, sadly, not fiction. The GMJ Intelligence Briefing is best when read together with the two other non-fiction books: American Military Might – Debunked as well as VOICES – War Crimes USA.

You will also read political studies in the Intelligence Briefing not to be found in mainstream Western media. That too, I am told, is shocking to many readers. America is detested intensely by many and hated by most, seen as a rogue state that needs to be destroyed for the better of mankind.

18

And this you can blame squarely on the Washington Swamp, your political class. They caused and own this miserable state of affairs but you will pay the price, not them, they are well protected. If ever the QME is needed it is right now, yes, the greatest irony of all time. (Note: In November 2018, my reservations and warnings, the GMJ research, got confirmed. "I'll never forgive Barack Obama for what he did to our United States military by not funding it properly. It was depleted. It was old and tired, and I came in and I had to fix it, and I'm in the process of spending tremendous amounts of money, so I'll never forgive him for what he did to our military. What he did made this country very unsafe..." Donald J Trump on 9 November 2018. "The United States has lost its military advantage to such a degree that it could potentially lose a future war with Russia or China. The US military could suffer unacceptably high casualties and loss of major capital assets in its next conflict. It might struggle to win, or perhaps lose, a war against China or Russia..." National Defence Strategy Commission to the US Congress, 14 November 2018. What you do about this remains to be seen. I take no joy from being vindicated, be that known.)

In Code Name Lise, we deal with the idea of sinking warships with shore-bound artillery. It can be done and was done in history many times before, but you need them close to you, almost at a dangerous close range. They must be ambushed unexpectedly and destroyed, or you will be in deep trouble as they call in heavy airstrikes or used their long-range weapons to maximum effect. And that is the biggest problem you will face in this scenario, the air threat. All modern warships are armed with helicopters and South African warships at times have the Denel Rooivalk attack helicopter on them. A helicopter that is deadly and feared with much reason. The question I wanted to be answered in this book was to see if a Rooivalk attack beast can be shot down and if so, how. They are armoured against

23mm shells, they are faster than an Apache and their pilots are aggressive fellows. You will normally not get close enough to shoot a Rooivalk down, she can see in the darkness and she has deadly missiles outranging any MANPAD or anti-aircraft gun. Her ECM and E-ECM systems are world-class. Thus, you need to surprise her, get her close enough and down her in the first few shots or you are dead when she counter-attacks. There is a way, a maskirovka. Foxtrot and his men crossed into Northern Kwazulu-Natal, South Africa, after the ambush in southern Mozambique where Angelique is almost killed during Code Name Phoenix. He wants his enemy, the naval squadron searching for him and his Q-ship, the EBS Orlando, within gunnery range to destroy them. If not destroyed, then at least severely damaged, before running hard to Mozambique before reinforcements arrive. Escaping would always be a problem as the Egg Breakers face overwhelming odds and with Angelique wounded, there are command & control problems. Something that is so crucial in modern warfare that I wanted to highlight it for you. I fear that the over complex lines of command we find in most militaries will lead to disaster at some stage. We keep forgetting history, it is sad. There is no excuse, you better know who commands where and when, the command line must be extremely clear.

I am at times accused by Deep State and their paid lackeys that I use Russian / Chinese intelligence in my books where I expose US and NATO weaknesses and or war crimes. The historian / author / analyst, be it known, cross-checks whatever comes across his path or the information has no value. He frequently finds the evidence / information that he needs for his books / exposés in "enemy" archives because he is not allowed by self-protecting laws to access the information in his own country. Or, and this is happening all the time, that what the mainstream is publishing is deceitful and half-truths. Let me give you an example taken from a BBC article regarding Donald J Trump's movements on 11 November 2018, "And he skipped an outing to a French cemetery that was filled with graves of US soldiers who had served in World War I." What the journalist fails to add is that it was raining that day in Paris and also foggy. The Presidential helicopter could not fly in safety to the cemetery and the presidential convoy would have caused immense disruption to the Paris traffic. For these reasons, the president did not go to the cemetery, not because he was afraid of the rain or has disrespect for the fallen soldiers. Quite reasonable, I would say, but not a word is explained further, a half-truth is left hanging there. Such is the propaganda that you are exposed to which is nothing to the effect of doctored pictures. Who will not recall Time Magazine faking an illegal alien child being dominated by the well-known "Scrooge" Donald J Trump? There are countless such examples doing the rounds and always when illegal immigration is approved of by the elite. It is thought-provoking that Hilarious Clinton got by far most of her votes in rich / affluent districts, you know, those people that will never compete with an illegal immigrant for a job. In Code Name Swan 53 we look at where the militaries are recruiting, the poor- and working class families. The mainstream liars also never tell you that the so-called "refugees..." read migrants, are 70% and more unaccompanied young males. All you see on the news is the women and children being tear gassed. When you see the shenanigans that the ruling class is up to, you fully understand their outright reluctance to be exposed. The Arch Liar, that is Winston S Churchill to you, not a man admired in my books for a great many good and accurate reasons, said that "history will be kind to me because I intend writing it..." And he did, and today you know what he wrote and precious little regarding his many faults. But is that accurate history or propaganda? In all conventional wars the ruling class ensures that the enemy archives are either destroyed or captured and locked away for 150 years. Anything and everything needed to be done to protect their "unblemished" reputation and interests will be done. But much has changed in the last decade with the internet becoming freely available. Research is now easier than ever and much more comfortable. Let it be known, I will look for whatever I need wherever it is to be found. I will quote from the BBC to Sputnik as long as the original article is based on something that I can trace to its source and not the opinion of the writer in which I am not interested in. Unlike the mainstream journalists, I do not use mysterious, anonymous and unverified "sources close to matter" or such crap. Whenever I read that, I dismiss it automatically as fake news with hostile intent to mislead and deceive. I also look carefully at the wording of official statements. Wherever I find "is confident," "are consistent," "are intended," "high probability," "no other explanation" and "we believe" I dismiss it outright as fake news no matter who says it or what Agency made the statement. See Code Name Moonlight and American Military Might – Debunked, where this is explained in detail. Sadly, these words too are simply ignored by the mainstream liars and they then make out as if the report / statement is gospel – see Code Name Swan 53 where their techniques are explained. My books are researchable and thus I am willing to invite you to check the facts for yourself. I know what you will find. It is insane to say that an author cannot look for information / evidence outside his own country or blame him when he does so. That would be a clampdown and suppression of free speech. Let me remind you of what German Pastor Martin Niemöller said after being released from a Nazi Concentration Camp: "First they came for the socialists, and I did not speak out – because I was not a socialist. Then they came for the trade unionists, and I did not speak out – because I was not a trade unionist. Then they came for the Jews, and I did not speak out – because I was not a Jew. Then they came for me – and there was no one left to speak for me." I hope you enjoy the GMJ Series. They are books worth reading if you like military history, romance, espionage and although the books have a strong South African flavour, the messages in them are directed towards the West. Keep in mind that the GMJ Books are written as a warning to those who may not understand what is happening in sub-Saharan Africa, the new battleground, as we speak. As such, the GMJ Series contain intelligence truths which some will dislike on principle, if so, I invite you to research my books. I believe the public should be informed. And that the warnings communicated in this book are of utmost importance.

**Description:** After sinking a South African Navy frigate in an epic gun battle in the Mozambican Channel, former Police Special Forces Company Commander, Geoffrey Foxtrot, now Egg Breaker Ground Commander, is heading down south with his fellow Egg Breakers intending to ambush a squadron of naval fast attack craft that is coming north to investigate the sinking of the frigate. To get them close enough and inside gun range, he "abandons" the Q-ship, the EBS Orlando, on a deserted beach, a maskirovka designed to bring the fast attack craft towards the ambush site. For political reasons, he must cross the border into South Africa and spring a naval ambush from northern Zululand and thus taking the chance of meeting with superior South African ground forces, a fight he cannot possibly win. To make matters worse, a South African Denel Rooivalk is escorting the naval vessels and constitutes a major threat, she must be shot down and quickly or she will destroy him and his men. With his wife, the former South African Secret Service Counter-Terrorism Head until she defected in Code Name VFO565, a pregnant Angelique Dawson-Foxtrot injured and dying from wounds received during an ambush in Code Name Phoenix, he needs to dig deep to accomplish his mission. The ambush takes place and the Egg Breakers try to escape with the Q-ship, but they are found by Gripen fighter jets and sunk. As the men swim for their lives, they are strafed mercilessly but rescued by friendly forces. The job is not done though, Foxtrot and Geelslang make a HALO jump into northern Nigeria to escort a prisoner out. Angelique is induced into a medical coma to save her and Foxtrot's unborn twins, Lise and Odette... one more burden on Foxtrot that already lost a wife in the War on Terror. If you wish to read about Covert and Special Forces Operations in sub-Saharan Africa, the GMJ Books are the place to start. You will learn about covert operations, Special Forces techniques and military history not known outside the select few. Code Name Lise is the 4th book in the popular GMJ Series.

As you may know, a surprising percentage of GMJ Books are suppressed, yes, they use that ugly word, suppressed by mainstream publishers, see my blog http://www.georgemjames.com/gmj-blog/put-god-first-and-see-what-happens-the-immediate-suppression-of-your-books for more details. This is not about royalties but freedom of speech. It is a very big deal when any book, conservative or liberal, is suppressed without legal justification. We added dozens of audio clips at https://www.youtube.com/channel/UC89xiDq-jbHsIDVsgvUtfAQ and http://www.georgemjames.com/author--video.html where you can listen to GMJ talking about his books. I hope that you enjoy them. If you like the GMJ Books, please take the time to write a good review online, it is the only way to spread the word on the messages they contain. Again, thank you, my readers are important to me: http://www.georgemjames.com/gmj-blog/angeliques-song.

Thank you,

George M James

2015

*"My failures have been errors in judgment, not of intent."* Ulysses S. Grant

**Chapter 1**

**South African Mozambican Border, 25 February 2014, 10h05**

We invaded South Africa early in the morning or perhaps I should say we crossed the border into northern KwaZulu-Natal, a province right next to Mozambique where the Zulu Nation lives. An invasion, by definition, is with the armed forces of another country, not a bunch of "right-wing terrorists" as the Egg Breakers were now called by the liberal press. To be sure that designation, "right-wing terrorists," was ironic if not plain idiotic but with journalists that is often the case. They don't do research and listen slavishly to what governments feed them. In fact, the Egg Breakers started as a deep undercover organisation known as Directorate F of the South African Secret Service (SASS) to safeguard the new democracy against right-wing terror. All the men were carefully chosen and all were ex Special Forces, whether from the Police or the Army Unit and all went into Africa with curt orders to "...piss off and start a new life. The correct authorities will be in contact if needed."

So we did, my mate Geelslang and I went to Mozambique though we were also known to operate in Nigeria and other places. Others went to every country south of the Saharan desert. For a good few years nothing much happened. We establish spy networks and ourselves in business doing what any newly emigrated man would do. It was good time, almost a holiday for us but we were concerned, not about right-wing whiners - they all whimpered and scampered off to Australia where they still are but the new wave of radical Muslims we started to see in our spheres of interest. First came a few to scout around, then the Mosques rapidly increased and the Imams arrived. After them came the foot soldiers to guard the important ones. Yes, they were setting themselves up. We warned repeatedly without avail. Then in the late 1990s we received the code word "VFO565" which activated us from our sleeper agent status.

We started to work with the highly trained and dedicated South African Secret Service (SASS) field officers to see what the Muslim lads and others were up to or so they explained to us anyway. What exactly the SASS agents were up to only they knew for it soon became clear that we had different views on the subject. By this time the right-wing threat has all but disappeared being a bunch of has been drunks to start with. No one in his right mind wanted to go back to what we had under Apartheid. Yes, you hear them whining on the internet and around the camp fires but mostly they are just that, whiners and whiners never do anything but whine. No, we were up against dedicated (I would hesitate to say "radical") Muslims. As much as we wanted to believe in the liberal wet dream - the new South Africa or Rainbow Nation we soon ran into inconvenient truths.

The South African government, after Mr Mandela retired, rapidly became just another African government which the right-wing whiners always warned about. They gave important jobs to incompetent old mates called "cadre" employment. They stole millions via that age old liberal redistribution of wealth called corruption and still it was not enough. They decided to take sides on the War of Terror which was a fateful decision. In a way, it can be admired as they stuck with their old cronies, Russia (the former Soviet Union), Red China, Palestine and the rest on whom the West usually frown. They certainly showed loyalty towards their old mates even if the loyalty was totally misplaced from some viewpoints. This siding with their old mates was no surprise to us who knew the country and our old enemies, now the elected government. They were traditionally supported during their "struggle years" by these countries and when they got a modern

26

and well-armed country like South Africa after winning the one-man-one-vote elections - fairly it must be said - they quickly became power mad. They became even nastier than what they were before. Now they could be arrogant too, they had the tools of the trade, so to speak.

Apartheid South Africa was always feared by its neighbours and with good reason. It was not a normal African country then and it is not one now. In many areas, it is a powerful, modern and able place. For instance, there are more electricity, roads, railways, industry and military power than the rest of Africa, Egypt included, combined. When the new lot got to power they inherited a disciplined, powerful and modern Army, Air Force and Navy steeped in tradition based upon the British Army (very ironic - the Afrikaner dislikes the Pommies more than anything else in the world). The inherited Security Forces were also highly experienced in counter insurgency having won every single engagement against them for decades. This military strength alone made them the new kids on the block and they acted it out once they realised what they had. If the surrounding African Nations expected a friendlier South Africa, they were sadly mistaken. Almost overnight South African troops were everywhere from the DRC (Congo) to Lesotho either countering a coup d'état or acting as "peace keepers" under United Nations or Africa Union flags. This was not by chance; they wanted the troops out of South Africa to prevent any untoward ideas of kicking them out of power. That is what usually happens in a newly independent African country, the military takes over and execute the elected ones. Then they elect themselves to be President for life. That is until the next General executes them and so is life. Here it never happened for the Armed Forces never had such intentions, it was and is unthinkable. Then there was the South African Police Force, a much feared organisation with excellent informant networks and the ability to fight as crack mechanised and light infantry. Their subsequent actions to destroy the police and sell all their Casspir armoured personal carriers to India (another old and new mate) showed clearly how much fear they had for the police. They did their very best to destroy the unyielding discipline until the new police attempt became a joke and object of much ridicule. They tried the same with the Army, the Air Force and in a much lesser extent the Navy. Those first years were turbulent years and many thousands of professional soldiers left in disgust. At the turn of the century they woke up to the fact that they would need professional Armed Forces if they wanted to stay the local Super Power and dominate everyone else. They bought new fighter jets from Sweden, the SAAB JAS 39 Gripen which rates well against the more famous F18 Super Hornet. They bought new German Type 209 1400 diesel-electric submarines which cannot be tracked by any known means underwater. These ultra-silent boats replaced the old French Daphne class the Navy had since the 1960s. On the Army front they made sure to bring some of the discipline back to the Forces and got rid of the worst offenders. However, they left the police to stagger from one management crisis to the other. Ah yes and they stole millions from kickbacks from all the above. The merchants of death were only too glad to pay the bribes requested. But a few army units stayed as sharp as they always were. In particular, the Paratroopers and the Special Forces Brigade did not drop their standards. Nor did the submarine service or the new surface fleet...it takes professional sailors to operate modern warships.

The surface vessels were also catered for and the Navy got a few new frigates to show the flag at the same time as when the new submarines and Gripen fighter jets arrived. These ships are ultra-modern, heavily armed and very good at hunting submarines down or to engage a surface fleet with their Exocet missiles. They are officially used for anti-piracy patrols but did more hunting of Western submarines than anything else. This would play a great role in what happened later (see Code Name Lucy and Code Name Ghost for how such ships are used). For close inshore work they rebuilt the old Apartheid era fast attack craft and called them "Offshore Patrol Vessels." Actually, they were now changed considerably to be "inshore vessels." The aft surface-to-surface missiles were removed and replaced with two large ski-boats and the ships painted with black radar absorbent paint. As my former SASS handler and now my loving wife, Angelique Dawson, pointed out, that could only mean that they decided to go on the offensive (Code Name Pour Angelique). Those ships have only one purpose and that is to land and retrieve Special Forces and that only happens when you attack or observe something to attack later. Such ships are never used defensively (see Code Name Casselberry). I was planning to get one such ship into an ambush and sink it in the next few days or hours.

The unofficial war, it could not be called anything else, between the Egg Breakers and the South African Government started slowly as both sides took a stand on the War on Terror which was irreconcilable. All Egg Breakers sided with the West and the new lot entered into a rather silly truce with the Muslims. What it came down to was to invite them to southern Africa and some right into South Africa on condition that they leave the country alone. They could use it as a safe haven and a place for rest and recuperation. This offer was immediately accepted as the Jews were chasing them out of the Middle-East and North Africa. The well-known British "white widow Samantha Lewthwaite" did hide in Johannesburg, South Africa for a while. The London Tube bombers did have South African links and passports and there are many other examples which made the West suspect that a truce was operating. The problem was what to do about it. The Muslim lads were hiding everywhere feeling safe. In any other African country, a SEAL or SAS team would simply launch a snatch or assassination raid and sort them out. In South Africa, they faced a military enigma (see Code Name One Alpha and Code Name Casselberry on what will happen to such a team, they have no chance). Firstly, the place is covered by radar and any unauthorised flight, even at low level, would be picked up and the modern Gripen fighter jets scrambled. They would certainly try to shoot such a helicopter down or force it to land - a major humiliation for the West. Secondly, the Type 209 submarines were always on the prowl and God knows where for they cannot be tracked under normal conditions. They are ultra-silent. The Royal Navy tried twice and was seriously embarrassed. Then there are the vested South African spy networks, patiently built up by the Egg Breakers and handed over to SASS control. That made official operations very difficult as they are everywhere in Southern Africa. Always watching and waiting and reporting.

What outsiders forget is that Africa is not empty, even in the middle of the Sahara Desert you will find someone who will report the movement of any Special Forces Team, whether it is an official or covert one. In a failed country like Somalia that would not be a major problem but in South and southern Africa it would have deadly consequences. The Teams would be hunted down and exterminated as the rescue helicopter would never be able to reach them without being shot down. Worse, such an action of invading its shores would be seen as an act of war and in fact it is one under international law. Nothing would then prevent the nuclear submarine or carrier from where the attack originated being sunk by the Type 209 submarines and or any other means necessary. It is legal to react to an armed invasion. There is also no doubt that the South African Navy is capable of sinking a carrier or nuclear submarine. Back in 2007 during "Exercise Amazolo," the USS Normandy, FGS Spessart, HNLMS Evertsen, HMCS

Toronto, HDMS Olfert Fischer and FRP Alvares Cabra were taking part in a joint naval exercise of the South African coast. Each one of these NATO warships was "sunk" by one such submarine, the SAS Manthatisi. The submarines are a game changer able to inflict serious loss. This would be completely justifiable in a court of law. If it then escalates as it will, the South Africans have their BRICS partners in reserve. This made them even more obnoxious than usual.

No one knows if the BRICS nations (Brazil, Russia, India, China and South Africa) have a secret mutual defence agreement with each other or not but certainly neither Russia nor China is that troubled about the War on Terror. They, together with India, are also nuclear armed as was Apartheid South Africa. It is known that both China and Russia have many thousands of MIRV nuclear tipped missiles pointing towards the West. No one is about to find out if such a treaty clause exists and hence an official raid would be out of the question. Besides the sheer distances involved, the chance of World War 3 breaking out is simply too great. To be sure, the South Africans will lose such a war in the end but they will inflict serious damage and cause uproar amongst the Western liberals who see the country as their wet dream of democracy. This also made long-range cruise missile attacks unlikely and some would be shot down anyway. They do have such a capability with their own missile defense systems but the main obstacle was the stated intention to declare war on anyone who attacks them. That part cannot be prevented by diplomatic means - they are obnoxious people when riled and shooting a cruise missile into a country is an act of war. What will the USA do if a Russian submarine launches a few cruise missiles into Las Vegas to kill a dissident? The South Africans feel the same way, if you attack us, we will respond immediately and have the means to do so.

With the risk of war too great to launch official teams, only covert operations remained and that ran into immediate problems. The whole of southern Africa is under South African influence, both economically and also military. Operating in Africa, for a Western Intelligence Agency, is very difficult and traditionally never done before at this scale - southern Africa was not that important. The Western lads simply don't get the conditions or the people and believed, very wrongly, that money would buy them what they wanted. That attitude caused resentment and frankly, no African trusts them. We know they will run for home afterwards leaving us to face the righteous wrath of those who survived. It happened in Vietnam, Iraq and Afghanistan that the loyalists were left behind. No, we were not impressed with such an impressive track record of constant and cynical betrayal. Nor were our leaders, they warned their men against helping the West. Let the Muslims and Christians sort out their own problems. Just leave us in peace. In other words, neutrality which is the last thing the West can afford in a counter-terrorism war.

Still the Western Agencies tried and ran into trouble almost immediately. The few covert teams sent in were found and sorted out. Paradoxically, it was the Egg Breakers who found them and made them leave after a few bruising encounters where the undercover lads were physically assaulted and told to leave or face much worse. All African nations are good at counter intelligence; they have to be since they don't trust their own that much. It is as hard to operate in as was the Soviet Union in the old days.

The West soon became wise and realised the answer was the disgruntled Egg Breakers who did not support the Muslim Truce and never will being mostly Christians themselves. They certainly did not like nor admire the Palestinians or Gaddafi in the old days and sent many warnings over the years about the existence of the truce. All were Afrikaners or had Afrikaner sympathies which ironically never had much hatred against the large Muslim community - the two groups left each other alone for hundreds or years. Historically, when it came to counter-terrorism, in Africa, there is no one else who knew more and could operate anywhere being Africans themselves. Best of all, they were already established and in place. But there was a serious obstacle...the Afrikaner traditionally dislikes anything to do with the UK lot and the UK lot is seen by the Americans as experts on Africa. Something they most certainly were up to the 1960s when most African States became independent. Since then they lost all ability to operate in Africa. The Afrikaner via the Apartheid State replaced them and was not about to take orders from them. This aspect severely complicated matters.

It is rather strange, the well-known Afrikaner dislike of the English or Pommies as they are called. As with all good traditions it is not really known why they dislike the English so much. They fought two wars against the English and lost the second one, unfairly so in their opinion. The British Army murdered almost thirty thousand of their women and children in concentration camps. Of course, they probably never meant to murder the non-combatants or so they said. Nor did the British Empire declare war; the Afrikaner did and promptly invaded the then British Natal Province as well as the Cape Province. This pre-emptive action caused what is known in British military circles, with much horror, as the "black week." They were almost chased out of southern Africa before their time. Before that the Afrikaner fought them at the Battle of Muizenberg in 1795 when the Royal Navy attacked and took control of the Cape Colony, then a Dutch possession. This was during the Napoleonic Wars.

As can be expected from a breed of independent farmers (called boere, the Dutch word for farmer) they took a very dim view about their defeat under

Dutch officers and made a promise never to trust a European dandy to command them ever again. A few decades later, in 1834, they simply left and migrated north to establish the independent Boer Republics of Transvaal and the Orange Free State across the Vaal River. They wanted nothing further to do with the English or Queen Victoria and said so often enough.

The two new Boer Republics were called model Republics for the time with railways, telegraph, electricity, and the Boer Kommando system to fight its enemies if needs be. There was no professional standing army. Every burgher (citizen) was expected to form a commando within his community and act as highly mobile cavalry. At this they excelled, being crack shots and hardy riders. Only the Transvaal Republic kept a professional artillery regiment and of course, the highly proficient ZARP or Zuid-Afrikaansche Republiek Politie (Police).

The policemen, as with most African countries, were soldiers first and carried the line on parades. They would fight in numerous battles and are still remembered for their gallantry at Battle of Dalmanutha in August 1900 where they were destroyed as a unit. After that they fought on as individuals and pointed out that 74 policemen cannot stop 1500 professional English soldiers though they kept them at bay for almost a day before they were overrun suffering fifty percent fatal casualties. No medals were issued; the Boer Republics did not believe in such things. A man did his duty towards God (the Christian one), his country and then his family and so it was. They did not even have a uniform and chose their own leaders by popular vote. During the three years of the Second Anglo Boer War they caused the British Empire more than 300 000 casualties which was for the time, horrific. But they stopped fighting when they realised that their women and children were far in the process of being wiped out. The war had to be stopped.

They also had their own ideas on democracy which was not strange for the time and much more enlightened than most. No black man could vote being a savage in their opinion and unable to understand democracy anyway. Extraordinarily, the coloured man (not black, the Afrikaner distinguished between the two - with this is meant "mulatto") had the vote in the Cape Colony up to 1954. Back in the two Boer Republics they followed the principle of the "noble savage" though of course, they knew from bitter experience that the savage is not by nature a good person or anyway not into what they thought noble civilised behaviour should be. They fought and won many a battle with the locals all the while telling the British Empire to piss off. They may have been subjected to the Queen at some stage but they ain't now and so it is. To ensure that London got the point they bought considerable quantities of weapons, Mauser rifles and Krupp cannon from Imperial Germany. They imported mercenary officers from Imperial Russia and Germany to teach them how to use the cannon - the rifles they already knew and were generally crack shots. Most hunted from the age of six years and one shot meant one dead springbok or a hiding for wasting ammunition.

The brightest of their sons, except for a few odd ones like Jannie Smuts who later became a Field Marshal in the British Army besides Prime Minister, went to Dutch and German Universities. Especially the University of Leiden was the first choice for everyone from lawyers to medical doctors. When the Union of South Africa came into being, in 1910, the national flag followed the Dutch one with a small Union Jack and the two former Boer Republic flags in the middle. This then was the flag under which South Africa became hated as the Apartheid Republic.

The legal system followed Roman-Dutch law, not English and the official language was Dutch though most Boers could speak decent enough English when not in public. Even today they would not easily admit having any

English blood in their veins though many do. Through the centuries many an English lass fell for a charming broad-shouldered Boer who took her home to teach her decent Afrikaans and the Afrikaner culture. Hence today you find many Afrikaners with Scottish & Irish names and no idea why they have it. They just know; it is instinct, that they dislike the Pommies on sight. Being called English was and is a great insult.

It was gold, almost ninety percent of the world's gold reserves, which brought the two wayward Boer Republics back to the British Empire. Once gold was discovered where Johannesburg is today, it was a matter of time. A new Afrikaner term came into being "uitlander" which translates to a foreigner...a non-Boer and mostly white trash from the UK. It is mostly not a term of endearment and as big an insult as "kaffir" would become later years. These "uitlanders" caused many troubles at the gold and diamond mines where they worked using cheap black labour, something which is forgotten today by the same mining houses they created. The mining houses still exist but ran to London when the black man finally got a vote in 1994 and Mr Mandela became president...obviously some liberals voted with their feet and others with their cross at the ballot table. Many a war was caused in Africa by the same mining houses though the focus went from diamonds to oil.

It is though ironic to the extreme that since the 1902 defeat, the Boers, who now became known as the Afrikaner, modelled their own Armed Forces on the British Army and fought with distinction in the First World War, Second World War and Korea with the British Empire. The most famous Battle of Britain fighter pilot was an Afrikaner, Sailor Malan (and soon very unpopular for his stand against Apartheid). The police also fought as infantry gaining much experience. There was no way the policemen would be left at home. Military wise it did not stop at following the British ranks and regiments. The Afrikaner, by his very nature, never accepted that Europeans would know more about Africa than he who was born here and lived here for hundreds of years. They would take a good look at what worked in Europe or anywhere else, even the Middle-East Israeli Wars, and adapt it to local circumstances.

This led to them developing landmine proof vehicles which are still copied forty years later. They built and flew a fighter jet called the Cheetah from leftover Mirage 3s which subsequently won every engagement against the much vaunted American F15 Eagle during exercises in the early 1990s. Their Kukri helmet aiming system is still copied and used by the Russian and other major first world Air Forces (they stole the technology via a Soviet Military Intelligence spy called Dieter Gerhardt, a former South African Navy Commodore). By 1976 the Apartheid State had nuclear weapons and the capability to deliver them - the new lot may still have that capability though they deny it. The nuclear weapons were given to the Americans to destroy or play with just before Mr Mandela took over in 1994. Something which is resented because it showed clearly the West did not trust the famous human rights leader with such weapons.

It should be clear that the Afrikaner was always difficult and tricky to handle. The new lot is not much better - they are every bit as arrogant as their predecessors and soon started to flex their muscles annoying many neighbouring States. However, in Africa, the Afrikaner Egg Breakers were the only logical choice to snatch and kill the Muslims if they could be convinced to do so. In the end that convincing part was not that difficult but complicated. They did not want to know, though they suspected that the whole Egg Breaker concept was a British MI6 front. They still don't like that idea. And then there was the Angelique factor, my wife and former SASS handler once known as that "Bitch of SASS."

She controlled all counter-espionage, which included counter-terrorism, operations. That encompassed the Muslim Truce whilst working for SASS as their top spymaster. There she came up with an idea to mortify the West by capturing one of their mother ships with the kidnapped (snatching of terrorists is in law kidnapping) Al-Qaeda operatives. Essentially, she conspired to cause them the biggest humiliation ever - it would have toppled governments and kept all covert operation on ice for decades. It would also have safeguarded the truce as no one else would have tried to break it.

I infiltrated the MI6 operation on her behalf and snatched two Muslims with the help of my mate, Geelslang. We delivered them to one Major Graeme Something, formerly of the Royal Marines who operated from a mother ship just off the coast of Mozambique. He would have a fatherly chat with the snatched ones and we disposed the bodies afterwards. Well, the sharks also had to eat and there was no need for prisoners. Once they were squeezed dry enough, they had to go to paradise. In a way we did them a favour and I am sure they would agree if they had a chance to think about it. After all, they wanted to die a martyr and now they did.

We were not the only snatching team. Although working in cells in our own areas we suspected, rightly as it turned out, that Graeme had other Egg Breakers helping him. All went well for a month or two, the Al-Qaeda lads were being snatched all over Africa when suddenly the Egg Breaker teams started to disappear. At that time Angelique got detained and sent me a secret message, it was in a code only we understood, that she was compromised and I better run away.

It was for me, the worst news possible. We were not married then. Through the years we looked at each other in unprofessional ways but it was only during that operation when she was already a widow and I, a widower, when we realised her obnoxious ways could perhaps be cute also. She is unlike any Afrikaner girl I ever saw or heard of. Slim with a firm chest area with startling green eyes and brown hair which she wore shoulder length unless parachuting. When parachuting, on my insistence, her hair is cut shorter into a nice bob. We don't want her hair to get entangled in the parachute cords and her neck broken before she even hits the ground. Contrary to evil speculation from jealous men she does sometimes listen to me, as she should, me being her husband and all. Besides that, she entirely deserved her nickname as the "Bitch of SASS" for her ways which were and are different.

Firstly, she was not that impressed with our Special Forces & Egg Breaker background. As far as she was concerned, she was the boss controlling us and we were just a strategic tool for her to abuse to complete her objectives. This was of course true of all spymasters as far as it went but for an African male such a woman would always be difficult to tolerate never mind to love. After all, she is rated just behind the cattle (an honourable position, I assure you) in our tradition. As could only be expected from her, being an only child and "otherwise" she took great exception against such ideas and would become violent if prodded too much on her rightful place in society. After all these years of blissful marriage I decided she is right.

I did try my luck a few times before our souls found each other on a beach in Mozambique. I must have been crazy or in love or both. Prior to that, it was a bit dangerous to try your luck with her although many tried to break through her barriers. She developed a violent reaction to unasked for attention and turned out to be very handy with her knees and a devastating right hook she learned somewhere. She kept the Egg Breakers and her own gang in place through sheer willpower and personality. I was treated differently which I suppose now was the first sign of affection. She got into the habit to place well-aimed kicks on my shins when not paying proper attention when she spoke. Unfortunately, that happened often. Her eyes are dangerous. When I stare into them, I always sort of lose track of everything. She would then become terribly annoyed and revert to her obnoxious ways.

The shin kicking sort of stopped now since we got married. As her husband such acts would be frowned upon. Mind you, I make sure to stand a few yards away ready to duck and run when she gets mad which is not often as she has calmed down considerably after our twins were born. Angelique was the best agent and spymaster SASS ever had but she was still snatched by them and severely maltreated during the subsequent interrogations. Geelslang and I rescued her and subsequently assassinated her boss, one Ramish Malesedi for the insult of ordering her maltreatment. He died when a 20mm sniper bullet exploded in his chest. He was not alone; his bodyguards died with him and within sight of the SASS headquarters in Pretoria East to prove a point. Next time I will level their buildings completely. I made sure to have a nice private heart-to-heart with one of her torturers who happened to fall into my hands. He regretted that lesson in good manners so much that he ended in a mental institution which shows he was weak willed to begin with. I will get him there too if my wife so desires but she does not at this time so he is safe enough with his nightmares. Perhaps that is good news for him as next time around I will cut his remaining eye out. Then it will be his fingers one by one with a garden plier. Last time I only broke his fingers, all of them, with a handy plier which Geelslang brought with. As well as a few ribs and, of course, we castrated him for good measure.

They had every reason to be angry, the SASS lads. Angelique turned out to be a double agent working for the French DGSE or foreign intelligence. She did so for almost 28 years. It was in a way logical for France was never seen as an enemy by Apartheid South Africa where we grew up. Any country that disliked the Pommies would be the Afrikaner's friend and we used French built Dassault Mirage fighters and helicopters to kill our enemies.

The garlic eaters are also dangerous and feared more than any other country in Africa. The French don't talk and don't draw lines in the sand...they simply act and will cut your balls off if your views are uncivilised enough. The only line is your heels as they drag you to your destiny. They don't need to play at being gentlemen like the Pommy Hooligans do - they bloody well know they are. I suspect she was recruited for DGSE in the Comoro Islands whilst working undercover as a diving instructor (she is a shit hot diver, better than Geelslang and me) by one Colonel Bob Denard, a well-known French mercenary commander. However, when I asked her about the old goat, he was a horny Frenchman; she became predictable, meaning violent. Obviously, whatever happened, she had a soft spot for him and attended his trial as a token of support.

During her time in the Islands she was a teenager, having finished school two years before the rest of her class mates and something of a "wunderkind" gone wrong (to the Intelligence Service and not directly to University). Her father, a former police general whom I failed to rescue after his capture, was a very big name in intelligence circles. It was not my fault, the failed rescue, I did what I could but he had departed by the time we dropped on them. I refused orders to desist and did the next best thing which was to execute every surviving terrorist. None survived to tell lies in court. My mate Geelslang was second in command of the rescue team. That was where I saw Angelique first, on a picture with her dad in his wallet when we searched his body.

The French got a star agent and through the years gave her the rank of colonel and made her a member of the Legion of Honour besides other awards. This meant she was, by French law and military tradition, entitled to be saluted by members of the French Armed Forces no matter what their own rank. This also meant she outranked me who left the police as a very young major and I have to walk a pace behind her if we follow strict protocol which we never do. She would simply grab my hand and that was that and so it is. As her husband and soul, it is my right to be next to her side at all times and I will not surrender that privilege. She is never alone anyway, except in our bedroom, her French bodyguards - all former Special Forces and Foreign Legion lads, are always around her giving everyone except our twins the evil eye. Their evil eye includes me which I am fine with. We have an "understanding." If they fail to protect her and survive, I will kill them. It is written in blood.

Regardless of my "understanding" her bodyguards (I call them affectionately "thugs") became part of the family. They adore their "ma chérie Colonel Angelique" as they call her and especially her Frog Minder became something of a favourite uncle to our twins. It is not to be wondered at; the bastard is always there and has a surprising knack with kids. From what I know he grew up in an orphanage and joined the French Army at 16. After a few years of excellent service in an Armoured Regiment he graduated from the Saint-Cyr Military Academy and then came into his own in the Foreign Legion as a paratrooper before joining French Army Special Forces. Thereafter the DGSE grabbed him and the rest is history.

He has been with Angelique ever since he was first assigned as her DGSE liaison officer and head of her bodyguards. We had our tuffs through the years. He once allowed Angelique to jump from an Antonov-124 with shoulder length hair making me roar in anger until she landed ten yards away smiling sweetly at my antics. He landed a few yards away and within range to be shot but by that time Angelique and I were already kissing and I forgot to shoot him. And then there was the time she got shot in her fore arm because he did not physically restrain her from rescuing one of her bodyguards out of a burning truck. I was not amused, but then, Angelique is difficult to control at the best of times and outranked him. Still, I wanted to shoot him in both arms so he could get the message. Thing is, he is what is known as the debonair type and has a typical thick skin that only Frenchmen have as a natural endowment. Every time he screws up, he just smiles and shrugs and lights a Gauloise and so it is. You cannot stay angry with such men for long and would soon grin back and laugh it off. I know Angelique cares deeply about him in a motherly way which is funny for he is older than her.

It was during her subsequent debriefings after her escape from SASS (which took almost a year) that she revealed her master plan to embarrass the West. Her revelations caused shock waves in our community, almost as much as the news of her marriage to one of her Egg Breakers, me. We suddenly understood why the Egg Breaker teams were disappearing. SASS took the time, in conjunction with the Special Forces Brigade, to ambush them. Their next target was the mother ships which they could track via satellite. That was only prevented by promptly withdrawing them to safe waters.

The Pommies realised that unless the nuclear attack submarine guarding the mother ship is authorised to shoot, their bluff would be called and they would be boarded. And if the submarine shoots at a South African Navy warship trying to rescue the kidnapped Muslims it would start World War Three. So the mother ships sailed to safer waters and away from the African shores. Predictably that stopped snatching operations and the valuable intelligence so gained dead in its tracks.

Something extraordinary had to be done and was done. They recruited Angelique from DGSE or got the DGSE to release her to undo her own master plan. They asked her to play chess with herself. Exactly what the deal was between the DGSE and the rest I would not know but she took command of the Egg Breaker operations to destroy the SASS truce. Her Frog Minder acted as some sort of a liaison officer between her and DGSE. I am sure that DGSE then dealt at a much higher level with the Western Governments.

Later on the Pommies, via their senior officer, Sir John, reinforced the Egg Breakers under my command. They used ex-Special Forces lads from a London based company called Sandrine who were place directly under Egg Breaker command since we knew the area and they did not. Besides, we don't take orders from Pommies. We went on the attack hunting down the SASS led teams and snatching the Muslims where we could and assassinating them where they were too well protected. Our idea was to get them out of southern Africa and cornered in South Africa where we fancied our chances.

There was no way that the West would back down and leave the Muslims in peace - not after chasing them out of North Africa into Southern Africa. As could be expected, the SASS lads reacted equally violently and placed a TWEP order on her, myself and Geelslang and his medical doctor wife who was innocent of our activities. Dr Thandiwe runs a medical clinic at our place in Northern Mozambique called the Ukuthula Ranch. Her only crime besides being married to Geelslang was that she treated Angelique after we rescued her. Such an insult could obviously not be ignored by us and we swore they would pay in blood.

Long since denied by the liberal wankers in government or hidden under sinister terms like "wet work" or "permanent removal from society (an Apartheid term)" a TWEP order translates to "terminate with extreme prejudice." It is an out and out assassination order. Whoever sees her and got a shot would take it and be promoted if he succeeds. If he fails and we get hold of him, he would die a dreadfully pro-longed death for his arrogance. There is a reason why she is so well protected by her French thugs. They tried several times to kill her and I have no doubt they will try again in the future. During the process we killed a lot of them in return and we also sunk two of their silent Type 209 submarines and one frigate, the SAS Amatola. We did this to open the oceans for the official snatch teams and they swore revenge. The end of our war was not nearly in sight. They were stubborn and had to relearn the meaning of fear.

The last attack on Angelique, now pregnant with our twins, took place only yesterday when a rogue (they should not have been in that area) SASS patrol ambushed our convoy. She escaped with a shattered fore arm and I continued south to launch an audacious attack. It was not in revenge as it was part of an overall strategy. I intend to sink one of their fast attack craft and do some other damage too, if possible.

Angelique, her remaining bodyguards and the seriously wounded were evacuated for proper treatment. I did not expect to see her anytime soon. In fact, I did not even know where they were at that stage except that it was somewhere in France. Her departure suited me; I was always cynical to have her in Africa whilst the Egg Breaker versus SASS war was ongoing. Even with the best close protection you only need one lucky punk to get through. They came too close this time. We got saved by a bit of luck. Geelslang, he was an altar boy in his youth, declared it to be the hand of God. That may be so and I am grateful, certainly I had a premonition and stopped the convoy just outside the death zone. Hence, we only lost one SAMIL-20 that stopped in the death zone and the Unimog with Angelique's thugs in. That was an act of incredible courage. They deliberately drove the unarmoured Unimog between her Casspir and where the SASS men were shooting RPGs at it trying to protect her from harm. I can still see the Casspir dragging itself with its front wheels, the rear ones were shot out when the Unimog placed itself next to it. Yes, perhaps Angelique was right to rescue the driver from a fiery death. We gave thanks to God during the burial ceremony of those who fell during that ambush. We said the same for the other side too after taking pictures of their faces for later identification. Our list was growing rapidly.

The fact that they shot at a clearly marked Casspir ambulance to get Angelique was noticed by Geelslang, me and all our lads. Such action is calculated to anger us...we did not abuse the Red Cross sign to protect Angelique. It was the only armoured vehicle we had available and which could fit her, her frog Minder and some of her thugs in safety. Angelique was driving it - she likes driving armoured vehicles and big trucks. They were shooting continuously at it to get her. We would remember this act of barbarity in the future. Obviously, the niceties and rules of war did not apply to them. Problematically we were ruthless enough in our ways but not enough to shoot at the Red Cross...we do not do such things. However, would now seriously consider it. As with all things in life you start with the best of intentions but it ends in something else.

The border crossing itself was nothing spectacular - there is only a normal four feet high wire fence. We merely pushed it flat and drove over it. There were no border guards to bother us. In the old days the crack police counter insurgency units patrolled the fence every day to look for spoor and if found, would track the insurgents down and either arrest or kill them. These days they are too fat and lazy and the counter insurgency units were

46

disbanded twenty years ago. None of the new generation except for the remaining small Special Forces platoon had any training or inclination on what to do with such things. We felt we were safe enough from police intervention and the locals were quite used to smugglers. They would keep neutral and stay away from heavily armed soldiers as they would believe us to be for we were towing anti-aircraft cannons (or if one, we were towing one field gun.)

The Army and Air Force did enter our thoughts as they were capable of mounting a surprise attack if given enough warning. I worried about the few SASS lads who escaped our counter ambush attack. They could have run back to South Africa as fast as our vehicles could move. Luckily their long-distance radio was useless to them - we had it in our possession and were keeping a listening watch on it. They themselves could not do much to us but they would have reported that the notorious Foxtrot is heading south with heavy weapons the moment they re-established contact. That meant our time on the ground was very limited and we knew it. At one stage I seriously gave thought on cancelling the mission but decided not to. Time will tell if I am right or wrong in this decision. Who dares wins said SAS founder and first commander, Colonel Stirling, so long ago. Well, we will see. Our own motto was, at the Army Regiment anyway, "We fear naught but God."

The road, not that it was worthy of that name, was a very sandy track where our vehicles had to use low range to get through. We also lowered the air pressure in the tyres which always helps a lot in soft sand. After the previous day's ambush we were reduced to the three SAMIL-20s towing the ZU 23-2 cannon and the armoured Kwêvoël towing the M46 130mm field gun. These were former South African Army vehicles which we got on auction and rebuilt. They were uniquely suited to the conditions and would confuse the locals even more. All of them still had their original paint scheme on. Geelslang was still driving the Kwêvoël with his usual aplomb. It was by far the heaviest, being armoured and towing the eighteen thousand-pound M46. However, that was what it was designed to do and it was a mean looking vehicle with an oddly V-shaped cabin and thick bullet proof windows. He had a light machine gun, the old Soviet RPD mounted on his left and one on the roof. We would be able to put a lot of lead down if required. The men were awake and waiting for the first signs of trouble.

The burned out Unimog and SAMIL-20 were left next to the road. Africa is full of such wrecks and it would not really attract any attention. Their onboard radios were destroyed by the flames. We retained the SAMIL-50 carrying most of our personal equipment. The Kwêvoël, being landmine proof carried the reserve ammunition and the M40 106mm recoilless rifle we captured from the SASS patrol. The problem was we had barely enough men to man these weapons but I expected the crew of the EBS (Egg Breaker Ship, an internal joke) Orlando, with whom we were rendezvousing to act as infantry or at least loaders. The shooting part we could do ourselves.

Our ambush point was just over a mile from the international border on the South African side. We had a good idea where we wanted to go but checked our GPS devices every now and then because the last couple of miles were cross country. I recalled the days when you would have to walk away from the vehicles because the old magnetic compass would be affected by the metal armour. Then you kept on walking running with the convoy following on your heels. The other way was to fix a point in the distance and just get to it. Once there you would fix another and so it went. These days the GPS made life so much easier.

We would escape back or hoped to, by driving on the beach which was the most direct way of doing things. We did not use that method of entry because we wanted to approach the area from the land side without leaving any tracks on the beach for the enemy to wonder about. We reached the ambush spot shortly after ten in the morning. The flat white sandy beaches looked quite idyllic and not at all warlike. People would pay good money to sit there staring at the sea. Fortunately, none were there; we were a bit further north than where the usual tourists hang out. As always in high summer it was very hot and humid but you got used to it. In front of us, looking from the sea towards the land was a broad, about two hundred feet, stretch of beach and then the large African bushes where we unhooked our ZSU-2s and the M46 field gun. The spots were designated by Geelslang who had an eye for such details. We took every known precaution to camouflage the guns and it was a good thing we did so. The vehicles retired over a small dune to be out of sight from the sea for the time being.

I stood on the armoured cab of the Kwêvoël. "Foxtrot to Graeme, come in over." I used our pre-determined frequency. The answer came back almost immediately. A man like Major Graeme Something would have a very decent radio operator at all times and keeps a close watch. He would also know we should be in the area and expected the call to confirm it. I was convinced he would be just outside visual range steaming south to reach us.

"Foxtrot this is Graeme. I read you fives. Authenticate please.... Juliet Charlie Three Eight?"

The fives meant he could hear me clearly and the signal strength was good. It bloody well better be with the state of the art radios we were using. They would automatically scramble and jump frequencies for additional security. The chances of our signals being intercepted on a closed circuit on that FM frequency were very remote. We could take the chance to talk directly to each other for a short period of time.

I glanced at the code list to find the corresponding phrase. "This is Foxtrot, authentication...Mike Four One."

"Foxtrot this is Graeme, I heard you ran into trouble?"

Graeme sounded concerned. He fell in love with our Mozambican liaison officer and she was inside the same Casspir ambulance as was Angelique when the attack took place. The last time I saw her she was good but in considerable shock having emptied her pistol valiantly at the enemy. That took guts, the general public don't understand this but when the bullets hammer and shriek off the armour plating your first instinct is to hunker down and stay down. It takes real guts to shoot back and especially with a useless pistol. I would make a point thereof to tell Graeme she did well but really needs a decent rifle next time. A pistol is not designed to help much under such circumstances.

"Graeme this is Foxtrot, affirmative on your last, it was not a big deal."

I wondered how he knew about our incident; we kept complete radio silence until now but I gathered that Angelique would have reported the incident before allowing herself to be drugged to have her arm operated on. That also meant that Graeme now had de facto command until she could regain her health. It was a bit of a problem, although a personal friend and the best hooligan the Pommies could produce in many years, he stayed a Pommy. He could command but only via DGSE instructions for we would not take orders from MI6 directly. I hoped that it would not take Angelique long to get back. He confirmed that.

"Foxtrot this is Graeme, I have command and a message for you...all three of your family members reached hospital safely."

It was nice of him to let me know. He could only mean Angelique and the unborn twins. I had no other family except my mate Geelslang who I already knew was safe, he was standing next to me listening in on the spare earpiece. At this he showed his ivories. He saw I was worried about Angelique. My first wife died in an IED explosion in Iraq whilst working as a DGSE counter terrorist specialist. She was of Algerian stock and a devoted follower of Allah, the Merciful. Her version of Islam was not the least what the radicals' said it was. She told me of a merciful God who would never condone what was being done in His name. Those virgin hunters will get the surprise of their lives one day.

Geelslang almost hated Angelique when she was still our SASS handler and not my wife. The way we looked at each other at times, highly unprofessional and like "two goats in love" irritated him to no end. Such things are not acceptable in his world of perfectionism. He never trusted her and had good reason for that. We had to run for our lives, for five long days and nights, from a crowd of homicidal maniacs hell bent on slaying us because her communication lines were broken and we were badly compromised. It became so bad that we formally hugged and said goodbye twice to each other before being rescued by submarine. He offered to TWEP her himself, me being unable to understand she is evil and "otherwise" and frankly, dangerous to our health. Needless to say, I flatly refused and had to threaten him with death if something malicious should happen to our "Bitch from SASS." Since we got married, he calmed down significantly and even considered her to be a distant relative. Much to his initial distress his wife and Angelique clicked like long lost sisters and are the best of friends.

"Graeme this is Foxtrot, we are where we said we will be. What is your expected time of arrival? We are prepared and Lise is waiting."

The last part was the code name we gave this operation, Lise, after one of Angelique's all-time heroines, a Special Operations Executive agent who won the George Cross in Occupied France during the Second World War. I was not too happy about the name but as always Angelique had her way.

"Foxtrot this is Graeme, our ETA is four hours from now. I confirm Lise. Out."

That gave us just enough time to set up the ZU 23-2s where they could cover the landing and surrounding area. We made sure that they had enough ammunition stocked close by. We expected a short but fierce fight.

The EBS Orlando was a smallish vessel of just over fifteen hundred tons. She was a former US Navy vessel designed to land a tank company on hostile shores. We got it second-hand and converted it into a Q-ship by adding three ZU 23-2 automatic cannons and the M46 130mm field gun onto it. The armour was upgraded; frankly it had none to begin with, by placing two foot thick Hesco walls around the bridge and through deck where the vehicles would have been parked in the old days. The concept, though old, worked well. We sunk the new South African Navy frigate, the SAS Amatola by spreading the word that we were a mother ship holding the captured Al-Qaeda lads. When they came within point blank range to board us, we opened fire and kept on shooting until she turned turtle. They did get a few shots in and put up a valiant fight but we had the advantage of surprise.

That sea action caused an uproar. The new lot in Pretoria swore revenge and made wild statements of us shooting at them whilst under the Red Cross flag which was just not true. We had a flag flying during the battle and it had a red cross on it but it also had the Egg Breaker symbol in the corner. It was for all intents and purposes a Crusader Flag with the added Egg Breaker symbol. Not that it mattered, they said a lot of things but the fact remained that we sunk the pride of their navy on the open sea. Naturally they responded rather aggressively and sent a whole squadron of ships to find and sink the EBS Orlando. It was this squadron we hoped to ambush or rather elements of it.

We knew the frigate would stay offshore as the water was a bit shallow for it. Once they found the Orlando, and we would make sure of that, they would come close to investigate. We knew where the squadron was, a friendly nuclear attack submarine was shadowing it all the way and informing us. We also knew it had two fast attack craft and the supply ship SAS Drakensberg with them to ensure extended operations. From the submarine's observations we detected that the SAS Drakensberg had a deadly Rooivalk attack helicopter on board and the frigate an Oryx transport helicopter. We concluded that the two fast attack craft would have their full complement of Special Forces onboard. Those ships were hunting Egg Breakers, not submarines or pirates. They gave the game away by threatening too much and leaving their Super Lynx anti-submarine helicopters at home. In my view that was a mistake and indicated they were reacting to us which gave us the upper hand. We gained what the military calls the "battlefield initiative."

The presence of the Rooivalk helicopter bothered me more than anything else. It was superbly dangerous to us. Some experts rate it above the better-known Apache Longbow and I took special precautions against it. We would see if my precautions would work out the way I hoped. I certainly expected it to act aggressively and attack us. In fact, I hoped it would and was glad they only brought one with them, as usually they hunt in pairs. That would have made life much harder and I would have called the operation off.

Using the EBS Orlando as bait after she sunk the SAS Amatola was not our original plan. Our first idea was to sail the EBS Orlando out to deep water and scuttle her. That would have been easy since the Mozambican channel between Mozambique and the huge island of Madagascar is on average nine thousand feet deep and the ocean is a big place. She would not have been found and even if found, so what? Nothing would be salvaged or left to be salvaged. Nevertheless, we decided, it was my idea and approved by Angelique as commanding officer, to leave the EBS Orlando exposed on a secluded beach and when the South Africans investigate, as they would, to ambush them and cause even more damage. Thereafter we would retire back into Mozambique. For complex international law reasons, we had to open fire whilst on South African soil and hence we crossed the border earlier that morning. For the same legal reasons, the EBS Orlando would be beached also on the South African side to clear the Mozambicans of all wrongdoing. They preferred to stay officially neutral in this fight.

They were not that neutral to be honest. Few African governments were. It would be better to say they were positively neutral towards us and our sponsors who had the aid money they got used to. They wanted the Muslims out of their territory as they were not even asked about it and had nothing to do with the South African / Muslim Truce. Many were fairly upset about the arrogance of making such an arrangement in their country.

As a senior intelligence official said to me, they desire to rebuild and live in peace. This war is not their problem and as long as we leave the Mozambican citizens alone we can do within reason what we please. That is as long as they are not embarrassed or forced to explain our presence. It was the usual deniability we were used to and respected. This aspect the SASS lads forgot, they got so arrogant about being powerful and the regional bully that they forgot to keep to the African tradition of showing proper respect to your hosts. It is a mistake that no Egg Breaker would ever make, we believed in our traditions. Furthermore, we operated undercover for two decades. We knew better than to anger the local lads and have long since established cordial relationships. We did that by being humble as only a strong man can be. We had nothing to bluff about. We had already proved what needed to be proven...we knew we were selected men entrusted with great responsibility. Living and working in the shadows had become second nature.

Just after 13h00 Geelslang saw her first. He had uncanny eyes. She was just a spot on the horizon but he did not even need binoculars to confirm it. He just said, "there is the Orlando" and pointed straight east. She must have sailed all the way to the meeting point and then turned 90 degrees west or towards land.

We walked down the beach and waved at the small vessel as she approached. She was still bearing the scars of the Amatola fire fight which took place only ten days before. Her left side was scorched and the bridge area pocketed with small holes, where hundreds of 35mm shells had hit her. Some penetrated the Hesco barriers and caused casualties. Geelslang himself still had stitches because of it but then so did I above my right eye.

The scorch marks on her side was our doing. As the M46 130mm field gun fired shell after shell into the Amatola the superhot gasses coming out of the muzzle brake caused the paint to scorch and finally burn. Not that it stopped them from shooting. They kept a steady rate of a shell every ten seconds for ten minutes. The heavy seventy-pound shells exploded right inside the Amatola causing her to burn.

The EBS Orlando looked different though. She was not the same ship as what the Amatola survivors would remember. Her port navigation wing was gone. Graeme blew it off so that the M46 could be hoisted down when we landed a few days ago at a secluded beach just north of the small Mozambican town of Xai Xai. There we met with Angelique and a convoy of trucks to tow our weapons down south to the ambush spot. I suppose, it is always easier in hindsight to be clever, as we could have kept the weapons onboard and retrieved them at the ambush spot but the problem was what would have happened then? With the crew and the Egg Breakers there were simply not enough vehicles to transport everyone and everything back to Mozambique. We would then be forced to run all the way which was silly. We could not sail away with the old Orlando - we believed that she would be destroyed in the coming battle. She was beached as a sacrificial lamb to bring the enemy to our guns which would be onshore, and not on the ship as the enemy expected. I still believe it was the right decision to tow the weapons overland to South Africa, despite the ambush. We needed the heavy firepower they provided. It was the rear most ZU 23-2 that unhooked and gave us covering fire. They saved Angelique's ambulance Casspir. I have no doubt that it would have been shot out if not for that automatic cannon fire. The ZU 23-2 destroyed the rocketeers; they had two RPG7s with them, just as they closed in on the kill.

I was leading the counter-attack at that stage as is the standard anti-ambush tactic. You execute a flank attack which we did successfully. I then looked back towards the Casspir, which was crawling away to safety when she got shot. I was convinced Angelique had died. A very unpleasant feeling which would not have bode well for any prisoners and would have changed the course of the Egg Breaker war, as I would have chased the three escapees down and tortured them to death. After that, well, someone in the presidency would have suffered for my loss. Such an insult is not to be left unanswered in my world and way of thinking. After the IED incident where my first wife, Marwa, died, it took Geelslang and I one year to hunt down and kill every Muslim who was even remotely involved including one who gave them shelter. He kept on saying he did not know but so it was and he died a horrible death for his lack of knowledge. We could not torture many of them but did the second best thing, which was to kill them in front of their families, a great insult in our tradition. So the SASS lads were lucky that Angelique escaped with only a shattered fore arm.

I noted that the starboard navigation wing was also gone. Graeme must have blown it off to make the vessel more evenly balanced though that had nothing to do with weight but appearance. Old Commodore Octavius, the Orlando's captain and we suspected, father of Graeme, made other changes. He had tarpaulin barriers or fake walls erected creating the illusion of a higher free board than usual. We struck this down as we wanted the Orlando to be recognisable. It was hard to believe that only four days had passed since we last met. I made sure her name was still painted on the aft above the stern and on the bow.

"Foxtrot to Graeme. Can you spot our toys?"

I asked over the short-range FM radio when they were still a good few miles offshore. After all, the direction they were coming from was the same as would our enemies in due course. I hoped they would only see the pristine white beach and small dunes with African bushes behind it.

"Foxtrot, that is negative on visual and negative on radar and optics."

The warships would have much better radar systems but picking up a small piece of metal like a cannon hidden in front of a dune with only its barrel sticking out is not that easy in real life. Perhaps with infrared or thermal imagining but only after that barrel got hot shooting and then it would sort of be too late. The threat was still the mark one eyeballs of the two Rooivalk pilots but we would deal with them. They did not know, since we had never used it, that we had a good supply of the latest French made Mistral Missiles with us. They were short-range surface-to-air missiles or MANPAD as it is known and I hoped to give the Rooivalk the last surprise it would ever have.

I saw the Orlando come to a full stop about two hundred yards offshore and drop her beach anchor as if she wanted to winch herself to deep water again. Again I felt the admiration and affection we had for Commodore Octavius. The man must have been in his seventies but still as sharp as a Swiss clock. He missed nothing. The maskirovka was that the Orlando beached here and the crew could have gone either to South Africa (highly unlikely and another reason why that is exactly what we did) or to Mozambique (where we were not at this stage). They would think that most probably something went wrong with the ship; perhaps it was damaged by the Amatola's guns and could not get off the beach again. There were many scenarios but this is logically what the squadron commander would think. He would then have a choice. He could stand offshore and shell it to pieces but doing that would take away the great prize of showing the rogue pirate terrorist ship to the world. We also had a way to combat that idea which I would implement later on. The frigate would not be able to come too close as the water was too shallow although we expected the fast attack craft to come within a mile or two which is all we needed. They would come into range and we would sink them or at least damage them seriously enough to prove a point.

To the naval commander, the Orlando would look obviously abandoned. The bow doors would be open and the ramp lowered as if she had launched vehicles. So he would first send his Special Forces lads to capture and take control of her whilst the Rooivalk circled around keeping away from the Mozambican border but looking for the Orlando escape party. The Special Forces lads, they are as good as any other similar unit in the world, could approach the Orlando in one of three ways. They could fly in and fast rope down or they could approach with their ski-boats or they could swim in. Of all the scenarios the first one was the most likely. It was fast and effective and had an element of surprise against non-Special Forces types. Obviously, they could see that the guns were removed and that the Orlando did not pose a major threat. She could be taken easily.

Twenty minutes later the old ship came to her last halt and the telegraphs tingled to switch the engines off. The bow doors opened and we were greeted by Graeme and Commodore Octavius who were standing there waiting for us. They were smiling, as well they should be, it is not often that you get the chance to play pirate for your country.

"Permission to come aboard, Sir?"

That was Geelslang the traditionalist amongst us. He commanded the Orlando during the Amatola battle and I was in effect the gunnery officer controlling the guns. He roared the traditional request as we walked closer.

"Permission granted, Peter" replied the Commodore graciously, his white hair and beard blowing in the wind. He liked Geelslang very much and later said the man had no equal as a sailor. That was quite a compliment from a man who served for decades with the Royal Navy. What exactly he did with them I could not even begin to speculate about.

"Peter" was Geelslang's real name which few dared to use in public. The Commodore was one of the few men who could use it without obtaining his wrath. Besides his father and his wife no one else did except me when I wanted to rile him a bit. Not even Angelique used it in the old days when they hated each other.

We walked onboard and gave each man a firm handshake as was our way. None of that weird French cheek kissing was for us even though I could call myself a citizen of France because of my marriage to Angelique. The grateful Republic gave her citizenship with her rank and medals which made our twins automatically French citizens too.

I still cannot get used to this cheek kissing and often look at Angelique's thugs with astonishment. That however is nothing to what the locals say when they see grown white men kissing each other on the cheek. Their shocked comments range from speculation on unnatural acts to a sad click of tongue which is the African way of shaking your head in disgust or disbelief and frequently both. Mind you, these days the older thugs were beginning to understand the local languages and customs and so we had to be more careful as they sometimes knew when we were taking the Mickey out of them and react. Mostly they are quite easy going regarding such things but like most Frenchmen, all in fact, they get fanatical when national honour is at stake.

On the other hand, as Angelique pointed out, the locals got used to them and their strange ways so perhaps the answer is somewhere in between. I fear the day when our twins will bring some lads from the Sorbonne where they are studying to the Ukuthula Ranch but as Angelique said, we will deal fairly with them. She had an unholy glint in her eyes when she said that and I don't even want to think what those lads will have to go through. They will soon realise that I am not the dangerous one but Madame Foxtrot is everything you should not tangle with.

"So what happened? We only heard you ran into trouble and that Angelique was shot."

That was Graeme wanting details as was his right. With Angelique indisposed the burden of de facto command fell squarely on him. I hoped she would be back soon as I trusted her a whole lot more than him. We may be good mates and all that but he stays a Pommy bastard.

"We were ambushed by a rogue SASS patrol that recognised Angelique and opened fire. We were fortunate; only one vehicle was inside the death zone and immediately destroyed with its occupants. The rest of us could extract ourselves and launch a successful counter attack."

The loss of so many men really irked me. It was not the Egg Breaker way to lose men although it was inevitable at times. I sounded angry to myself.

"I heard Angelique left the safety of the armoured Casspir to rescue one of her bodyguards? What the hell is wrong with her?"

He asked it in a peculiar fashion as if she was a normal girl and I would be able to keep her on a tight leash. I looked at him with raised eyebrows.

"Do you mean physically or mentally?" I replied a bit sourly for I did not approve of her actions no matter how well meaning or instinctual they had been. Still, I was glad she could not hear me saying this. Her reaction would have been predictably violent because she knows she is always right and I always wrong and that one day I will realise it. It did not take her more than a few minutes after being shot to get obnoxious with me. Luckily, I had a captured enemy soldier to attend to and a way out before it became serious.

To say I was mad was not quite true; I really wanted to shoot her Minder for allowing it to happen. I was bloody furious.

I shrugged. "She is what she is Graeme. Angelique will do what is right or what she sees as right and so it is. She said it was instinct. The man was unconscious and the truck burning and she acted to save him. You know how she is. The bullet went straight through her left forearm and shattered it. I suppose they were using dum-dum rounds."

Actually, they were not but it would have been legal under the laws of war if they did, for no war officially existed between us. We could use what we pleased and certainly the Egg Breakers used what is known as hollow points. It is the best way to kill a human being. The argument was anyway a bit academic. From the 1960s when the American M16 rifle came into regular use the balance of the bullet was changed ever so slightly so it would tumble through the air making it a dum-dum round even though it looked like a normal full metal jacket round.

The Soviets complained bitterly as the famous AK47 round does not do that and is in fact much more legal under the Genève Conventions than that of the M16. When no one listened they promptly and unsurprisingly did the same with their AK74 which fires the smaller 5.45x39mm bullet. It also tumbles and hence causes much more damage than what it would have done otherwise. Now it was the Yanks turn to complain but that was the pot calling the kettle black. Every nation since then has followed the same design. Hence the South African bullets followed the same pattern, that calibre, the 5.56mm NATO tumbles after a certain distance. You can clearly see it on the paper targets on the range - the bullet leaves a large hole where it goes through tumbling or sideways.

"Well the French are quite pleased with her deed" said Commodore Octavius who now spoke for the first time to me. "Just marvellous, the things that girl does. You are a lucky man Foxtrot."

I did not reply, because of respect for his age and senior rank that I would prefer her to be less marvellous in the things she does whilst pregnant. As she now has a shattered forearm and had to be flown out for treatment leaving a Pommy bastard in de facto command. On the other hand, that was Angelique and she would not change. It is one of the things I love about her so I smiled and said she is indeed marvellous and I am a lucky man.

I also did not mention to the Commodore that her "marvellous incident" caused me many sleepless nights. I keep seeing her flying backwards after being hit by the bullet (I initially thought this was due to the explosion when an RPG hit the Unimog in front of her). That vision would stay with me for many years and I would wake up to find her sleeping next to me and calm down again. I know for a fact I aged ten years in that moment though she denies that, perhaps two years and besides I was already grey when she married me so there. Get a helmet and stop this liberal nonsense of complaining all the time! No doubt it is by chance that I see her sometimes rubbing the scar when she looks at the pictures of our twins or are in their room when they are away.

"At any rate, your girlfriend acted very bravely too. She emptied two magazines into the general area of attack." I could still see her shocked face whilst holding her empty pistol with the slide open. I noticed this at a glance as I doubt if she even knew she was holding it. It was a terrible time for me; I was looking at one of Angelique's thugs trying to stop the bleeding on her arm. Simultaneously I was searching her Minder to shoot him but the bastard had disappeared doing all round defence with his lads.

Graeme grinned broadly at this and ignored the old Commodore's raised eyebrow. He obviously did not know about the less than professional relationship between the Graeme and his Mozambican Intelligence Officer. Well, Graeme can explain himself.

"Oi, I have been thinking about that Foxtrot. She will need a decent rifle next time. I am sure I will be able to teach her the basics at the Ukuthula Ranch."

He seemed quite pleased with this idea and they spent a considerable time on our shooting range afterwards. However, I somehow doubt if shooting was done all the time since we did not hear the shots. Angelique was polite enough to say that perhaps they were shooting and we simply did not hear it. My reply on this ancient wisdom of shot not being heard made her blush. She countered that grown-ups can do what they please. We were also young once in case I forgot. Nah, I did not forget and offered to show her how young I really felt. And that was the end of our working day too.

"They shot at a marked ambulance, at the red cross." You could hear the anger in Geelslang's voice. Such things are simply not done.

"I say old chap that was rather uncalled for. Don't worry; I am sure we will take revenge in due course. I hear you have a prisoner?" Graeme went on, all business again.

"Yes we captured one Special Forces lad. He was wounded in the foot and both arms but is good enough. We intend leaving him here to be found. Better news is that we also have their long-distance radio and are monitoring it. Besides the usual situation report requests nothing much is happening but that means nothing in itself."

"Yes, and I wonder if it could somehow be tracked?"

He had a valid point. All Special Forces have an emergency beacon in their vehicles able to send a signal that they really need to be evacuated. It was very possible that the radio was sending such a signal and if so, it was very much to our advantage, we wanted to be found.

"Angelique has a way to track those teams. How? I would not know. I assumed it was the burst transmissions and it probably is but I am not sure."

In reality I suspected she could switch the emergency beacon on and off. It was known in our world that a computer could be switched on and off remotely even if not on the internet. This could be done by a directional radio beam although you have to be relatively close. Or by using a standard landline telephone but that was already back in the late 1950s. It is old technology that the shrewd lads of MI5 first developed. They then sold the system to the astonished Virginians; the UK lot being still impoverished at that stage from winning the Second World War. We don't like MI5, of course not, they are Pommies and glorified policemen but you have to give credit where it is due. We are much better at drinking and slaying but not so good at gadgets and reading other people's mail. Something they seem to excel at. The two groups don't mix well and it is said, I heard it more than once from reliable sources, that they consider us to be something brushed with tar...not quite what is expected of polite society old fellow, hooligan behaviour and all that. Thing is they want to capture spies and we are spies in essence. Yep, we don't like them much.

"Well we need to get the ship rigged for destruction. I suggest we offload all extra ammunition and what we need first. Thereafter we can booby trap the rest and ensure that the 130mm shells detonate with it. That should blow her to pieces." Commodore Octavius said this ruefully, he and Geelslang really like the old Orlando.

"I suspect she will be shelled first anyway. Why don't we offload the 130mm shells first so we know we have enough? We can always return and rig the remaining 130mm shells as added explosives. I don't want to run out of shells in the coming fight."

When we left the Orlando a few days ago we decided to take only the bare essentials with us because of the weight restrictions of the vehicles. Now we could offload everything making sure that we don't run out of ammunition in the coming fight.

"I agree. Peter, see to it that we offload as quickly as possible. Foxtrot, what about my men?"

The Commodore would always and firstly take care of his men. That is the way the Royal Navy bred them decades ago when he was a boy sailor called a midshipman. In those days they still had ships to show the flag with. Today, not so much, they have for instance no real aircraft carriers and have lost the ability to fly fixed wing aircrafts from them. Even when their mighty new Elizabeth class carriers are finished they will need the Yanks to show them the ropes. As an Afrikaner I thoroughly enjoy their discomfort but it also makes me sad - even the Pommies deserve better than Blair and company. Africa owes them a lot including fair legal systems and infrastructure.

"Commodore, I need your men in this coming fight. They will act as loaders for us and afterwards we will evacuate all of you into Mozambique and then out of Africa." I answered quickly.

"We are yours to command then. So be it. Major Graeme, we need to get that signal out to force the situation. Do we proceed?"

Graeme looked at me. I was the ground commander even if he had overall control subject to what DGSE orders us to do. The Egg Breakers elected me as their commander and will not take orders from a Pommy. I thought about our situation. The guns were in place and Geelslang would offload the couple of tons of ammunition within an hour. I could already hear the rumbling of diesel engines as the SAMIL-50 and others drove into the hold and started to use its hoist to load the ammunition crates. Everyone knew this needed to be done very quickly indeed. They were quite busy and besides that, it was damn hot down there. February is the hottest month in Mozambique and unless used to it you will suffer a lot. I nodded in agreement.

"Commodore, please activate the emergency beacon of the EBS Orlando."

Graeme and the Commodore could be very formal with each other on occasion and I suppose this was one of them. Once that beacon, all ocean-going ships have one, is activated it would act like a homing beacon for every ship in the vicinity. They would immediately know that the Orlando was in difficulties and come to investigate. Since the inception in 1982, the distress radio beacons have saved more than twenty-eight thousand people. We were hoping the South African Navy Squadron would be on the scene first. They were not too far away steaming hard north to where the Amatola was sunk. They would soon get their chance to attack the Orlando. Sooner than what they thought when they left Simonstad Naval Base.

We walked to the bridge and watched him turn the switch sending a continuous signal. It was done. Code Name Lise was now officially underway and could not be stopped. Win or lose, it was going to happen. Someone was going to respond to it. I noted the time; it was exactly 24 hours since the ambush and I wondered if that was a good or bad thing.

It was the American General Eisenhower who first claimed that the legendary German Field Marshall Erwin Rommel was mistaken to counter-attack immediately and in piecemeal formations whilst gathering sufficient forces. According to Dwight D Eisenhower you should only attack with strong formations even if that means waiting a couple of days and then hammer away with overwhelming superior forces. Otherwise the piecemeal attacks will be swallowed in the cauldron and have no effect on the eventual outcome. In this he and the difficult but brilliant British Commander, Field Marshal Montgomery, were in complete agreement. General Eisenhower proved his point at a place called Bastogne during the Battle of the Bulge in December 1944. He flatly forbade the overly aggressive General Patton to counter-attack until he had enough forces to destroy the Germans. Gathering them took a couple of days. General Eisenhower and Omar Bradley had long since worked out that the German Army could go nowhere without capturing American supply depots. And so it was and exactly what we hoped the South African Commodore would not do. We wanted him to attack us piecemeal, to send his fast attack craft ahead whilst he followed with his frigate and the fleet replenishment ship which was much slower and had to be protected.

This was normal navy doctrine; you protect the slower vessel which then controlled the speed you could cruise to wherever you wanted to be. You have to stay close to each other. If they do that the frigate's superior search radar and optics would be neutralised. I doubted if our enemy would see through our bluff and had to wait as General Eisenhower demanded all those decades ago. The man would feel he had the Orlando trapped and a job to do and the two fast attack craft were well armed for their small size. Each had a powerful 76mm deck gun, not as new as the frigate's newer model but still effective as well as two 20mm Oerlikons with .50 heavy machine guns as backup. On a close enough range they could take care of themselves and speed is armour. Hence, they would be released and rush into our trap.

We were more worried about the frigate's twin 35mm automatic cannon than the 76mm OTA Melara cannon on all three warships. The 35mm twin gun was hard hitting. We experienced that first hand with the SAS Amatola clash and had excellent optics. In a fair duel with our smaller calibre ZU 23-2s we knew we would be in serious trouble - they outranged us. Reversely the 20mm Oerlikons on the fast attack craft were not really a fair match to our ZU 23-2s. We outranged them and were firing from prepared positions. We fancied our chances. Certainly our aiming optics were better, more modern and better calibrated than a fellow strapped into a Second World War Oerlikon.

Thermal imaging would be a further complication and much to our disadvantage. We knew that the Rooivalk attack helicopter and the frigate had scanners able to pick up heat sources from many miles away. Human beings are not that much of a problem - Africa is full of them and you cannot just shoot at them but military type trucks may be a different story. They needed to go. I decided to take the bull by the horns.

"Commodore, I want you to take the trucks away and across the border into Mozambique. Once you are there you cannot be attacked by the South African forces and will be able to come down south and meet with us or we will run to you but only in an emergency. We really want to take our heavy weapons with us and for that we need those trucks to be in perfect working order. They cannot be part of the coming battle and perhaps be damaged."

As expected, the old Commodore did not take kindly to this idea. "I say old chap, first it was Peter chasing me off my bridge and now you are chasing me to safety. This is not done old fellow. I can load a gun as good as the next man."

I doubted that but was too polite to say so. The magazines for the ZU 23-2s weighed more than what I thought he could possibly load on a continuous basis but with Pommy bastards you never know. They are a hardy breed and not to be taken lightly. The 130mm shells weigh about seventy pounds each plus the charges which were admittedly much lighter. I looked at Graeme for help and he immediately agreed that this was an excellent idea...who else could be trusted to rescue us when the time came and that settled it.

I gave the Commodore the GPS reference where the trucks should wait which was two miles inside Mozambique under fairly large trees...the only ones in the area normally more known for its flat bushes. He was not completely safe, you never knew with the South Africans and by law they did have the right to cross an international border when in hot pursuit. There was a crucial difference though, if he left before the attack there cannot be any legal justification for a hot pursuit operation against him. It was a technical point but one which would make the difference in condemnation and reparation claims at that useless liberal organisation, the United Nations.

I took the time to carefully scrutinize the beach and our hidden guns. As far as I could see and I looked really hard, everything was normal. Yes, the offloading vehicles left tyre marks on the beach but so what? Many vehicles do so even if it is illegal under South African law to drive on a beach. I knew that the incoming tide would take care of most tracks but most importantly, it would be expected that the Orlando's vehicles have left her - the vehicle ramp was down for all to see. Or perhaps she was loading vehicles. Who knew what Foxtrot would be up to? That did not bother me as much as would have a convoy of vehicles towing guns. I hoped that the three escapees hadn't reached a place where they could report us but even if they had, they only knew we were heading south. Not what we were up to.

Geelslang signalled to me that he loaded what was needed and started to drive to the guns, offloading the ammunition. A SAMIL-20 immediately approached the Orlando to load the crew's kitbags and cat which I did not know we had. I just shook my head. If only it could talk.

"Commodore, I propose that you follow the beach north. There is no river to cross and if you keep on the hard and wet surface, your tracks will be washed away in minutes. Once you reach your waypoint, turn left and go inland for one mile. The GPS will lead you but you will note the tall blue gum trees. Do not move from that spot under any circumstances but if you have to, here is the secondary rendezvous point. If we are not there by this time tomorrow, get out and get back to London. Do not attempt to cross the border into South Africa. Sir, do I have your word on this?"

"Yes Foxtrot, good luck." He turned and walked to the beach without looking back. I knew his soul was crying for his last command. He was still feeling hard done by which was typical of the man.

The men were waiting for Graeme and me at the beach. They formed a small circle around us. I have always believed in keeping the lads informed as to what we were up to and what we thought would happen. In the end such tactics lead to better results.

"Gentlemen, we have come a long way since we got the old Orlando in Djibouti Harbour a few weeks ago. We sank the SAS Amatola as we said we would and now we are going to sink another South African Navy warship or perhaps two of them." At this a few cheered and smiled knowingly, yes, if given a chance they will become legends. We did it once and hence will do it again.

"We have suffered grievously and lost too many good men during the sea battle and the subsequent ambush. Let us have a moment of silence for our brothers in arms." I bowed my head as did everyone removing their hats. It is a military thing which civilians don't get. After a minute Geelslang said "Amen" and I continued to explain what was happening now.

"The Orlando has one last purpose, to act as a sacrificial lamb. We have activated the distress beacon and we expect the enemy to investigate. They will most probably come by helicopter first and drop Special Forces onto her. The enemy has a squadron of ships approaching. According to our information and it is accurate, they have one frigate, two fast attack craft and a fleet replenishment ship. I guess that the frigate will stay far offshore because of her draft but we expect the fast attack craft to come close enough to engage them. That is what we hope will happen but as you know, they may also approach with ski-boats or just shell the Orlando to pieces from a distance."

The Commodore looked most unhappy about the last part but so it was. I continued. "I have a stratagem for that last scenario, to prevent it. As you know we captured an enemy soldier as well as the patrols long distance radio. I plan to place him, suitably tied down on the Orlando and let the enemy know he is there. That may prevent the offshore shelling but cause the first wave of soldiers landing by helicopter to rescue him and gather evidence to be used for propaganda purposes against us."

I did not feel too bad for the captured lad. Angelique only ordered me not to kill him on the spot, not to keep him alive forever. If his mates want to shell him to pieces knowing he is there, well, that is their problem. If they can

72

shoot at a clearly marked ambulance, I can use their lads as hostages. They are serving evil anyway.

"Now much will depend on what those helicopters do. We know they have an Oryx troop carrier with them and one Rooivalk attack helicopter. We expect both to arrive with the Rooivalk giving top cover. Gentlemen, I want that Rooivalk shot down more than anything else. It has the ability to kill us all. We can still run away from the warships but not from the Rooivalk."

One of the lads asked, "Foxtrot will we know when the helicopters launch?" I looked at Graeme who stepped up as expected.

"Yes and don't ask me how but thank the Silent Service next time you see them on leave." He grinned and the men grinned with him. He was a natural born pirate and men would follow him to hell and back. It was important though. We knew that a nuclear submarine was keeping the squadron under observation but did not know they would risk sending a signal once the helicopters launch. This was good news.

"The Rooivalk is armoured against the standard 23mm Warsaw Pact ammunition but I doubt, our intelligence lads say so, that it will hold out against depleted uranium shells. However, I want you to change your loads from last time. Let us have a mixture of depleted uranium, armour piercing and tracer. Leave the high explosive shells for the ships and don't be bothered for now with the Orlando. Get that Rooivalk down."

They nodded in agreement. Every gun would shoot at the Rooivalk first and the Oryx second. It was only armed with two FN Mag light machine guns and had no chance whatsoever against entrenched ZU 23-2s. Not when it was over the sea unable to duck behind a tree or hill. The moment it flew into range it was for all intents and purposes destroyed.

"Ok, I want our missileers to take a hand in this. If at all possible we will shoot missiles at both helicopters simultaneously. I want you to use the Mistral MANPAD we have and shoot two missiles at the Oryx at the same time as we open up on the Rooivalk with the guns. I expect the Oryx being unable to dodge both missiles and go down within seconds. We will get her when she is most vulnerable, that is hovering for the team to fast rope down."

"Remember lads, both helicopters have warning devices against the tracking. This should not bother us as the Mistral works with infrared homing and emits no electronic signals but they will detect the flash point of the missiles igniting and take immediate avoidance action. The good news is that we know that the Mistral has a 95% chance of hitting what you aim at even with flares deployed but lads, that is only so when aimed properly the first time round. Do not mess up here for the Rooivalk will retaliate immediately. Those of you who fired at the Oryx, you must change immediately after that to the Rooivalk no matter what. Even if the Oryx survives..." at this I smiled, it would not, "switch to the Rooivalk. Guns, note that the Rooivalk will take immediate evasive drills and probably dive down to sea level. Follow her and keep shooting."

The gun captains grinned at this. As long as she stays inside the ZU 23-2s range she would be tracked and mercilessly shot at until she is no threat to anyone. They got the picture all right.

"We have four Mistral MANPAD surface-to-air systems here but only sixteen missiles. Two will fire at the Rooivalk and two at the Oryx and after that, no matter what happens to the Oryx, all of the missiles will go after the Rooivalk. Lads, is that clear?"

They all agreed that was clear. They would shoot down the helicopters and so it was. I knew how good they were with the MILAN anti-tank rockets. Though the guns did enormous damage it was the MILAN whose pinpoint accuracy prevented the Amatola from escaping or retaliating seriously. It took out all their offensive weapon systems right in the opening sequences of the fight.

"Now once the helicopters are down the Special Forces lads will be trapped on the Orlando if they have fast roped down. They may also still be in the Oryx so keep a good lookout for them. They are as well trained as any of us and will react much quicker than how the sailors did during our last battle. You can bet your last penny they will attack us but if trapped on the Orlando I will give them a chance to surrender. If they refuse to do so I will blow up the Orlando with them and the prisoner onboard. The charges are already rigged and Major Graeme here has orders to blow the Orlando if something should happen to me. Is that clear to all? You blow that ship and the Special Forces lads on it. The Orlando is no threat unless the charges don't explode at which time we will deal with it."

Graeme chuckled good naturedly at this. He was very good and experienced with demolitions. It would blow all right. I had no doubts about that and it would be spectacular. Geelslang left two thousand pounds of ammunition in the hold for just that purpose. I hoped they would understand and surrender but doubted it. Such men don't surrender easily. It was more logical that they would either attack us or go into escape and evade mode back to the sea. Like the SEALs these men were more than comfortable in the water.

"What about us?" That was the M46 gun crew asking a bit plaintively. Up to now they were only spectators and most unhappy about it too. They knew what damage their field gun did to the Amatola and wanted to be part of the action. Their gun captain, a grizzled ex-SAS warrant officer stared at me waiting for orders. There was a lot of good natured rivalry between the crews and the men.

"I am glad to hear you ask that question. You lads and the MILAN teams, after they shoot down the helicopters with their Mistrals, will engage and sink the fast attack craft. We know the depth of the ocean here; they could come in quite close..."

"Say one mile offshore minimum before it becomes tricky" says Commodore Octavius from the side. He studied the fast attack craft details and would know to the inch how close they could get without being stranded. Even at that range it would take serious guts from their commanding officers. It was really close to the shore but if the helicopters are shot down they may throw caution to the wind. They were specially picked, like the submarine commanders, to be aggressive. They will attack and shoot back, I had no doubts.

"And we have a seventeen-mile range" remarked the gun captain. "High Explosive shells again? I noted we have fragmentation-high explosive shells in abundance. Would that work against the fast attack craft Commodore?"

"Yes, splendid old chap, splendid. The fast attack craft is not armoured and our problem would be to shoot right through them. What we want is explosions inside them. I suggest, if Major Foxtrot agrees, that the MILAN lads take their 76mm guns out as they did with the Amatola. At the same time the M46 can aim at the bridge area. Lads, it does not really matter where you hit them but the bridge is always good. They don't have missiles anymore and no close-in-weapons either to stop the MILAN missiles. They may try, I would have, with their 20mm Oerlikons but it is virtually impossible. That is why they normally operate by stealth only, at night and over the horizon."

I spoke again liking this news. "I agree completely and will switch the guns to the fast attack craft as soon as the helicopters are down. As with the Amatola I expect you to shoot and keep on shooting until I give you the order to cease fire. Do not stop shooting even if they are burning or retreating as I expect them to do. Remember we also have a captured 106mm recoilless rifle if you run out of MILAN missiles. Do you know how to work it?"

I looked at their faces. They said they knew and had already lined it up. The question was would it aim properly? We had not test fired it yet and would not until we needed it. We have to remember; it is a Korean War design and has a short range of about fifteen hundred yards. After that it is highly inaccurate. Still, they would sort that out when the time came. They would not fail.

It was an honour to serve with such men and ironic that only two of us, Geelslang and I, were genuine Egg Breakers. The rest were Graeme's lads from Sandrine, the unofficial SAS Regiment though many were former Royal Marine Special Boat Squadron lads. For political reasons it was very important that only the Egg Breakers commanded the operation. Practically I knew that Graeme or any of the senior Sandrine lads could replace me with the same results.

"There is no real need for our heavy machine guns at this range but keep them handy and if you have a shot, take it. Set it and the RPDs up to cover our front just in case the Special Forces lads storm us from the beach. Geelslang will cover our rear with a few claymore mines. We do not expect an attack from that side but you know we won't get to be grey unless we cover the basics."

Geelslang said he will place more than just a few claymores there and that was a fact. He had close to forty of the nasty weapons hidden away. I felt confident that the claymores would buy us enough time to reinforce that flank if needs be. He had a great reputation with the men, Geelslang, being much more approachable than me. I simply don't have the personality to lead a sing along as he did with Graeme backing him up.

"I need volunteers from the Orlando crew to reload the guns for us. It will be hot, dusty and dangerous and will require on the job training." I lifted my hand as most stepped forward "I also need five men to drive our vehicles across the border under command of Commodore Octavius. Once across you will wait for us to join you or we will call upon you to fetch us. There is no shame in this, it is crucial to save the vehicles or we will have to run all the way to Maputo which is a hundred miles up north - just follow the coast and keep the sea on your right shoulder."

They all laughed at this and after a while five men stepped up and gave good natured waves of goodbye to those of us remaining behind. Commodore Octavius gave Graeme a hug which must have cost both of them dearly but no one laughed. They had also seen the family resemblance. He then turned and saluted the EBS Orlando and then us who returned the honour. Then he got into his vehicle and drove off leading the way with Geelslang's armoured Kwêvoël. The three SAMIL-20s and one SAMIL-50 followed him and they made good progress across the firm wet sand. The vehicles all had permanent four-wheel drive systems (six-wheel for the Kwêvoël) and would easily cope with the conditions even with inexperienced sailors driving them. I turned to the rest of the lads now sorted into groups of gun crews and one strategic reserve of about ten men.

"Our escape plan is as follows. If we go on the run, we would cross the border into Mozambique and reach our vehicles where Commodore Octavius is waiting. The rendezvous is at..." I spelled out the GPS co-ordinates "and the back-up on that is at..." I gave the back-up GPS co-ordinates.

"You will note the first rendezvous is amongst some high trees and the second one three miles further inland. Get to that point and wait for each other. Be aware that there may be SASS patrols and they may follow you across the border. The locals will not help you and you cannot depend on the Mozambican Army to rescue you. They have an extra-ordinary fear, well deserved I can assure you, of the South Africans. In every clash during the last forty years they came off second best. They are also neutral and don't want to be involved. We don't really exist in their minds."

"Gents, if worse comes to the worse, ditch your weapons and I mean all of them. You don't want to be caught with weapons by the local police. Get yourselves to Maputo, you have your escape kit with enough money for a taxi and call this number..." Graeme took over and explained the unlikely scenario of them being chased out of the country. It was needed, such information is very important for moral. We all were trained in how to escape and evade and we know first-hand what to expect if caught. Having a well thought out escape plan was comforting to us. We knew from experience how far and fast we could run when needed and it was faster and further than most.

I continued after everyone entered the numbers in their GPS devices. "Ok, I don't believe this will be needed but if so, you know what to do. It is only a mile or two until Mozambique but I will say it again, the South Africans may be following you - they have that right under international law. Try not to do anything to embarrass our hosts. Conversely, if all goes well, and it will, we will recall the trucks, hook our guns and move out in an orderly fashion. Thereafter you will exfiltrate home or be dealt with as Major Graeme needs you. The rest of the Muslims are still entrenched in southern Africa and they still need to get thrown out by their necks. Do you have any questions lads?"

One stuck out his arm. "How are Colonel Angelique and the rest of the lads? Do we know?"

"Yes, I understand they made it safely to the airport and were airlifted to a French Military Hospital where they are being treated. There were no further casualties or deaths. Thank you for asking, our twins are also fine."

A cheer went up when they heard this. Many quietly approached me to raise their anger at the idea of shooting at an ambulance with a pregnant woman inside. It was the older lads who had kids themselves who were the most upset. Welcome to my world lads. We have no rules but one and that is to win, each and every time.

"Are we clear? I will use the same gun commands as on the Orlando. That is 'A' 'B' & 'C' for the ZU 23-2s and the M46 will be 'D' as always. The MILAN lads, whether you fire your Mistrals or your 106mm will be called MILAN or Mike to hide what you are. Keep the radio waves open and wait for my command to shoot. I say again, do not stop shooting unless ordered by me to do so. If I should become incapacitated Geelslang will take over and after him Major Graeme and after that you better be running for the border."

They laughed as I expected and left for their gun positions. Soon everything was as quiet and peaceful as it was when we arrived. Only now the Orlando was lying sadly awaiting her fate. I walked with Geelslang to the wounded prisoner who was in a much better condition than how we found him yesterday. He was a very fit lad to begin with and responded well to our expert medical treatment. I spoke in Afrikaans.

"Kyk hier my ou, ek het belowe om jou veilig te hou en te oorhandig aan jou eie mense. Ek is 'n man van my woord. Sien jy daai skip? Ek gaan jou op hom los. Vasgemaak maar in goeie kondisie. Ek is seker jou maats sal jou kom red. Het jy enigiets nodig voor ons jou skuif?" (Look here, my man, I promised to keep you safe and to hand you over to your own people. I'm a man of my word. Do you see that ship? I am going to leave you on it. Tied but in good condition. I'm sure your friends will come and save you. Do you need anything before we move you?)

He just stared at me with something between hatred and admiration in his eyes and shook his head. He would know that both Geelslang and I were seconded to his unit before he even finished grade one. We had excellent reputations as operators then and now. He did not trust us an inch and believed his orders that we were wanted right-wing terrorists who blew up two submarines, one frigate and assassinated or murdered many others including members of his unit. Still we did not kill him outright and Angelique saved him by ordering us to let him go in peace. This was not what he expected. We were a bit of a puzzle to him as were the other Pommy bastards we commanded. There were quite a few black men amongst them besides Geelslang who was a Zulu. This did not bode well for any far right-wing racist theories. Likewise, it takes a good fighting man to recognise another and at least we had earned that kind of respect.

I nodded to the men. "Ok bring him with" and started walking towards the EBS Orlando.

They picked him up and carried him to the Orlando where we made him quite comfortable in the captain's cabin. It was big and airy and he had a water basin next to him. We also left enough food to keep him fed for a week but chained his uninjured leg to the bed, locking it with a rather large chain and padlock we found in the bosun's store.

"Die sleutel vir die slot is op die brug bo-op die kaptein se stoel. Jy kan die water drink, dis veilig en die kos, soos jy sien, kom uit geseelde blikke wat voor jou oopgemaak is. Ons sal nie weer ontmoet nie maar sterkte en ek hoop alles werk uit vir jou. Jou mense is reeds laat weet waar jy is en ek verwag hulle binne ure hier. Totsiens." (The key for that padlock is on the bridge on top of the captain's chair. You can drink the water, it's safe and the food, as you have seen, comes from sealed cans that were opened in front of you. We will not meet again, but good luck and I hope everything works out for you. Your people have been told where you are and I expect them here within hours. Goodbye.)

I turned my back and stopped in the door when I heard him say something. "Majoor, dra asseblief my waardering aan Kolonel Angelique oor en waarsku haar ons sal nooit ophou solank die eliminasie opdrag geldig is nie. Sy is nogsteeds nie veilig nie." (Major, please convey my gratitude to Colonel Angelique and warn her that we will never stop as long as the TWEP order is valid. She's still not safe.) He looked at me as if he wanted to say more but the words never came.

"Ek sal so maak...wees rustig...ons verstaan hoe dit werk. Hierdie oorlog was nie ons keuse nie en jy moet miskien mooi gaan dink oor wat hier aangaan. Moenie dieselfde foute maak wat ons onder Apartheid gemaak het

82

nie. Tot later dan." (I will do so ... take it easy ... we understand how the process works. This war was not ours by choice and you should perhaps take a good look at what is going on here. Do not make the same mistakes that we have made under Apartheid. Until later then.)

I suppose I could have explained better. That we too followed orders under the old regime and never questioned it. After all, our reverends, teachers, parents and everyone else assured us many times we were right and that communism had to be stopped. These days it sounds so stupid but that was how it was then. We believed. So we kept on fighting a war which should never have started in the first place. No TWEP order could ever be legal; it was murder as no judicial oversight took place. In fact, there is no legitimate death penalty in the new South Africa and ordering a person murdered is as illegal as it gets. I knew from bitter experience how the system worked. By following our orders blindly meant that we were easily betrayed by our so-called leaders who could not run for pensions fast enough once the end came. But then again, I had no time to give a history lesson and simply walked away before he realised he was being used as bait.

It was time to put the second part of our maskirovka in place. I winked at Geelslang and picked up the microphone of the captured SASS radio. It was still, against all regulations, at the pre-set frequency. I knew that if I press the microphone it will also send a signal of our whereabouts. In fact, I was counting on it and had it mounted on top of the forecastle so they could get an exact fix. We wanted to be found.

"Speskop, this is Foxtrot."

Speskop was the name of the Special Forces Headquarters in Swartkop Park nature reserve outside Pretoria. That is where all Special Forces operations are planned and controlled from. Obviously in this operation the final say would be at SASS Headquarters a few miles to the north east but I thought it logical that the patrols would report to their own first and SASS second.

Foxtrot, this is Speskop, go ahead."

The reply came quickly which was impressive. We were just over four hundred miles away and had the eleven thousand feet Drakensberg mountain range between us. I supposed the signal bounced off the stratosphere and back to earth again. South Africa was and is a world leader in military radios and has been since the middle seventies.

"Speskop, I have one of your operators. He is wounded and waiting for you to fetch him at the following co-ordinates. Are you ready to copy down?"

"Foxtrot, this is Speskop, go ahead."

These lads were obviously either expecting the call or used to people breaking into their radio networks. Of course, the escapees would have reported the missing radio and hence headquarters would have monitored it whilst switching all other operations away from it. It is standard procedure and expected of me to contact them. I have done so before on captured frequencies.

"Speskop, your lad is on the EBS Orlando which is beached at 26869291 latitude & 32887331 longitude. He is tied down in the captain's cabin with enough food and water to last a couple of days. Note the captain's cabin is below the bridge. His wounds are treated and he is in no immediate danger but the wounds are multiples."

"Foxtrot, this is Yankee Two Zero."

Yankee Two Zero was my old mate from the Ukuthula Ranch attack, now a brigadier in the Army; we last saw each other when he took a pot shot at me

84

near the Simonstad Naval Base. This was no problem to me, I tried to kill him too but he was clever enough to disappear from view. Next time I hoped to do rather better.

"Go ahead Yankee Two Zero."

I needed to hear this but I knew he was trying to keep me on the air. There was no technical need for that but old habits die hard.

"Foxtrot, thank you and we will meet again. We will take care of our lad in due course. Do you have any other messages?"

"Yankee Two Zero, I hope so and have indeed another message for your superiors."

"Go ahead Foxtrot; we will relay your message to them."

"Foxtrot to your superiors, Mrs Dawson (Angelique's SASS name) sends her regards. From me, fuck you and better luck next time. We are coming south to sort you out. Be prepared to meet your forefathers soon."

"That is copied Foxtrot and will be relayed. To what effect I have no idea but you will soon find out. Yankee Two Zero out."

Perhaps he did not want to keep me on the air after all. I grinned at Geelslang and Graeme who were tugging at my sleeve. I like playing mind games with my enemies. I know the mere threat of me coming down south will keep them under lock and key for months. They were not brave during the bush war and were certainly not now as they got obese from eating too much.

Graeme spoke urgently. "We have confirmation Foxtrot, the Rooivalk and Oryx took off forty-three seconds ago and are twenty-seven minutes away at cruising speed. They will arrive, unless they change course and if so, we will know, from the south east."

He pointed but nothing was in sight yet. Still, we took off at a mad rush for the dunes. I prayed that my plans would work. If not, we would be dead.

*"Then Asa called to the Lord his God and said, "Lord, there is no one like you to help the powerless against the mighty. Help us, Lord our God, for we rely on you, and in your name we have come against this vast army. Lord, you are our God; do not let mere mortals prevail against you."* 2 Chronicles 14 v 11*

## Chapter 2

### Beach just south of Mozambique, 25 February 2014, 16h08

I believe that the South Africans made a huge mistake in how they select their attack helicopter pilots. Unlike the British Army and the Americans, the attack helicopter pilots were Air Force men. They had no specialist infantry training or outlook and hence simply did not think as infantrymen. This was a major disadvantage when fighting ground forces. They are not able to figure us or the deception out until it is too late. If I was piloting those helicopters, I would have arrived from the west. That is from the rear of or landward side and not from the sea. They might have survived then, as the chances were good that they would have spotted the guns, although that is not for certain either. We did camouflage them thoroughly and knew better than to move with a helicopter circling around. As long as you don't move and they don't use thermal imaging you have a good chance of not being spotted. It also helps if you have a known "pirate vessel" nearby attracting all the attention. Ironically, nothing prevented them from taking that route; they had enough fuel and could land anywhere if they ran low. However, they did not and betrayed their lack of operational experience by taking the most direct route to the Orlando. It was also obvious to me that Graeme's submarine was tracking them constantly on radar or perhaps even visually. The attack boat skipper had balls of steel. Under any other condition they would have slipped away quietly under the waves and left us to our fate. I realised again that the new lot down south had no real comprehension on what power the West had available. It was beyond their comprehension. Whatever, they were about to find out what strategic initiatives really mean.

Once again Geelslang spotted them first. He had eyes like a hawk and could see better than any man I know. The three of us, Graeme to his right, were lying on top of a dune, hidden under a bush and slightly behind the guns. This was our command post and gave us a decent view over the Orlando and into the crystal-clear waters of the Indian Ocean. The lads formed a protracted battle line below us, about three hundred yards from end to end starting with the M46 130mm field gun to the north or closest to Mozambique. We placed the field gun there because we did not expect a land attack from that side but could perceivably be attacked from the South African side, or southern end of our line. Hence a fast firing ZU 23-2 was placed on the southernmost end of the line. This was gun "C for Charlie" as we called her crew when still on the Orlando. If needs be, she could be turned south and defend the line from any attack. Next to her, moving northwards towards the M46 (called "D for Delta") was "B for Bravo" gun and then "A for Alfa" gun almost in front of us.

The MILAN lads were stuck between "B" and "A" guns but behind them high up on a dune which luckily had quite a few bushes which they used to great effect for camouflage. They asked to be placed there so that the missiles have time to arm as we were a bit too close to the Orlando where we expected the helicopters to hover. Furthermore, with the missiles scanning down towards the cooler sea water; a solid infrared lock on the warm engines was guaranteed. That made sense to me and so they established themselves about sixty yards to my left and rear.

In a way our ambush line reminded me of the old Zulu war tactic of forming a buffalo horn formation. The older more experienced (and less fit) warriors were left in the middle engaging the enemy first. They would draw them in and into the ambush. The younger men formed the points of the horn and those regiments would surround the enemy with rapid flanking movements.

A Zulu regiment, or Impi, is able to move many miles a day and is the second most frightening sight in the world. You would struggle to escape an advancing Zulu Impi even when on horseback. They are known to run down cavalry formations. From thereon, once surrounded, it was the end of their foe as they moved in with their short assegais and slayed everyone in sight.

In many ways this tactic was followed by great military commanders during the Second World War and even during the First Iraq War. The tanks would race around the flanks to cut the enemy off, forming a cauldron from which few escaped. The Falaise Pocket in Normandy, August 1944, is the classic example of this method. In military terms it is known as the "strategy of indirect approach" made famous by Heinz Guderian and much lesser so, by the Pommy, Basil Liddle-Hart. Naturally, here we had a coastline and a ship to be covered by our guns - our choices were limited but we stretched the flanks as far as we deemed necessary to prevent mass casualties and to give each gun a clean field of fire. This would prove important as the battle progressed.

I left the headquarters reserve, about ten men and the medics, behind the second landward dune to warn us of any attack from the rear. I did not actually expect the enemy to be able to launch one this quickly but took no chances. You never know and I heard later that they wanted to drop paratroopers behind us and between us and the Mozambican border to lie in wait for another ambush. How they would have done that without us seeing them floating down, I don't know, but cutting off escape routes are normal counter-insurgency tactics. Fortunately for them, they had to fly a good seven hundred miles to get to us and that took much longer than what they had. The Hercules transport aircraft were not immediately available either being based in Waterkloof Air Force Base, Pretoria, a good three hundred miles away from the elite Parachute Battalions in Tempe, Bloemfontein. Many, about half their fleet was anyway not in South Africa but supporting the Africa Nations troops in the Congo and other places. Boris made good money flying such missions before the Gripen incident when he smuggled Angelique and me out of South Africa. (See Code Name VFO565).

The paratroopers are the finest light infantry once on the ground and had an enviable reputation, well deserved, for toughness. During the bush war they were the first choice to serve as fire forces and did excellent work. Getting on the ground may have been their problem here if they had attempted that drop. We were well equipped to shoot slow transports like a C130 Hercules down and would have done so. But the fact is the drop never took place. It was one of those "what if" discussions done over the barbecue fire years after the actual event. The country not being on a war footing was simply too slow to mobilise. In my own view, as commander of the opposing ground forces, they would have been wiped out and would not have been able to stop us from reaching safety. The ZU 23-2s, when used against infantry, are deadly.

In the old days it would not have been that easy for us. The crack South African Police Counter-Insurgency Units had bases not too far away and could have been on the scene within a few hours and most probably much quicker. They were armed with normal infantry weapons and their highly mobile Casspirs which they knew how to deploy most effectively. However, I believe that we would have destroyed them too; we had heavy weapons which they did not have. That is once we were entrenched. On the other hand, they would not have stormed us directly but ambushed us on the way back to the border or just after crossing it for they would have known where we were. Their delaying actions might have caused us considerable casualties. Happily, this was also a "what if" scenario because the new lot, in their great fear (not wisdom, fear) sold all Police Casspirs and made sure that the new breed could not perform such tasks. It was a very dumb move.

The last factor was the South African Air Force. They could scramble ground attack aircraft. The Air Force Base Hoedspruit was only three hundred miles away but they had a problem, to get to us they would have had to fly through Swaziland or Mozambican airspace. A violation which would have been protested if nothing else, therefore the actual route was almost double that distance. We were not too worried about the Air Force being able to react quickly enough or able to hit us with rockets and cannon fire. Not with us being a few miles from safety and having the means to defend ourselves. That is why I chose this spot. We were ready.

"Foxtrot to all, radio check. From Delta downwards please."

"Delta, five."

"Charlie, five."

"Bravo, five."

"Alfa, five."

"Mike, five"

The last was the MILAN team behind us using the call sign "Mike." We were using the individual radios that each man carried. Signalling would not be a problem for us. Five means the signal is clear, perfect in fact. Nor would the radios be intercepted many miles away. They were designed for close-in work between members of a patrol and not for longer distances. It is a basic security function.

Geelslang nudged me and I saw them for the first time. "Foxtrot to all. Enemy is in sight to our right. There are two helicopters; the Rooivalk is on our left and slightly above the Oryx. All guns and Mike...you are authorised to track them visually but not to shoot. Let them come closer, lads."

The Mistral MANPAD had a maximum range of 4 miles and the missiles were able to travel at 930 meters per second when at full speed. Such speeds are as fast as some bullets and they can also pull ten times more g's in manoeuvres than any human pilot can. Of course, this only happens after igniting them about forty yards in front of the missileer and they won't last forever. I would find out in a minute or two how it feels to be close to where the missile ignites - something I am afraid we did not think of but so it is. We all make mistakes and learn from them if lucky enough to survive. Experience is always a bitch which is hard to please. Next time I will remember to keep the missiles well away from me.

The helicopters were approaching steadily and were now about a mile away. The Rooivalk suddenly started to climb which slowed her down. The big Oryx approached flying fast but low, just a few feet above the water. She was painted in the standard South African Air Force colours, meaning camouflage but had no markings which I could see. This was another indication they wanted to use her for clandestine operations against the Egg Breakers. Why else would they remove the new lot's jockstrap flag? Superficially at least she still looked like a Puma and the camouflage made her really stand out over the water.

The Rooivalk was in its usual camouflage with the jockstrap flag at the tail. Its origins cannot be hidden; no other Air Force in the world had them since the Americans made the deal to buy their overrated Apache subject to other aid and weapons systems. It was a plain and simple old-fashioned Yankee blackmail which cost the British Army the Rooivalk deal back in the 1990s and hundreds in South Africa lucrative jobs. The Yanks made it clear that unless they bought the Apache, they would not get submarine and aircraft carrier technology later on.

The Pommies improved the Apache substantially by fitting home-grown Rolls Royce engines. In Afghanistan the American made Apaches had to ditch their optics mast because their engines were too underpowered for the high altitudes. The Royal Air Force had no such problems and an immense advantage because of it. It is also notable, as Graeme once said; that only the American made Apaches were shot down over Iraq and Afghanistan. Would the South African made Rooivalk have done better? Who knows? It would have been substantially cheaper though and had the same weapons systems.

The Oryx was a South African improvement of the old French made Puma transport helicopter. It had uprated engines, navigational equipment and most importantly, filters to defuse dust and a lower heat signature. When configured to the troop carrying role, as this one was, it could carry up to twenty armed troops. Her side doors were open and the Special Forces men were sitting on the floor with their legs dangling outside. That was the way we did it as well and it was a wonderful feeling as the trees rushed by a few feet below you. The rest would be standing behind the lads in the door. The thick ropes were already fastened to the side. The crew only had to throw the ropes out and seconds later the men would be on the Orlando as they fast roped down. Flying that low in the water gave me an idea to be implemented immediately. We would change our tactics. I had enough confidence in the lads to know they would respond magnificently. The decision took less than a second to make.

"Foxtrot to Mike and Bravo, change of plan. All the Mistrals switch to the Rooivalk. Bravo Gun, when that Oryx flares to offload the Special Forces team; you shoot it in the belly and keep on shooting until it is destroyed. The rest of your guns concentrate on the Rooivalk. Mike and Bravo, acknowledge."

"Bravo affirmative."

"Mike affirmative."

The Oryx was now less than two hundred yards away from the Orlando which made it approximately three hundred yards from us. The Rooivalk was behind her climbing to about a thousand feet, probably to get a good look and to be able to dive down giving covering fire if needs be. Thus far everything was according to plan. They were operating as expected following the manual.

It was time. The Oryx suddenly popped up, her engines screaming for more power. She was flaring just above the Orlando to lose speed before going into a hover and the ropes (they have weights at the end to uncurl) went out of the doors. They would be down in seconds. I unleashed hell.

"Foxtrot to all guns and Mike. All guns and missiles are free; guns are free...shoot shoot shoot!"

The last part of the sentence was drowned out as the Bravo gun opened up with a steady stream of tracer rounds right into the exposed belly of the Oryx. The crew had no chance and the aircraft emitted flashes of orange fire balls as the shells hit it. They tried to weave to the left but the tracers

94

followed them thudding home all the time causing enormous damage. A few men were thrown out of her or perhaps they jumped as I would have done no matter what the height. I saw them falling or rather tumbling in slow-motion. She slowly lifted into the air in a final attempt to get away before crashing down hard on the fore deck of the Orlando where she exploded into a huge fireball. The tracers then stopped for a second as they acquired the Rooivalk and started again.

By this time the Mistrals had launched with a very loud whoosh noise and were flying over our heads. I noted after my initial surprise when they ignited in front of me, that they were not fired as a salvo but with one second breaks in between. I heard and saw the flashes as they ignited one after the other streaking towards the Rooivalk. When I asked the lads about the time delay, they explained that the Mistrals would then arrive at the same rate making it impossible to dodge them all as they all had a solid lock to begin with. They had practised this technique, which they said was unique to the French Army, in simulators many times before and it always worked.

Whether that was unique or not it was a most impressive sight as they raced towards the Rooivalk one by one. For a while it looked like they would overtake the tracers from Alfa and Charlie ZU 23-2s who were firing short bursts arching towards the Rooivalk. The missiles and the shells were merging in a deadly laser type display which was awesome to watch. Then the third stream of tracers joined the fray from Bravo gun. Even in daylight the bright green tracer rounds could easily be seen looking deceptively lazy but in fact travelling at close to the speed of sound. There was nothing except a major miracle that could save the Rooivalk.

I will tell you this, only the very best pilots qualify for attack helicopter gunships and these lads were not slow to react. In the few seconds they had before the Mistrals arrived, they dropped like a stone to the sea and were hidden behind a mass of flares which may have been released automatically for no human being can react that quickly. It was still pumping the flares out when the first Mistral hit. They also opened fire on us with their 20mm chin gun but not too accurately as there simply was not enough time to aim properly. By our count they got a single burst off before plunging into the sea. I suppose it was more of a desperate attempt to distract the gunners and keep our heads down for them to escape. Yet, they were up against experienced professionals who knew they had one chance and one chance only. The weight of shells going towards the enemy always equals the same weight in armour. The lads kept on shooting as they did with the Amatola ten days before. The surprise factor once again worked in our favour. I vaguely wondered how long it would take them to understand what they were up against and realise we wrote their manual many years ago. We knew what they were going to do before they even did it.

Geelslang later confirmed my impression that it was like a super imposed video game with the missiles streaking past or at least keeping up with the 23mm shells. They were making clear white contour trails through the sea air and were easy to follow with the naked eye. I willed the missiles on for what seemed to me like ages but in reality, was only seconds. Each one worked as designed. They exploded one after the other with bright white flashes that we could clearly hear above the roar of the ZU 23-2s.

The missileers later disputed amongst themselves exactly what took place. Each claimed his missile hit first, obviously, but the general agreement was that the first two Mistrals scored a solid hit somewhere in the vicinity of the Rooivalk's engines or port engine anyway. They knew that because a long

96

orange flame emerged at the back as the engine destroyed itself. Some claimed they heard the starboard engine increasing power to compensate but that was impossible and fancy thinking. It would have done so, no doubt, as the engine management computers do it automatically but it could not have been heard with all the noise.

Whatever happened, the Rooivalk never really recovered from the self-imposed dive or rather never had a chance to do so. It just kept on going down. I am convinced that the dive was initiated by the pilot for it was too fast for anything else. It was a power dive, not a drop from the sky.

The next two mistrals exploded by the proximity fuse and the shrapnel seriously damaged the hydraulic pipelines. The Rooivalk started to emit grey smoke which drifted in the air afterwards smelling something awful. We also saw the many smaller holes in the fuselage when inspecting it afterwards and made our deductions on what happened. At the same time the 23mm shells hammered into the canopy area killing the pilots outright - we found their bodies still strapped in their seats. They died instantly before they hit the water and could not have suffered much. As anticipated the depleted uranium shells punched large holes through the armour. You could put your fist in some of them. Our theory was correct.

The ZU 23-2s did not cease fire when the Rooivalk hit the sea with an almighty splash. The sea was less than three feet deep at that point so it did not sink but stayed upright for a short while. Because of the shallow beach water, the top part and most of the helicopter stuck out while its rotors were still spinning madly. We fired no further Mistrals but the 23mm shells kept hammering into the now immobile Rooivalk. I quickly grasped that it was only the water preventing it from exploding and it presented no further threat. At this very moment the first MILAN anti-tank missile struck it just below the rotors and that was the end of the rotors which blew complete off hurling to all sides including us. Perceptibly Mike Team dropped the Mistral launchers and grabbed the MILAN for the coup de grace. My respect for them and the MILAN system grew anew. It was done in seconds and without any orders from me. They knew what had to be done and did so efficiently.

"Foxtrot to all. Cease fire, cease fire. Helicopters are destroyed." I shouted into the microphone.

The engagement took less than two minutes and was the first Rooivalk to be shot down by enemy fire but not the last. Next time it would be much more difficult for they never operated alone ever again. Next time they would be a lot more aggressive and dangerous.

The sudden silence was deafening. I stood up and gazed almost in wonder at the scene in front of me. The Rooivalk was smoking a hundred and fifty yards away with the lower half three feet under water. The rest including the canopy was sticking out but there was no sign of life and the engines were silent. They must have been either shot out or the water drowned them or something. It was a surreal sight against the peaceful turquoise Indian Ocean and white beach in front of us. The spray glinting of the broken canopy glass and fuel was leaking out forming a pool around the stricken attack helicopter. It could be smelled a fair distance away.

The Oryx was gone. Nothing was left of her after the explosion but there were bodies in the water. A few were swimming towards land or me. This was a problem for they could and would start shooting. No Special Forces lad would take such an insult of being shot down without any warning, lying down. The survivors immediately opened fire on me and Angelique came very close to being a widow again. What saved me were a couple of contributing factors. First Geelslang angrily reached up and pulled me violently down and away from the bullets. I lost my footing and rolled down the dune to safety. I heard Graeme shooting back with his L85 Individual Weapon. Then all the RPD light machine guns and the ZU 23-2s opened up. That was that for the survivors. They had no cover and died bravely before they even reached the beach. Their blood floated in with the waves and mixed with the white sand. It reminded me of pictures I saw of D-Day. Not a pleasant sight.

When I finally reached the bottom of the dune, I was a bit more careful and took a running dive for cover much to the amusement of Graeme and those who saw it. The danger from the enemy soldiers was already gone and my actions a bit unnecessary but I did not know that. All I remembered was the bullets swishing past me. Still we had no peace for at that moment the M46 boomed across the beach for the first time. The sound echoed all along the shore. They were firing at the first fast attack craft one and a half miles away. And the fast attack craft was firing back furiously. Her 76mm gun was spurting flame every few seconds as they returned fire. Obviously, this fight was only half won. They saw the carnage and decided to take remedial action.

It is not a negligible shell, that of the 76mm OTA Melara. It fires a twenty-seven-pound high explosive shell for many miles and at a fast rate too. Fortunately, the fast attack craft had the older versions of the famous Italian naval gun. Their optics controlling it was also not really up to scratch or perhaps we were just lucky but they missed us completely with those first salvos.

Well perhaps saying they missed us is not quite true. They were aiming at the Orlando and the shells fell around her. I figured out later they probably had the gun already aimed at her and simply opened up when the helicopters got shot down. The ships positively looked sinister with their black radar absorbent paint and covered in grey smoke. Every gun on those fast attack craft from the 76mm to the two 20mm Oerlikons were firing nonstop and where they missed the Orlando the shells thudded into the dune around us. This was getting dangerous and uncalled for. I remembered the Commodore saying they could approach to about one mile before it would become tricky for them.

"Foxtrot to Alfa and Bravo and MILAN. Open fire on that fast attack craft closest to us. MILAN and Charlie on the second one, shoot at will."

I said it as calmly as I could. It was not really necessary for the guns were already arching their tracers towards the closest fast attack craft. The MILAN lads, as wide awake and professional as ever were also tracking it and soon a MILAN crashed into the 76mm deck gun destroying its working parts. As a precision weapon the MILAN really had no equal and could stop a main battle tank at that distance. The unarmoured gun turret had no chance but of course, the MILAN could not actually sink a ship. Not even a smallish one like a fast attack craft which is only 450 odd tons fully loaded. But it could delay and hurt them and did.

The first fast attack craft were in trouble though for the first 130mm shell hit it squarely on the bridge area and exploded inside the superstructure. It went out of control with black smoke coming out of the numerous holes caused by the ZU 23-2s who were hammering away in short bursts. The heavy M46 shells were exploding time and time again against the ship leaving dark brown clouds of cordite all around her. There was no doubt that she was in deep trouble and then it got worse, she ran aground and became motionless.

Being stationary in any gun duel is probably the last thing you want. You need to keep on moving for speed is armour. As long as you can move you can duck and dive and swing to make life difficult for the opposing gunners. Once the fast attack craft was stranded it was beyond help. The M46 shells slammed repeatedly into her and the 23mm shells hosed her from side to side destroying the fire control radar domes and everything else. The only logical thing left to do was to abandon ship and her crew started to dive overboard swimming towards the second fast attack craft that incredibly came to a dead stop to pick them up.

I admire bravery as much as the next man and rescuing their sister ship was a brave act. It was also foolish for now we switched all guns and everything we had onto her. She tried desperately to hide behind the first attack craft but could not. The placement of our guns was now coming into its own leaving a clear line of fire for the M46 and the two southernmost ZU 23-2s. She too was soon burning furiously and foundering about four hundred yards away from the first wreck. As with her sister ship she was now stationary, drifting and burning and awash. With her flags still flying she went under the water with a huge cloud of steam raising into the air. The water was reasonably deep there, according to Commodore Octavius, more than six hundred feet. There would be no real chance of salvage.

I gave the order to cease fire when I saw the bright orange life rafts deploying and men jumping into it and overboard a few minutes before. Luckily for them the wind was blowing them away from the shore and into the ocean away from us. Presumably they would be rescued by the still approaching frigate and fleet replenishment ship. They were not yet in sight though.

"Graeme, how far is the frigate away?" I shouted across to him as he walked down with his Individual Weapon held loosely in his hand.

"Ninety minutes Foxtrot." They were far enough away to not bother us. Just to make sure the sailors were picked up I contacted Yankee Two Zero again. I wanted to needle them into a state of mind where they would act illogically. Those sailors would talk and be the best propaganda we could possibly have.

"Yankee Two Zero, go ahead."

"This is Foxtrot; note that we sank two fast attack craft at the same location as where the Orlando is. There are a few crew survivors floating towards Madagascar in life rafts. You are advised to start search and rescue directly."

"Yankee Two Zero, copied. Where are my men?"

"Foxtrot, the wounded prisoner is still on the Orlando but since your navy decided to shell the ship, I have no idea on his status. The assault team died when their Oryx was shot down. You can police the scene yourself. As far as I can see there were no survivors."

"Yankee Two Zero, copied. We will meet again."

He sounded angry and upset as he well should have been. This was the second time I told him his men died under my guns.

"Foxtrot, for your sake I hope not. Out."

I turned to Graeme standing next to me. He was looking at me curiously for we were speaking in rapid Afrikaans and he could not follow it. He knew a few Afrikaans words, mostly insulting ones used to describe him like

"Rooinek and uitlander." I explained briefly and asked him to get the Commodore back so we can hook up our guns and they can leave the battlefield before the Air Force arrives. They also needed to disarm and remove the claymores. We had need for them in the future.

"Oi and where are you going then?"

He looked at me with a raised eyebrow field officers use when talking to a wayward marine who made a move on the Colonel's Lady the night before. It conveyed so much that it was worth copying.

"Geelslang and I are swimming out to the stranded fast attack craft to seize the code books if they remained intact. Thereafter we will meet with you here, it won't take long. We can all move out together but don't waste time. I am sure that the latest insult will lead to desperate counter moves. And once inside Mozambique we need to move and keep on moving. Remember the vehicles must be refuelled in Ponto do Oro first."

I replied rapidly for I was in a hurry. The frigate was approaching and I did not know what the Air Force would do after the latest insult.

"Ok but I suggest you take a few men with you Foxtrot. You never know what remained alive on the ship."

He called a few lads by name, they have served together in the Royal Marines and off we went. It was not much of a swim; in fact, we walked mostly through thigh high water until the last hundred yards when swimming became more profitable. We were in a hurry though and wasted no time but the swim was enjoyable after the heat of the day. I hoped no sharks were around.

The fast attack craft, I could see her name was "Isaac Dyobha" when we got close, was lying less than a mile offshore. She was named after a chaplain in the Native Labour Corps who died during the sinking of the troopship SS Mendi in 1917. He was not alone, 646 other men including 607 black South African soldiers died with him that day. The ship was cut in two by another vessel. There was heavy fog and the other ship, the SS Daro, cowardly, kept on steaming leaving the men to die. A Royal Navy destroyer, HMS Brisk, did its best to rescue the men but it was too late for most of them. You have to remember the dying men were almost all black and volunteers. Most of them could not swim and knew death was coming when standing on the tilting decks. They were far from home, close to Le Havre in France and decided to die like men. What happened next is the stuff of legends which men still talk about in awe when the incident is discussed.

The Reverend Dyobha is a hero to me and many others. His prayer or words, some say it was a prayer, is very famous among South African military men. As they were dying, he roared to his flock: "Be quiet and calm, my countrymen. What is happening now is what you came to do...you are going to die, but that is what you came to do. Brothers, we are drilling the death drill. I, a Xhosa (man), say you are my brothers...Swazis, Pondos, Basotho...so let us die like brothers. We are the sons of Africa. Raise your war-cries, brothers, for though they made us leave our assegais in the kraal, our voices are left with our bodies." And so it was, they died with great dignity for the English King in the hope of getting a better dispensation at home. Many are buried in England where the war graves are still kept neat and tidy as can be expected from the Pommies. Such acts of kindness are noted by warriors. It took decades, up to 1995 before this act of bravery was officially recognised and today we have the Order of Mendi for exceptional bravery. For the new lot that probably means to be able to resist a bribe for longer than ten minutes but for military men it means a lot in terms of leadership. His words became widely known as the "death drill." It was ironic in the extreme that the current flagship of the squadron from which they detached to hunt us down was the SAS Mendi, a new Valour Class frigate. She was still too far away to play a role but would later rescue many of the survivors and prove to be a difficult customer.

The Isaac Dyobha is not by any means a big ship but swimming in the seven feet of water in which it ran aground it certainly looked formidable with the sides towering ten feet and more above us. I was scratching my head wondering what to do when one of Graeme's lads started to pull himself up against a rope hanging by the side. He was a fit lad; broad shouldered and went up that rope like a monkey. We were impressed but then he was at least twenty years younger than Geelslang and me. Still, there was no way in this world we would admit to being old and over the hill so we busted our lungs but got onto the deck a short while later. That was where I decided that the life of a farmer would suit me better. In my youth I climbed ropes ten times higher for fun but this one was tougher or perhaps it was just age. I was wheezing a fair bit. Geelslang also suffered. He still had his multiple wounds which he got during the Amatola battle ten days earlier. Some of the stitches tore loose during that climb but it could not be helped.

The four Royal Marines with us were used to such things as boarding ships. To them this was no big deal and waited rather impatiently for us. Then they spread out and formed buddy teams moving directly towards the bridge with their Individual Weapons ready. Geelslang and I followed rather more slowly. It was in shambles. The M46 shells weigh seventy pounds each and exploded inside the vessel which was not a big vessel to begin with. There were fist size holes made by the fast firing ZU 23-2s everywhere. I was not surprised to see numerous bodies lying in grotesque positions where they died. It was carnage.

"They were not ready for us, it is tragic."

As usual it was Geelslang who noted the finer details first and pointed to the upper torso of one body. His deep voice sounded strangely out of place, as if we were disturbing the departed. It was uncanny and gave me cold shivers.

"Yes, I see, this was bad leadership, they were not at action stations." I replied knowingly and a bit disgusted myself. This was not what we expected.

When a warship goes in battle a few things happen. First, they close all the watertight doors to ensure that no flash fires could take place and flooding kept localised. The lads down in the magazines know that the magazines will be flooded if any danger exists of them blowing up. In many cases, it is known from the survivor accounts, they flooded the magazines with themselves inside it to protect their ship. I have no doubt I don't have the guts to do so, it takes a braver man than me. I would leave first or prefer the quick death of an explosion above that of drowning.

During battle, all sailors wear a flash proof hood designed to give some protection (it is more psychological) against burn and fire. Lastly, they hoist a battle flag that is much larger than any standard flag. These lads were not wearing their hoods. It meant they did not expect trouble or at least, were not at battle stations. Though it would not have made any difference in the end it angered Geelslang who was the ultimate professional warrior. He lived by the rulebook when it came to certain things and this was one of them. Every available tool and piece of equipment designed to protect your men's lives should be utilised in his book. It was perhaps a good thing that we found the captain dead a few short steps further. Well, we deducted it was the captain since he wore the two and a half stripes of a navy lieutenant commander who normally commands such vessels. His head was shot off though.

We finally reached the bridge or what was left of it. The radio room was just behind it. The codebooks were in a massive safe and the safe was locked. Next to the chart table we found a young officer and searched his body for the keys. It was not on him. We searched the captain downstairs and it was not on him either.

"Do you have any ideas?" I asked Geelslang who was the smarter one between the two of us.

Time was an issue here. We could not afford to stay much longer for the vehicles were already returning and hooking up the guns. The frigate was also approaching, cautiously but coming hard. We had to get done or leave empty handed.

Geelslang gave me a look of pity and knelt down to place the plastic explosives he brought with him on the hinges and around the lock. "Yes Foxtrot, you just stand there and watch me blow this safe open. Unquestionably they would then know that we stole the codebooks but that cannot be helped."

"Why not destroy her completely afterwards? We can rig the remaining fuel tanks; she operated on diesel did she not? Start a bonny fire and all that. There is no one here who would mind."

I looked at the grinning Marine and nodded in agreement. That made sense, burn her down and hope no one notices the safe was blown.

"Do you need anything to implement your idea?" I asked quickly.

"No sir, you just stand there and watch me burn this ship to the waterline now."

He had a typical Welsh accent I would normally look down on. We don't like Pommies but this one was different. I must have gone soft being in their company for a month. He was a corporal in Graeme's platoon at one stage before Sandrine offered him better prospects for adventure. A natural leader and always polite though the "sir" part meant nothing in itself...a Royal Marine will call a tree "sir" if it moves and looks stupid enough to be saluted.

"Ok off you go then but just make sure we are all off the boat first before you start your fire now."

I had to salvage some of my authority. They were getting as bad as Geelslang and I realised we had a nice esprit de corps going here. Up to now I was under scrutiny. Yes, they respected my Special Forces background, the South African Units have rather good reputations but it was still a test of leadership forced under battle. Such men don't just follow orders, they expect to be led in the right direction and as highly experienced professional soldiers they would know which way is right and which way is wrong. Thus far I went the right way and we did what we said we would do. That counted a lot. I also cared deeply about lives, my men's and the enemy's unless they did something to Angelique.

"Aye, sir, see you on the beach in ten minutes then." He started chuckling and disappeared down to the engine room with his mates. I only saw now that one was wearing a large bag which I presumed contained explosives. If I had seen it sooner, I would have swum a bit further away from him.

108

We waited a minute to make sure everyone was far away. Geelslang inserted the detonator and walked to me. "Let's go! and remember to keep your mouth open. It is for the shock wave you know."

I gave him the evil eye and opened my mouth but said nothing. It was standard demolitions procedure. According to the theory the shock wave then causes less damage to your eardrums. I remember when he first came to the unit after Selection. We were much younger then and he floored a white constable who called him "skaapsteker" which is the Afrikaans name for an ugly but none too dangerous snake. However, it also means or can be translated to a "sheep shagger" and he reacted with a powerful left to the chin.

We had our own, direct, ways of sorting out insults. As was his right he demanded a boxing match with this fellow. As his platoon commander I instantly granted his request and looked forward to seeing the fun as the other lad was a known boxer. He did quite well against our main enemy, the Army lads. It was no contest. Geelslang utterly destroyed the man in the first round. I have yet to see anyone move that fast. I counted three lefts and a tremendous right uppercut in the first seven seconds before his opponent went down for the first time. Deeply disappointed and thinking it may have been a fluke we had a rematch and the same happened again. Since then no one called him anything else but "Geelslang" which is also a snake, a very dangerous one. I also enlisted him in bouts with the Army where we made good money in side bets. Unfortunately, the war heated up and we went on operations and had no further time for boxing matches.

However, his love of boxing never died. Today, Geelslang teaches boxing at our place called the Ukuthula Ranch which is in North East Mozambique. Where he also doubles as the local pastor on Sundays thundering out great services but it is his boxing which made the local kids flog to his ring. For poor African lads such a skill is vital, it may even lift you from poverty and at the very least it can give you respect. Even our twins were known to spar a bit at Geelslang's gym. Good training against Frenchmen with romantic notions, I explained, when they asked why they should fight instead of just obey.

I am proud to say they had an unsurprising natural ability in the ring. They inherited it from their mom, Angelique, who stood watching critically shouting advice much to Geelslang's annoyance. Undeniably they were not scared of blood which is the first lesson in boxing. You have to know you cannot duck and dive all the blows and will be hurt at some stage. They soon became the terror of all boys who did not really know whether they should laugh or cry or just humour them. The results were entirely predictable. The lads got the living daylights knocked out of them before swinging back. Mind you, now that they are grown and proper ladies, they don't often put their boxing gloves on anymore. They told me the other day they know they can always shoot the bastard or call mom.

That last bit would make any lad think twice on what good manners are. Being shot is much less painful than what Angelique would do to him and one look is usually enough. Through the years quite a few became extremely polite much to our mirth. Yep, they all obtained a sudden urge for old world standards and manners when on the Ukuthula Ranch. I am sure their parents also approved of our number one skin cut hairstyle they hurriedly adopted to please my wife. It is as Angelique explained, not the in thing to look like Absalom (and they better know who that Biblical figure was). You know he hung in a thorn tree by his hair until he died and there are, as anyone could plainly see, many thorn trees on the Ukuthula Ranch.

The explosion shook me out of my reverie about the good old days and we rushed back into the radio room. The safe door was hanging by a thread and a good kick made it fall on the floor. We grabbed all the contents and left without looking back. We had eight minutes to get back to the beach where Commodore Octavius was waiting for us. The guns and M46 were hooked up and the SAMIL-50 was driving towards us. Well the water was not too deep to begin with but it did seem odd, a big truck driving towards a ship. You don't see that every day.

For once I was ahead of Geelslang and grabbed his arm just as he prepared to dive overboard. "You know the first rule of jumping mate? Yeah, look down before you jump! The water is almost gone."

The tide had gone out and it was only about three feet deep. We could see the bottom clearly and waited for the SAMIL to come next to us. Then we jumped the couple of feet onto the load bed where Graeme stood grinning like a pirate.

"I say old chap, first time that happened to you?"

He looked fairly pleased with himself but men like that always do. Nothing, and I mean nothing, ever gets them down. They smile in the face of death and angry women.

"Nah, we do this every day. Now let us leave as your lads decided to burn her out. Have you seen them?"

"We are here, sir. We have five minutes to get away."

The Welsh voice came from above me and I looked up to see them jump over the rails onto the SAMIL. So we left or rather tried to. The vehicle stalled and left us right next to the warship which was about to burn and well explode in the next few minutes. I don't really know the record for starting a SAMIL-50 again but we broke it. Within seconds the engine was purring and Geelslang shouted to the driver to put it in low range and keep the revs up. Whilst moving it is not a big deal but once stopped the tide would eradicate the sand from under the wheels. The vehicle then settles and can get stuck in the sand. It is an old off-road trick not to stop in the sea bed for more than a few seconds at a time and if you must, to hook up a boat or whatever, then engage in a low range to get yourself out again. It takes a lot more power than what you would expect, as water does not move away as air does. Water creates more drag that will slow you down and increases the amount of power needed. The driver did exactly that and we moved off leaving the old Isaac Dyobha to her fate. A short while later, while on the beach, a deep rumble came across the water and the Isaac Dyobha shuddered. Then a flame shot into the air for a hundred feet or more. She instantly became a roaring fire burning in great black pillars of smoke. And then the explosions began as the ready use ammunition started blowing.

I raised my eyebrows and the happy Welshman replied with one word "thermite." We nodded in admiration; so he knew how to create a mini fuel air explosion. That was very well done and Geelslang immediately got into a highly technical discussion on exactly what he did. Such knowledge was an art to be shared with your mates. I also noted that Graeme did not ask for the codebooks. He probably guessed we would only give them to Angelique.

Commodore Octavius stood waiting next to the Kwêvoël onto which the M46 was now hooked. Each of the three SAMIL-20's had their respective ZU 23-2 and the SAMIL-50, which we were on, was quickly loaded with kitbags and other equipment. The convoy was ready to depart South Africa. It was now just after three in the afternoon. We were five hours inside the country and it was time to leave but I could see the Commodore had something on his chest.

"Graeme, I have an idea which you and Foxtrot must make a decision about."

He went on without waiting for us to answer. "We can leave with the Orlando. I went through her and she is in fairly good shape. The shells did not do much damage and the Oryx crash burned her only superficially. She will float and can sail away if we wanted to do so."

Graeme looked at me who nodded in agreement. I said. "Yes, I think that would be a great idea for it would leave no real evidence behind. If you could sail it out and sink it in deep water it would really help on the propaganda side of things. That was our original plan anyway. No Orlando means no sob stories."

"Commodore, how long will it take you to get her out of here? We are under serious time restraint for the frigate is not far away. We cannot afford to have her captured with you onboard. It will defeat our deniability claims." Graeme did not sound worried but concerned for he needed to decide based on the advice he was receiving.

"It will take five minutes to start her up...my engineers are already doing so in fact and then we can be off. There is no chance of the frigate catching us. We will scuttle her before that happens. Just give the word and we will leave. It will be easy."

As confirmation of his words we all looked towards the Orlando. There was indeed smoke coming from her funnel and men scurrying about. It could be done and would help our cause. It was for me an easy enough decision. The old ship deserved better than to die on a beach. Obviously, I did not know what was coming or I may have made a different choice.

"I agree but we really need to get a move on and leave this country." I said it to Graeme who after all had the final say now that Angelique was indisposed off. Well, sort of, he still needed to adhere to DGSE advice but for the moment he had tactical command.

I felt tired, the last couple of days were fast paced and a lot had happened. I was wondering how Angelique was and, more importantly, if she would be OK lying wounded in bed without me comforting her. Call me old fashioned but it is a husband's duty and honour to be at his wife's side when she is ill or shot. Yes, we had to leave. I wanted to get to my wife and soul.

"Ok I tell you what. Why don't you go with the Commodore? I understand Sir John wants to speak to you anyway. He is on board the Astute who is to rescue the Orlando crew members. At the same time, you can visit the wounded that we dropped off. I will then lead the convoy back to Mozambique."

After the Amatola battle the HMS Astute, the latest nuclear attack submarine the Royal Navy had, surfaced next to the Amatola to take off our seriously wounded men. That was ten days ago and I did not know that the old horny goat was onboard. Perhaps he only arrived later.

Sir John was a retired Royal Navy nuclear attack boat commander and Graeme's direct boss. Through the years we had our differences. I tried to assassinate him before but he escaped by luck and nothing else. Since then he acted a bit wary around me with his bodyguards giving me the old evil eye. Angelique and his mom, a dear old lady, were the best of friends, God knows why and why the woman gave birth to him. The man was one hell of a good submariner. It has to be admitted that he ran some pretty amazing operations during the cold war and was a good spymaster since then. However, I really did not like him and did not trust him either.

"Fair enough but Geelslang will go with you and the convoy. You lads don't know the Mozambicans as well as we do and that is what the Egg Breakers do best, liaison with the locals where we have some influence. Let us meet at the Ukuthula Ranch in the near future then?"

"Eh, perhaps you should leave the SAMIL-50 here until we winch the Orlando off the beach. Just for in case, as she has settled in quite nicely now that the tide is out."

The Commodore was already walking towards the Orlando leaving a bemused command group behind. This did not sound as positive as we had understood it to be.

"Oi, Commodore, I thought you said it would be easy" shouted Graeme to him but the old Commodore dismissed him with a wave. He was already concentrating on getting the Orlando back into the ocean.

I frowned at Geelslang. "Geelslang, get the convoy back to the Ukuthula Ranch from where we can redeploy. Once you cross the border keep on moving as I expect a sneak air attack or at least some sort of an attempt to retaliate. Your fuelling station is at Ponto do Oro and I am sure you will be met by Senhor Feradi's men."

He nodded, shook my hand briefly and climbed into the armoured cab of the Kwêvoël. The engines roared into life and I looked at Graeme. It was time to say goodbye.

"Now I don't suppose you want to go with the convoy because you want to see our Mozambican liaison officer now do you? How far can I negotiate with Sir John anyway?"

"All the way, Foxtrot, you have full command on ground level. I only, ah, approve the strategic direction until Angelique is out of hospital. Regarding our liaison officer, you got that damn right mate."

He grinned and went on "However, I am also arranging for Boris to fly us to the Ukuthula Ranch with his Antonov-124. He should be back from France tonight. So it is not just for my own selfish reasons. Eh, you did say she did rather well old chap?"

"She did very well Graeme, you can be proud of her."

I recalled her shocked face. It also reminded me of the pool of blood next to Angelique with her thug medic working on her arm as she sat inside the Casspir looking very small and vulnerable. I felt the anger rising against the bastards who caused it. Someone is going to die for this insult.

"The Commodore has the rendezvous point and communication channels with Astute. You should be good and here is the remote control for the demolition charges. I am sure you would want to press the button yourself. Remember to add a timer on the explosives just in case it does not work as designed. I suggest that six gunslingers accompany you but as you know, we cannot really stop a determined assault with six men and rifles."

We shook hands; I took the timer and ran to the Orlando. The bow doors were closed just as I hopped inside and went straight to the bridge where Commodore Octavius was barking orders. The winch was already taking strain to winch us off the beach. I wondered if he had a presumption that it was not the end of the EBS Orlando when he dropped it a few hours ago. It

116

seemed like years. The convoy was already moving north, back to Mozambique following the hard sand just in front of the water. I did not expect much trouble for them and besides they were well able to deal with anything and anyone.

"Foxtrot, will you go down to the magazine and ensure that my son's Heath Robinson contraption does not explode prematurely. And we have a rather strange young man in my cabin. Chained, sir, to my bed, and he refuses to speak to me too. Told me, respectfully I must admit; to piss off and ask Major Foxtrot why he is there. After that rude conversation he just stared at me."

The Commodore shook his head in wonder about the lack of manners of the youth. In his day such things also happened but at serious risk of being sorted out afterwards.

Ah yes, the prisoner. I sort of forgot about him, well he could wait. I went down the hold and made sure to disarm the detonators in our magazine. I noted with approval that Graeme had a backup for every system and that it was straightforward. About forty pounds of high grade plastic explosives onto two thousand pounds worth of shells and cordite. Yes, it would be a great explosion when the time came. I took the detonators with me.

The ship started to move under my feet and I went up again stopping first at the cabin. The prisoner was not happy to see me again. I explained we will drop him as promised and as soon as we get a suitable place. Patience is a virtue even if too young and stupid to realise it right now, and no, it was not my intention to have him exposed to shells unable to duck and look for decent cover. In fact, I was as surprised as he was when the warships started shooting at him. That was not my fault and he can lodge a complaint with my mate, Yankee Two Zero, I presumed he knew him well.

I have no doubts that he did not believe me but that could not be helped. At that I climbed to the bridge where the Commodore was now busy destroying the distress beacon. It could not be switched off and was broadcasting our position. After a few well aimed kicks and blows it was in pieces. He looked quite satisfied at the mess. I wondered why he did not just throw it overboard but supposed the fast attack boat survivors would anyway tell the world we sailed off. In the end it would make no difference.

"Commodore, we need to drop the prisoner off at the first life raft we see. Would that be possible? He is not going with us on the submarine and I have orders to keep him alive." I was a bit anxious about this, I gave my word and so it was.

"Aye, we can do that. See there, Foxtrot?"

He pointed to the sea where our bow was now heading. "There is a life raft not too far away. Coxswain, steer towards that life raft on our port bow. I suggest you bring your prisoner up to the deck for the exchange."

I took the pre-caution to bring four burly lads with me and explained the facts of life to him. "We have a life raft in sight and you will be joining it. Do we need to tie you down again or will you be sensible? My men have orders to shoot you if needs be. Make up your mind."

He said he would be good. Just to get rid of us would be worth the mental anguish of being a part of the prisoner exchange, so I unlocked the chain and watched him being assisted to the deck. I noted that clouds were now forming and it looked darker than what it should have been. Even the water was turning blackish instead of turquoise. It made me shiver for no reason at all. I had such presuppositions before and it always turned out badly. This would be no different.

We stood waiting on the mid deck where the Oryx crashed. It was scorched black with a few parts still around. The prisoner was lying on a stretcher staring at the clouds. I saw that his bandages were freshly changed and wondered who bothered. It was not him for he had nothing to do it with. I heard the Commodore shout a command and telegraphs rang to stop the engines. We drifted towards the first life raft. It was fairly large; twenty-five men could easily fit into it but there were only eight men inside it.

"Ahoy life raft, stand by to receive a passenger."

I leaned over the rail whilst shouting. They looked at me with much hatred and probably expected to be shot.

"We have a wounded man here who belongs with you. I have no idea what his name is or where he is from but you are going to take him. Is that understood?"

"It is understood. Lower him down. Did you report our position on the open guard frequency?"

I saw it was a chief petty officer who answered. He was not the most senior but, in such times, the natural leaders come to fore. His insignia indicated he was once a submariner, the medical orderly or whatever they are called. Interesting, I wondered what he was doing on the fast attack craft and guessed it had to do with divers. Perhaps they wanted to salvage the Orlando if at all possible.

"Yes, your misfortune was reported and I am sure" at this I grinned evilly "that you have activated your own rescue beacons. The SAS Mendi is not too far away. We are leaving now for Madagascar. Do you need anything else?"

"Only a rematch Major Foxtrot, we will get you next time" says he.

This reminded me of the executive officer of the SAS Amatola who said the same thing under the same circumstances. They have some aggressive lads in the navy who could find a natural home in the fast attack squadron or submarines. (See Code Name Ndebele 14 where the concept is explained.) This was certainly one of them. I wondered how he knew my name but then it was all over the news and I worked extensively with the navy lads in the past. He may have easily been part of a crew in the old days when we were still the best of mates. I gestured to the lads to lower our prisoner down. Luckily the Commodore had removed the wire fences on the sides of the Orlando which we had installed to repeal a Special Forces counter assault on the way down to meet with the SAS Amatola. It was thus easy to lower the wounded man to the raft. Whilst he was being received, I considered the petty officer and my answer.

"I have sunk two fast attack crafts, one frigate and two submarines thus far. What do you think I will do to you next time?" I lifted my hand as he stuck out his chin aggressively to tell me what he thinks he would do to me. "And I saved as many of the respective crews as I possibly could, including this fellow who was part of an assassination team who shot at a marked ambulance. At the Red Cross and a pregnant woman, that is against all rules of war. In fact, it is a war crime in every country and was this in a war situation, he would have been executed for his action, end of story. What saved him was that my commanding officer, the expectant mother he shot at, ordered his life to be spared. Yes, I would be glad for a rematch. Any time and any place. You can tell that to your superiors. We will go on the offensive and destroy your silly Muslim Truce. We will never stop before that is done and I don't care how many of you will die in the future. It is written."

"What Muslim Truce?"

He sounded a bit taken aback. It was probably unfair of me to point out how many ships I have sunk. Sailors have an abnormal affection to the mass of steel and electric wire they call a ship and he would have served on some excluding the one I sunk only two hours from underneath him. It was an impressive record and cost the South African Government close to two billion dollars if you count the various helicopters in. The lives of the soldiers, spies and sailors were, of course, worth much more than that to their families.

"Do you even know why you came after us? Did they tell you we are far right-wing terrorists? That we want to overthrow the elected government of South Africa and re-stablish Apartheid?"

I could see from his face that was exactly what he was told but he could only stare at the scrawny Jamaican lad next to me. Like Geelslang he did not conform to the far right-whiner story. Such people don't mix with coloured men and don't have their respect either. Fear perhaps, but that is not respect. The Jamaican flashed his ivories but said nothing. He was enjoying this.

"You are still young and have no idea how much a government can lie to you. You would do well to remember that all politicians are born liars and former lawyers to boot, no doubt. When they open their mouths, they lie. Ask your superiors about the Muslim Truce of 1999 by which they gave Al-Qaeda the right to live and recuperate in South Africa. Ask them about the amendment of this truce in 2005 when they offered them safe havens in southern Africa under the direct protections of Special Forces teams with SASS commanders. And if they have not told you to shut up by then, ask them about the Egg Breaker or Directorate F program of which I am the current commanding officer. Then ask them why their greatest strategic asset, Angelique Dawson, turned against them."

I was mildly astonished how bitter I sounded even to myself. I have long since emigrated in my mind from South Africa and under normal conditions could not care less what went on there. I don't even watch rugby matches anymore because the quota system spoiled it for me. Reverse discrimination can never be right no matter how you spin it to sound all noble. Nowhere in the world had affirmative action ever succeeded and it failed here too. Besides that, they lost matches so regularly that it is a national embarrassment and our soccer team cannot even qualify for the World Cup. The pride of the green and gold was simply gone. Back in 1990 Mr Mandela was released, we who fought honourably in the years before that quickly knew we were lied to. Though he was guilty of terrorism and had a fair trial we never realised he had every reason to become a terrorist. It came as a terrible shock to us. We really believed in our chaplains, officers and political leaders. The Army system grabbed us at the age of fourteen via the school Cadet Corps. From there on it was a natural progression. I volunteered for the Police, then the elite Flying Squad, then the Dog Unit and Police Trackers, then the Police Special Forces Unit which had a selection failure rate of 90%. We fought for years and won every single encounter. We cost the Soviet Union billions in weapons and stopped communist expansion in southern Africa in its tracks. But we were still on the wrong side. No matter what we said or how we tried, we could never defend what we defended. That is why the Egg Breaker program was so imperative to me. For once we were on the right side of things. We regained our honour which was severely contaminated by the Nationalist politicians who could not run away from us lads in the Services fast enough. For a while things went well, South Africa was the liberal wet dream - there was a lot of hope. Then after Mr Mandela retired the new lot reverted to form and became just another African bunch of power mad crooks as the right-wing whiners in Australia (those who could afford to run) predicted. The Muslim Truce was the final straw as far as I was concerned. Any radical Muslim is the problem of every God-fearing Christian as would be any radical Christian to everyone else, including his own and Muslims. It is a religious war in which the much more powerful Christian countries showed a lot of restraint which cannot be condoned for pure military reasons. In prior decades the Christian soldiers would have killed and maimed indiscriminately and this nonsense would have been over before it even started to become important.

You have to wonder, if the roles were reversed, what would have happened. We know the answer. We only have to look at the threats issued through the years by Muslim Nations against the State of Israel. The answer is very clear and the reason why they will never win. You cannot force a man to believe, it is a matter of personal conviction and flogging him to death or cutting his head off will not endorse you to him or his family. Such actions are very puzzling for I know true Islam is not like that. My first wife Marwa was a Muslim woman and we spent many hundreds of hours talking about her love for Allah, the Merciful. Almost nothing these radicals sprout has any standing in the Holy Koran, a book I read many times and am able to quote from. In fact, the one passage "(And (remember) when the disbelievers plotted against you to imprison you, or to kill you, or to get you out; they were plotting and Allah too was plotting; and Allah is the Best of those who plot)" is my favourite. I use it a lot to explain why you need God on your side.

"I will ask." He said it flatly and I knew he would. I also knew he would not get any decent answers but that was also fine. "Do you have any information regarding the patient's medical condition, Sah? The doctors may ask?"

"Oi Mon, he can talk and tell you himself but we gave him morphine twenty minutes ago. The wounds in his arms and foot are through and through with broken bones in all of them. He is not allergic to anything or so he says. You may want to give him morphine again in six hours and keep the antibiotics up to keep infection away. Clean the bandages regularly and check his temperature now." My Jamaican answered in his distinctive accent. So now we knew who changed the bandages.

We sailed away leaving them bobbing on the waves receding into the distance. Not a further word was spoken despite what was reported in the newspapers. They would be rescued the next day. Our prisoner made a full recovery. He also resigned his commission. He was in fact the platoon leader and said he "does not believe anymore." Ironically Sir John's mob, Sandrine, employed him then and our paths would cross again under better circumstances. In his heart he was a very decent man and tried to warn me about them and Angelique.

The clouds were low on the horizon and we were two hours into our trip when the Air Force finally arrived. It was my old nemesis, the SAAB JAS 39 Gripen fighter jets. There were two of them. They had drop fuel tanks on and were configured for a long-range flight. From the time it took them to get to us I worked out they must have taken off after the second message to Yankee Two Zero. They were attacking with cannon fire.

Why they did not simply fire a sea hugging anti-ship missile I would never know. We suspected and though we never proved it, it became clear they wanted to damage the Orlando and slow her down enough so that the frigate, SAS Mendi could get in range. But even that made no real sense for the SAS Mendi had Exocets onboard which could be launched from a maximum range of 97 miles. They did not need to close in unless they wanted to capture the Orlando for propaganda purposes. It was the only logical conclusion.

Whatever their thinking was they had great fun at our expense. We were defenceless and did not even have a single Mistral aboard to fire back. The first time we knew we were spotted, was when one Gripen made a low and very fast run across us. She came out of the clouds and dived down to visually identify us whilst another circled around waiting her turn. I believe they had us on radar for a while.

With the next pass they took turns shooting at us with their 27mm Mauser cannon. It did negligible damage for it is too small to stop a ship and we took the precautions to stay away from the bridge area. It was anyway heavily reinforced with the Hesco barriers and the high explosive shells didn't damage anything vital. With the rudders locked and the engine room under the waterline the EBS Orlando kept on steaming placidly enough. Still it was very uncomfortable and rather frustrating. A few lads took pot shots with their rifles back but to no effect. A modern fast jet cannot be shot down by a rifle no matter what Hollywood comes up with.

I am sure it must have been puzzling to the pilots that we did not issue any radio calls for assistance or even try to bluff our way out. I mean, who would we have called and besides that, the radio masts were shot away by the fast attack craft. Our radar was not working and hence we had had no warning. The Orlando was dying but we did our best to ignore them hoping they would run out of ammunition or fuel or get bored. None of that happened. After expending a few bursts of their 27mm ammunition they came in low again and circled us for a few minutes as if waiting for something to happen. We guessed they were waiting for instructions.

We kept on sailing, hoping that they would go away or that we would reach the HMS Astute. Not that we expected her to do anything about the Gripens. She was not about to betray her presence and had no surface-to-air defense capabilities which we knew off. No submarine does and besides, we were the expendables. We were on our own but every mile closer is one less to swim. And we waited for darkness though, of course, that would make no difference to a Gripen either. They are able to see in the dark as well as in daylight.

Things got a lot more serious after the first two strafing runs. They dropped four Mark 82 five hundred-pound bombs on the fore deck. It was the end of the old ship. She had no armour and they penetrated deep inside her before exploding. You could actually feel the ship slowing down as the water came cascading into the holds. All our attempts, Second World War tactics, of swerving away came to nothing. They were just too accurate. The ship began to settle and only one thing was left.

Commodore Octavius made the decision. "Abandon ship, abandon ship."

I heard the Commodore shouting on the tannoy. It was one command I never wanted to hear but so it was. The Orlando's engines immediately went into neutral still powering the electrical systems. Men started to arrive on deck and dove overboard with their life jackets on. It was just before seven in the early evening and the sun was still out above the clouds. In summer time the sun would only go down in another forty-five minutes. Visibility was good and there was no reason for the Gripen to open fire again with her cannon. She could and did see that we were launching life rafts but, in all fairness, we did not strike our colours (there weren't any to strike) and the

126

rules of war apparently meant nothing to them. So they opened up on defenceless men swimming for their lives.

In the spy world the rules of war don't exist and you expect that but when engaging with the armed forces of a country with a reputation of keeping to the rules of war and they don't, you have to wonder what happened to them. No fighter pilot is an idiot; they are highly skilled and quite bright. They don't react in anger but work out the dynamics of energy versus movement as first set out by USAF Colonel Boyd. It is all about energy for fighter pilots. So for them to shoot at unarmed men you have to accept it is with the intention to commit murder. There is no other logical explanation. I recalled when that very same Air Force would drop leaflets warning of an attack before they would strike. Yeah, times have changed a lot and not for the better.

"Launch the life rafts boys and each man for himself. Swim away from the ship and get yourself into a life raft. Stay together now." I sort of figured that one out already but still worried about the scuttling charges. I asked Commodore Octavius about it.

"What you mean is that you want to arm the scuttling charges old chap? The Orlando is sinking. Get yourself overboard and no I am not leaving yet. The captain leaves last and all that you know."

He stood on the deck shaking his fist at the passing Gripens. I made a lifelong enemy that day. Commodore Octavius swore for one hour and seventeen minutes non-stop issuing horrible threats of revenge after I picked him up and flung him over the side. We were anyway the last to leave and so it was but the man was most unhappy and affronted.

When we reached the surface, I realised the waves, which looked so insignificant from the Orlando's deck, looked enormous when only your eyes are sticking out. The water tasted saltier than usual. When I wiped my brow my hand came away sticky with blood, I guess it was the old wound I got in the SAS Amatola fight ten days ago. Now opened again by shrapnel or perhaps a new one, I was too busy to notice. There was a lot of ricocheting with the cannon strafing.

The Indian Ocean is supposed to be warmer than the Atlantic and I am sure there is lots of scientific proof to that. However, when you swim away from a sinking ship and have Gripens with evil intent circling, you tend to worry about more immediate dangers. Like sharks and cannon fire as they came down low over the water. I watched them take turns to open fire on the yellow life raft and it immediately started to deflate. The men inside died a violent death with pieces of flesh being flung over a wide area. It was an easy target, being unable to hide or defend itself.

"Oi, you buttsharks, I will put you on my own dink list..." and so Commodore Octavius went on in between his curses directed to me. Not being familiar with Royal Navy slang I did not get half of it but the rest of the lads did. They brayed appreciatively at his efforts. "You fat sack, ESAD you bastards, and FOAD to you too!"

He roared and shook his fist in their direction. His white beard sticking out of the water as he stuck his chin aggressively out. I now knew where Graeme got his personality from. The old man's antics gave everyone a chuckle when they needed it most. At one stage I thought I heard him say "voetsek" which is the Afrikaans word used on dogs and has the same meaning as "bugger off" in its milder forms. Apparently not, he meant ESAD again and it stands for "eat shit and die" but that I learned much later.

FOAD translated to "fuck off and die" and so it went on but the Gripens kept diving down and shooting at us. When they came down the fourth time and the water started boiling in front of me as the shells hit I quietly said goodbye to Angelique and our unborn twins and waited for my fate. There was nothing else to do. We needed a miracle and I raised my eyes to the heavens for one. Truth be told I felt quite calm and heard Angelique laugh. It was, as always, a sound which made me smile and some say I was smiling serenely.

It was an amazing sight though, when the miracle came. One of the Gripens suddenly banked hard right towards the sun dropping flares all the while. I wondered what was up with him when I also saw the remaining fuel tanks dropping off. It somersaulted in the air and landed quite a distance away from us. He wanted desperately to be lighter and that meant only one thing - other fighter jets. But who could it be? The Egg Breakers did not count any aircraft amongst themselves which would frighten a Gripen into fighter mode. I watched fascinated on what was happening above us, not really believing my eyes. A missile streaked past us and turned violently towards the climbing Gripen. It seemed much faster than the Mistrals and rapidly overtook him. Within seconds there was a bright white flash and a parachute with the pilot dangling below it came down to land a short distance from us. Someone or something shot him down.

The men began to cheer hoarsely as the second Gripen went on full afterburner and rocketed away towards the west where South Africa was, fifty miles away as the crow flies. She too dropped her external fuel tanks for more manoeuvrability and tried a series of evasion manoeuvres bobbing up and down and left and right but she did not make it either. Two missiles tracked her down and exploded close to her tailpipe. Unlike the first one there was no parachute. She simply went into a spin and hit the water with a tremendous splash and disintegrated on impact. It was all over within seconds...

At first, I assumed the Gripens shot each other down and started laughing at the idea. Assuredly their attackers looked very similar. They had the same blueish paint scheme all air superiority fighters have these days. My angle of sight was not too good and waves were breaking over my face. Still I stared hard to see who saved us. Those lads deserved the biggest barbecue at the Ukuthula Ranch ever. Although they stayed a fair distance away, I recognised two French Navy Rafale fighter jets turning away. They were already speeding back towards their aircraft carrier and made no fly pass over us which must have been for security reasons. Angelique later told me they were called in by the HMS Astute who were watching us and saw the attacks.

Apparently the two Rafale fighters scanned the airspace for more targets and when they found none, returned to base. Not once did they break radio silence and there was no news announcements on either side. If you ask any of the other lads what went wrong with the Gripens they will tell you one "f flew into the water and the other had a flame out." The French, they were from the Charles de Gaulle, the big French carrier, will tell you none of their Rafales were in the area and the party they had that night in their mess was because the ship's cat was expecting. If you ask even more questions a couple of fairly big lads in suits would visit you to hear what your views are on the Republic and it better be to their satisfaction - they know how to deal with liberal journalists. The South Africans said months later that one Gripen went down on a routine training flight and the pilot was not recovered.

I knew the Charles de Gaulle was somewhere in the Indian Ocean doing God knows what. We landed on her when Angelique first returned to Africa during Code Name Pour Angelique the previous year. It must have been close for the Rafales were not carrying drop fuel tanks or perhaps they dropped them before the dog fight started. Regardless, it was good news for us and very bad news for our tormentors. Even Commodore Octavius stopped cursing to say that the "Frogs ain't that bad and three hurrahs for them now."

The men roared their approval but we still had other problems. We were swimming in four feet waves with seven thousand feet of water below us. Several of us and the lads in the now deflated life raft were bleeding profusely attracting sharks. And the Orlando stopped sinking. To be sure she was low in the water with the waves breaking over her but she was still afloat. That bothered me more than the rest combined. The ship really needed to go down and take all evidence with her.

Hypothermia was not the big factor here but several of us were beginning to shiver. The Indian Ocean is warm enough to survive twenty-four hours easily if you could swim that long and the sharks or tropical sun didn't get you first. We really needed floating devices and I started swimming for the Orlando. I knew there would be something on her able to keep us afloat. Anything would be better than nothing. I even wondered if the dropped fuel tanks would be floating and if so, if we could somehow get to them.

"Oi I say, Foxtrot where you going then?"

It was Commodore Octavius; his eyes were red from saltwater and his voice hoarse. He was still treading water a few feet away from me holding on to his life jacket with one hand. We went out of them rather quickly with the first strafing. Being able to duck under the water seemed much more important than floating.

"To the Orlando to search for floating devices Commodore, we cannot swim indefinitely and some lads are wounded. We may be in for a rough night."

"That includes you Foxtrot. Do you know you are bleeding?" He looked at me with narrowed eyes.

"Yes, I realised that and don't feel too good but that cannot be helped. Are you coming with, sir?"

He was in fact swimming like a dog next to me; he did not know any other style with only his beard sticking out. I started laughing much to his disgust. Perhaps I was also going slightly mad with all that had happened in the last few days and weeks but to me it was really funny. I only stopped laughing when I reached the Orlando and realised she was making horrible groaning noises. In a way that was much scarier than the Gripens strafing us for it sounded like a wounded animal. Commodore Octavius calmly explained it was bulkheads groaning under the strain of keeping the water out and also air pockets trying to escape. I really did not want to get onboard and would rather be as far away as possible but we had no other choice and climbed over the rail. Leaning back, I pulled Commodore Octavius onboard too. Several other men were approaching the ship but too many were just drifting face down or in their torn life jackets. They would never need a floating device again.

The deck was awash with water. She had a peculiar motion as if tired and not wanting to ride the waves which were more or less breaking continuously over her. I looked back and saw about a dozen faces watching us from the water. Six hundred yards further away the shot down pilot was in his dinghy bobbing up and down in the water. He had all the survival equipment we did not have because of him. We had also given a few of our own life rafts to the SAS Amatola survivors. Something I regretted doing now.

I wondered if I should take a pot shot at him as an abandoned Individual Weapon was lying at my feet. I picked it up and tilted it down to let the water run out. I then took aim at the pilot before anyone could stop me. Not that they would have. The bastard deserved it after what he put us through. Much to my surprise, the advanced combat optical gunsight was still working as well as ever. I suppose as it should have; it is waterproof up to 36 feet and here it was only under two feet of water.

The deck was steady enough and it took only four rapid shots for him to join his mate. The bullets all hit his chest. He made no attempt to get out or avoid his fate as I would have done by diving overboard. Perhaps the fellow was still in shock. The men cheered and I felt quite proud about the marksmanship. I did not tell them that I almost did not pull the trigger for the pilot looked suspiciously like a woman to me. I have heard of female fighter pilots. The Soviet Air Force had many female aces during the Second World War and these days you find women everywhere where they should not be. I also met a few American pilots, they called themselves aviators, who were stunning girls and being aggressive by nature my type too. Still, I made a vow never to reveal her gender to anyone except Angelique whose spies would have told her anyway. When I finally came clean, she just hugged me for a long time. No words were needed. It needed to be done.

Commodore Octavius was walking or rather splashing towards the bow and I joined him, still holding the Individual Weapon, more to make an end to myself if we should be trapped than for anything else. In the forecastle we found a life jacket box and started to throw the jackets to the men in the water. They gratefully put them on and subsequently bobbed up and down. So did we when we joined them soon after swimming for the second time away from the Orlando. Still the Orlando did not sink but drifted away. We also released a Carley float for the most serious wounded. The rest of us were around it. There are those who say that the Carey floats kill more than they save but that day it was worth its weight in gold. The nay-sayers obviously never had to rely on one or they would not have talked such crap.

"Tie yourself together lads. The Astute is coming."

I admired the Commodore for this piece of advice as the sun was now rapidly going down. How he knew the Astute would surface fifty yards away I don't know but she did an hour later and rescued us. Our blinking beacons must have stood out for miles with the type of equipment they had aboard. It was a great end to a very long day.

*"Before you kill a man you must be his friend." Geelslang, 1987 during Operation Moduler in Angola. He was acting as our chaplain, something he is entirely suited to do*

## Chapter 3

### HMS Astute, Indian Ocean, 26 February 2014

There are few nicer things in life than a friendly nuclear attack boat surfacing in the ocean to rescue you. Well, anything with Angelique and our twins is better looking but you know what I mean. She looked huge when I last saw her taking our wounded onboard but now she absolutely dwarfed us. We were almost too tired to cheer but made the effort to swim towards her. It was a matter of pride and we were not ordinary men to begin with. We were ex-Special Forces and have been tired before, worse in fact, during Selection. So we swam and dragged the crew members behind us.

The executive officer, they call him Jimmy the One, did an excellent job keeping her half submerged so we could easily find our footing on her relatively broad deck. It was rather uncanny to feel the deck below our feet and know she could go down again at command, safely with us inside. So different from the Orlando that would have killed us with her suction if that had happened.

"I say Orlando; please ensure your weapons are unloaded before coming down. We don't want accidents at this late stage."

That was the captain standing on his bridge or sail as it is called today. I looked around me and saw every gunslinger had his Individual Rifle with him. The survivors that is, for we lost half the crew with the strafing and three of the six gunslingers. They gave tired nods and turned towards starboard and went through the weapon checks. I joined them and suddenly felt surprisingly heavy with legs made of jelly. It was a rather strange sensation and I looked around in alarm wondering if I was shot and did not know about it. It was the Astute raising itself completely above the water line. Shortly after we were hanging on for dear life to each other as the water cascaded down the sides.

Commodore Octavius looked up to the captain and shouted the usual "permission to come aboard Sir" crap. We were sort of already on board and would shoot them to take us down below but certain things are engrained in ex-Royal Navy officers and people like Geelslang.

"Aye Commodore Octavius, you are welcome, Sir."

The captain snapped a salute at the old seadog which was nice of him. It was even better when he held it until the last man walked past him and down the first hatch. We responded in kind. It is a military tradition which goes back many hundreds of years where the knights would lift their visor so that they could be recognised. They used their right hand too because that was their fighting hand, mostly. You read of many left-handed assassins but that is where the tradition comes from. It is seldom that a nuclear attack boat commander and his lads salute civilians which were what we were, officially. It was a nice gesture which went down well with the lads.

The "sir" part always made my wife laugh a bit mockingly. It is from the old English word "sire" which she translated further to seed or loins. However, I noted she never objects when called Madame but knowing her by now I said nothing. I know what is good for me and us. I may not be the smartest around but I am not stupid either.

It was great to sit at the wardroom table safely beneath the waves and drinking the strongest cup of tea they could produce. It was warm and cosy and well-lit and I was at peace with the world. A few ignoramuses lifted their eyebrows at my cup of Earl Grey. That only showed their lack of understanding of South African Special Forces. We learned to like that drink whilst serving with the Rhodesian Special Air Service. That was before my time but you tend to follow your instructors and do what they do and if they like Earl Grey tea then so do you. Angelique loves coffee but recently I saw her drinking Earl Grey Moonlight tea. I am not sure why but it started after Sir John's mom came to visit us. Now she has it every morning at eleven and all of us must attend. Sometimes I wonder about her. It is an English tradition and we don't like the Pommies. As an Afrikaner girl she should understand that.

The medical officer was doing something to my head. Exactly what he was doing I am not too sure. He injected the area with painkillers before starting to prod around making odd noises or trying to sing. That burned like hell but what can you do? Perhaps he concentrated best when singing. I closed my eyes and remembered the time when Angelique bandaged my head. Her hands felt much more loving and caring than this fellow whom I seem to remember fell in love with her last time she was on the Astute. And she a newly married woman who thought her new husband, that is me, died sabotaging the South African submarines! Yeah, I did not like him much and wondered if he could speak French. French speaking men traditionally were Angelique's weakness in life and my own French was more working class than anything else. I gave him the evil eye now and then just to make sure he got the message that I knew of his desires in life. Mind you, he did a splendid job on our wounded lads. I took the time to visit them. Commodore Octavius, as the senior Pommy went with and it seemed that they appreciated the effort. Most were in good cheer and raring to get back to the fight.

The captain stuck his head through the door. "Commodore, would you be so kind as to come to the control room? You too Major Foxtrot, we have a situation developing here on which I need your input."

I got up immediately and followed Commodore Octavius before I got lost. HMS Astute was a big submarine with many ladders and passage ways. The doctor complained a bit but one look from the captain shut him up. It was really inconvenient for me too. Now he would have to start afresh and I was bleeding again. I stopped the bleeding with a bandage which I pressed against the wound. He came rambling after us to continue stitching in the control room. To be sure we got a lot of looks from the crew. At least he stopped singing.

I found Sir John standing next to the periscope. As a former, and may I say legendary, nuclear attack boat commander he felt completely at home. He apparently knew the captain well. He was a snotty or midshipman in his last command all those years ago. They were staring at a hi-definition computer screen as the periscope on modern submarines is not really what you would call a periscope. It is a mast with electronic goodies attached - there are no mirrors as in the old days. Everything was electronic.

"Good evening Commodore, Major. We found the EBS Orlando." Sir John looked at us and shook our hands briefly before continuing. "But so did the SAS Mendi."

"It was no easy task for we had to use visual means and rate of drift with dead reckoning to do so. The Orlando's engines went dead long ago and hence quiet which made our sonar sort of ineffective. We lost her when we surfaced to rescue you lot. And we could not use our search radar with the SAS Mendi around." The captain said it a bit defensively as if reading more into Sir John's words than what I did.

138

I understood his problem with tracking the Orlando. With no engines there is no noise and hence also no propeller noise. This made it much more difficult than normal unless you use a Yankee search or active sonar - something no submarine ever does without shooting torpedoes afterwards. It betrays her position. The Soviet Navy and others often used that tactic, just to drift and listen on their towed array sonar for Western submarines in their waters. It is very hard to detect unless someone slams a metallic door (common on ships) or in one recorded case, drops a spanner on the deck. Noise travels faster under water than in air.

The captain continued. "So we tracked the SAS Mendi and the SAS Drakensberg as we have been doing for the last week. They suddenly increased speed, steaming hard and then stopped. So we popped up and guess what, they are now lowering a boat to board the Orlando. See this picture here, it is a live feed."

The quality of the video feed was beyond excellent. Someone installed the very best of thermal imaging on HMS Astute and whatever it cost, it was worth it. We could clearly see the SAS Mendi lowering a boat and beyond them the forlorn shape of the old Orlando. She was still awash but would not die. This was indeed a problem of mega proportions.

"Why don't we sink the Orlando? I could swim out and plant a couple of limpet mines on her. Using delayed action fuses so they will explode long after we left." My suggestion was made without emotion. There was the EBS Orlando, she had to be sunk, and that was the covert way to do so.

Sir John replied first and it was damn insightful to see that cold brain calculating the odds. "I have another idea. Torpedo her before that boat reaches her. They would think, or they may, that she exploded by herself. Whatever they believe would be impossible to prove. There are seven thousand feet of water below us and we can spread the word that the scuttling charges went off in the nick of time. Once they board her they would be able to fabricate whatever evidence they like and say they got it from the ship before it sank. It would take too long for you to swim to her Foxtrot, we have run out of time. If the SAS Mendi was not on the scene, we could have boarded her ourselves and rigged her demolition charges but she is there now."

"I concur with Sir John, there is no other way due to the time limits."

Commodore Octavius looked glum. He loved the Orlando and was the one who stopped me from resetting the scuttling charges. Not that I blamed him, he saved my life and at that stage it was the only decision. We had to get overboard and did. It was not his fault.

"Technically I am in command here Sir John." I said it with a smile to take the sting out of my words for he was a touchy man at the best of times. "Hence legally, I need to make that request. Would that help your cause?"

"Yes, and you better make it damn quick Foxtrot." His gruff voice sounded not ungrateful but to the point. We had long since decided that I would take all the official blame for what was done on his behalf.

I turned to the submarine captain. "Sir, what you see there is the EBS Orlando. It needs to be destroyed to cover our tracks and your government's involvement in Code Name Phoenix as well as Code Name Lise. I formally request you to destroy her before anyone reaches her. I confirm to you that to the best of my knowledge there is no living soul onboard her. How you destroy her is your concern. Note that the SAS Mendi does not, I repeat does not, have her usual compliment of any Super Lynx helicopters onboard."

The captain was a smart man. He would not be commanding the Royal Navy's latest attack submarine if he wasn't and had certainly seen much in his twenty years at sea but this was unique. The last time a Royal Navy submarine launched any torpedoes in anger was against the Argentine light cruiser, General Belgrano in 1982. HMS Conqueror sank her with three American made Mark 48 torpedoes and told the world afterwards it was because of their bigger warheads. In reality he did not trust his Tigerfish torpedoes to actually work so he used the tried and tested method. Tigerfish, regrettably, had a less than 40% chance of hitting its target and should never have entered fleet service - it is one of the disgraces of the cold war.

He looked briefly at Sir John who nodded and he asked his executive officer to note my request in the log. That last part worried me for it would be deadly evidence against them. Not that I cared about Pommies in general but they had saved my life and that of my men. Sir John quietly said that the HMS Astute has two logs, that particular one will never leave the ship and besides, they are destroying a navigational hazard. That is if someone asks stupid questions in Parliament. Any warship from any country has the right to destroy a derelict ship drifting in shipping lines. As long as no one is on board they were covered by the law and should be commended for their actions. He himself sunk three such vessels and was very proud of it too. Commodore Octavius agreed with this. It is the way of the sea and the perfect excuse or anyway the best they could think of right now. Whatever, he agrees completely for whatever that is worth and they can write that down too.

"Now hear this, now hear this. We are going to action stations and sink a derelict vessel which is causing a navigational hazard. This is not a drill." The captain took command and said conversationally to his executive officer.

"Jimmy, what is the angle to the Orlando? Load four Spearfish torpedoes, we will shoot only two at the Orlando but reload immediately. And at all times keep a firing solution on the SAS Mendi. If she tries to interfere, we will sink her too but only if she attacks us. Is that clear?"

He completely ignored us from then on. The control room became very busy in the next minute or two. Submariners never see a surface vessel other than anything else but a target. Keeping a firing solution on the SAS Mendi was standard procedure and they had long since worked out what angle they needed to sink the EBS Orlando. It was a matter of getting permission and now they had it for the Orlando. They did not need any for the SAS Mendi. Any surface warship or even a submarine which attacks a nuclear attack boat belonging to Her Majesty should know that they will retaliate with deadly consequences. That too is a rule of the open seas.

"Aye Skipper, we have the Mendi in our sights. We will however not fire at her unless attacked and at your instructions. Wire-guided and proximity fuse I presume?" Here was one lad who was ready for command, nothing was going to rattle or bother him.

The Spearfish torpedo is a marvel of British technology. A heavy torpedo, it is used by the nuclear submarines of the Royal Navy (they don't have diesel-electrics anymore) and no one else. Not even the US Navy has something which even comes close in speed. Like all modern torpedoes it can be guided by wire or autonomously by active or passive sonar built into it. It exists because of the sad fact that during the cold war the West had no torpedo fast enough to be really effective against the deep diving and super-fast Soviet Alfa class nuclear attack submarines. This deplorable state of affairs was rectified with the Spearfish which has a top speed of more than eighty knots or 90 miles an hour. This is roughly double the speed which

142

any known submarines can achieve. With its six hundred and sixty-pound warhead and shooting distance of just over thirty miles it was the ideal weapon for the job. By using a proximity fuse it would explode under the keel of the target and break her apart. There is nothing better to sink a surface ship with. The torpedo somehow senses it is underneath its target and explodes. That creates a large "hole" in the water into which the ship falls and breaking her back or so I was explained afterwards. All I knew was it was very effective and very reliable.

I started thinking what would happen when the Orlando exploded, because she was going to. There was nothing in this world which would stop the Spearfish from doing their jobs. Would the SAS Mendi then attack the HMS Astute? They would struggle to do so for they left their Super Lynx anti-submarine helicopter at home, replacing it with the Oryx we shot down but theoretically they were close enough to launch their own homing torpedoes. The question was would they? You never know with the South Africans, they are aggressive by nature and used to bollocking submarines around. On their so-called anti-piracy patrols they did nothing but hunt for Western submarines to prevent them from landing snatch teams or retrieving them. It was a rather dangerous cat and mouse game which could have rapidly escalated to war. I cursed, not for the first time, the Muslim Truce which caused all this.

The technical talk between the naval men was a pleasure to watch. They had obviously rehearsed this thousands of times and new exactly what they were doing. It was a controlled fury sequence of events. Within a minute they were ready to fire. SAS Mendi's boat was still next to her and had not yet left for the Orlando.

"Sir John, I want to sweep the area with active radar to confirm that the Mendi was more than six cables away from the Orlando and in no danger. Would that be acceptable to you?"

The captain asked or rather stated it. He was not about to take orders from Sir John but he would listen to advice from the two senior officers next to him.

Six cables in nautical terms is about fourteen hundred yards. This was like shooting over someone's head. I prayed those torpedoes would work as promised as there was no margin for error here. If they went wild or rogue, they could be destroyed by remote control but it would defeat our cause and give the other side ample warning.

"You had better do that only after you fire the Spearfish before they race towards the Orlando and force you to self-destruct. I would do that. As you know they will immediately pick the torpedoes and the radar sweep up on their own passive surveillance systems. I agree though and would also advise you to record the actual sinking of the Orlando as irrefutable evidence. After she is sunk, do another sweep confirming the Mendi is still with us. Then go silent and deep and dodge whatever they try."

"I concur with Sir John."

Both Commodore Octavius and I said simultaneously as did Jimmy the One. It was not good tactical advice. Submarines like to shoot and get away before anyone realises what happened but here we needed evidence that no South African warship was attacked or sunk. Everything is recorded and I am sure, will be used for many years in future training scenarios.

"Ok you heard the advice. Radar...one sweep and then shut off but not down. On my command do one complete sweep and after the explosions, again, but on my command only. Is that understood?"

"Aye Skipper, on your command, one sweep and shut off but not down, then another sweep after the explosions at your command."

The petty officer was calm and collected. This was what he and his team do for a living. They shared a panel not too far away and were listening to every word we were saying whilst staring at their screens.

"Skipper, we are ready to fire at the Orlando, at your command sir."

Jimmy the One sounded bored but it was an act. I certainly did not feel bored but sad for I liked the old ship. Commodore Octavius was positively looking close to tears and ignored us staring at the screen. Sir John was grinning; the old goat felt the thrill of command again and probably wished he was twenty years younger. I wondered if those three "derelicts" were really that derelict when he sunk them. I knew of one case where the Soviets claimed a destroyer was rudely torpedoed whilst on a peaceful mission in its own waters. No one believed them.

"Ok, standby with your stopwatch, Jimmy. Torpedo room, shoot one" and five seconds later "shoot two. Radar, one sweep, commence, Jimmy, countdown to strike if you please. Give us ten seconds warning." He looked intently at the different screens. "Diving Officer, keep your depth. Steady as she goes." After that he leaned back and smiled a secret smile. I wondered what he was thinking of.

"Skipper torpedo room, two Spearfishes launched, aye. Torpedoes are running."

The voice came from above us, from a tannoy box which looked a bit old fashioned to me. I expected some sort of a jolt but there was nothing. Immediately the diving officer reported the boat is steady as she goes. It was hard to imagine that close to eight thousand pounds left the Astute and she did not move an inch in depth. Everyone looked so calm.

"Radar aye, one sweep only and powering down again...sweep done Skipper. The Orlando is still six cables west of the Mendi. It is logged."

He too sounded bored and I began to wonder about the sanity of Royal Navy submariners. Have they no nerves?

We kept a close watch on the screen. There was no way we could see the torpedoes. They don't leave any tell-tale signs like air bubbles - that stopped in the First World War already but there were definitive other signs that the torpedoes were speeding away from us. The reports came in fast and from all directions.

"Skipper, Sonar. All hell is breaking lose on the SAS Mendi. She went into emergency speed and is rapidly moving away from the Orlando. I suppose they heard the torpedoes in the water."

"Skipper, Radar. The Mendi has activated her search radar and is scanning for us."

"They have also doused all navigations lights." The last part came from Sir John still glaring at the thermal imaging screen.

"Skipper, Sonar. Mendi fired three noise makers and is slowing down again."

"Aye, that was expected...they don't know what is happening and took the usual precautions by dashing away and launching the anti-torpedo devices.

146

No problem lads, you can ignore their antics but keep watching and listening. Spearfish will ignore them. Jimmy how long before impact?"

I was secretly captivated with the SAS Mendi. We worked with her many times in the past (Code Name Lucy, Code Name Wrangler and many more, Angelique). Her reaction was out of this world and very quickly done indeed. Even the motor launch cut her engines as to give the sonar a fair chance to locate us. It must have come as a terrible shock to hear the torpedoes and at the same time being painted by radar. It only needs one sweep to launch the Tomahawk anti-ship missiles and though reputedly not on the Astute, they were withdrawn from service and replaced with long-range ones during the War on Terror, the Mendi could not have known that. From the thermal imaging she went to action stations and the twin 35mm close-in-weapon system on her helicopter hanger roof started to move poking this way and that. It was the gunners testing it before switching to full auto mode from where it would fire automatically on anything seen as a threat. Of all her weapon systems I feared that one the most. It was deadly at short range and designed to blow incoming missiles apart. Even the 76mm OTA Melara cannon on her foredeck suddenly turned sideways as if sniffing around - she too could fire very rapidly at an incoming missile if she had the right shells which they certainly did. I remember the MILAN anti-tank missiles slamming into the OTA Melara turret during our battle with her sister ship, the SAS Amatola (Code Name Phoenix).

"Skipper, Sonar. Yankee search from Mendi. I believe they have us. Range four thousand two hundred and eleven yards. No further active measures."

The Yankee sonar search is not used often as it betrays the ships' position and is only done to break the submarine commander's nerves or to shoot at the submarine. The whole crew can hear the sound waves lashing the

147

submarine and know that they are found. It is a horrible sound for a submariner. In war the next step is to launch homing torpedoes and the one fastest on the draw wins. It was at this moment when the captain of HMS Astute became an old man. He had to decide to shoot first at the SAS Mendi, who had him now by the balls or to quietly slip away. Under normal conditions he would have dived much deeper after firing - modern torpedoes don't need the submarine pointing towards the target. They will search for it themselves giving the submarine a chance to slip away undetected. Here he could not do that for we needed the video evidence on what was sunk. We had to remain at periscope depth where we were exposed to counter attack. It went against every instinct. Where do you draw the line? His command is much more important than the spy games we were playing. I would have dived away and bugger the video.

The man had nerves of steel. "Aye, no problem, Sonar, keep me posted." His calm demeanour spoke more than the actual words. The Skipper said it is no problem and so it was. Everyone relaxed again.

"Ten seconds, Skipper" says Jimmy the One who held an old-fashioned stopwatch in his hands. I looked for a moment at Commodore Octavius. Two tears were dripping down his cheeks and onto his white beard. Sir John was still grinning. He positively looked evil with delight.

The double explosions lifted the poor EBS Orlando clean out the water. The screen flickered briefly as the thermal imaging compensated for the sudden flash and then the Orlando was no more. She had disappeared from all screens including the radar sweep which was conducted within a minute after the explosions. She was gone forever and lies in small pieces at the bottom of the ocean. There were no cheers from the crew but a quiet satisfaction of men who had done a job well.

148

*"Oh my word, Foxtrot, get a helmet - that is life, make peace." Angelique, quite often to me*

## Chapter 4

## HMS Astute, Wardroom, Indian Ocean, 27 February 2014

After the old Orlando was blown to pieces, we immediately dove to six hundred feet and started to play cat and mouse with the SAS Mendi that tried everything but launching a torpedo or two. That was a smart move as the Astute kept a firing solution at her at all times. By this time, I was sleeping. My head started to hurt as the anaesthetics worked off and the doctor gave me a few tablets for pain which made me sleepy. Most of all I wanted to get to Angelique to see how she was doing. Perhaps by closing my eyes I could dream of her and an abundant life at the Ukuthula Ranch.

I knew it would not last, my peaceful sleep and all that. The next morning just after breakfast Sir John came in for a wee chat as he pronounced it. We don't like each other much and such wee chats almost always ended in bad blood between us. However, we needed each other. We were in a shotgun marriage and just had to make it work. It began civil enough with feedback on what we did since we last met in Djibouti and sailed south to sink the SAS Amatola. This amused him to no end. The man was a born pirate and technically minded on such matters. It was rather obvious that he already spoke to Commodore Octavius whom I believe did not care much for him either. I was just confirming facts and adding a few more details here and there.

"Ah, I understand that you and Geelslang stole the South African Navy code books from the 'Isaac Dyobha' then?" He asked without blinking an eye and since I had not specifically told him that I simply stared at him, not answering. There was no way in the world I would give it to him.

"It is our property you know, that codebook. Since you are in our pay, we want it." He stuck out his hand expectantly as if I had it on me and would give it to him just like that.

For a moment I thought of spitting in his hand like rumour had it the old Zulu King Dingaan did back in the 1830s. The spittle would then be smeared on his body as a mark of respect. It is an old African tradition which I will never try with Angelique. She is absolutely guaranteed to become "otherwise," tradition or not. Not even I am that brave or stupid or both. I once asked Geelslang about it and he started laughing, not so much at the idea of spitting at my issued girlfriend as she was at that stage but that I could believe the malicious rumour. According to him, a proper Zulu boy, if you did that to Dingaan you would have died soon after or wished you had. Still, it is written like that in the history books.

The Afrikaner doesn't like Dingaan at all. He murdered Piet Retief and another five hundred men, woman and children with surprise attacks. Most of the deceased were children meaning less than twelve years of age as we understood the term. After that age you are expected to go on commando, hunt for food and work on the farm if a boy. As a girl you would and should be married by sixteen and breeding kids but it was that way all over the world. It is written by the men who found the bodies, that the children who were not stabbed to death with the assegais were taken by their heels and viciously swung so that their heads were smashed against the rocks or the wagon wheels. The Afrikaner's reaction was typical of the breed; they got together, prayed about it, and attacked the Zulu Nation. This was not government acting but a group of people on their own initiative. Two years later thousands of Zulu warriors were dead and Dingaan deposed. He died soon after probably regretting having ever seen the Afrikaner then known as Voortrekkers. Certainly, his treachery is taught to every Afrikaner kid or used to be. These days that act of terrorism is probably applauded as part of the freedom struggle against oppression.

"Sir John, how many times do I have to tell you I do not work for you? And you are not my commanding officer. Even if I had the code books, I would not give it to you but to Colonel Angelique who is my superior officer. So you can piss off now."

I did not even try to be nice about it. This was getting boring. The man simply did not get it that the Egg Breakers will never work for the Pommies. With them yes, but they take their orders from me or rather via me because they selected me for the time being as their commander. And I only report to Angelique who represents France, not the UK lot. Graeme was in command for the moment but even he was subjected to Angelique once she starts sending orders again. Knowing her it would not take that long and I was surprised that she had not done so yet.

He was a proud man, Sir John, and he had much reason to be. Throughout his life he achieved more than most and believed himself very capable of dealing with difficult colonialists like me. He was dangerous too. With men like that, with their proper hooligan accents known as BBC Standard talk, we normally listen very carefully. We know, for generations, ever since the Empire started, how "otherwise" they get when you don't humour them. There was a time when the mere showing of the old flag in the harbour was enough to make the natives (and colonials are seen as natives by his type) behave. Gunboat diplomacy is frowned on today but back then it was all the rage. Every savage knew the great white queen (meaning Queen Victoria) would avenge her children if you get too uppish with them. These days they piss on the old flag and it is a shame. Even the Pommy bastards don't deserve such humiliations caused by weak liberal leaders bending backwards to the European Union to do the old country from behind.

Mind you, the one exception to the rule was always the Afrikaner. We had no harbours in our Boer Republics for them to show their flag and fancied ourselves. Whatever the great white queen could come up with we would answer with Mauser fire. We don't like them and that is that. They could beat us into submission by murdering our children and women in concentration camps but they would never break our spirit or desire to dislike them on sight. In Africa, during this Egg Breaker versus SASS war we did not need them...if needs be, we could always make peace and leave the Muslims alone. It was not our war to begin with. Absurdly, most of us would never be given a visa to even visit the Virginians or the UK lot who always assumed we wanted to, which we were not keen on. We liked our farms and Africa, this is home to us. Why would we want to be in a place where the sun shines three times a year and they write in bold headlines if the temperature goes up to 65F. It is rather pathetic to live like that on top of each other with more Muslims around than what is safe. A country which supports gay rights is obviously not going to be blessed by God. Our own great oracle, Siener van Rensburg, predicted this back in 1903.

"We can search you if you wish to be difficult Major Foxtrot."

His voice became low and threatening. He was not about to take this insult lying down. He used his rank to show me that he, as a retired rear-admiral, was the ranking officer here. He often tries that when we meet. Like a spoiled child. Why I would not know, I don't salute anyone unless first saluted and that does not include him. I am a civilian these days, a defence contractor if you wish, we don't do such things. Of course, I would salute Angelique if she told me to, but she won't. Why, I remember demonstrating to her once what really jumps to attention if I see her in a wet t-shirt or any other place. This reminded me that this old goat was a horny fellow on his third marriage with a much younger Indonesian girl (see Code Name Foxtrot). Yeah, he needed to be watched and spoke French better than me. I could feel the ire swelling up in me but kept cool. Sir John came close to being executed by us before, only Angelique saved his ass (yes, see Code Name Cadillac, Code Name Jen, Code Name Caribbean and many more, Angelique),

"Nah, you won't. Because you are smart, Sir John, you know that an officer never gives an order which he cannot fulfil himself and more importantly, is none too sure would be obeyed. I doubt if you would find anyone on this submarine willing to hold me down to be searched. Remember, Sir John, I am their field commander and we did wonderful things together. Their loyalty is not with you anymore. That would mean you would have to do the searching yourself."

I lifted my hand and he ducked quickly but I was only preventing him from interrupting me. "Sir John be warned I am very ticklish unless my wife is involved and will become violent if you try to search me. Note I would not want to cause you hurt and lower your esteem in front of our men but I will not hesitate to defend myself. This is rather silly; anyway, I don't have the code books with me. They went down with the EBS Orlando and the rest of my baggage. It is very unfortunate."

I did not go on to explain that I did not take the chance to bring them with me because I did not trust him. Once on his submarine he could do what he pleased and there would always be someone as willing to follow him as they would follow me. No submarine can afford a riot between two sides which we would anyway win. The sailor who can stand a few rounds with former Special Forces men is yet to be born - we were simply better trained and harder. Geelslang had the code books with him and would give it to Angelique in due course. The only item I brought with me onto the Astute was the L85 Individual Weapon I used to shoot the pilot with. That was now with the Master at Arms, as were the other weapons. He should have checked that before issuing such a threat.

Sir John stared hard at me, his piggy eyes glistening in the bright lights of the wardroom. Some of the other men were looking at us a bit strangely, they saw him duck and he was after all a very senior officer. Commodore Octavius nodded to me and I saw he was holding a heavy silver pot of tea he intended to use as a weapon if it came down to it. It was rather uncomfortable for a few seconds until Sir John started laughing. The man had a terribly annoying laugh too, like a hyena in heat.

"You are a rogue, Foxtrot, but so be it. Let us talk about Nigeria."

The change of direction caught me off-guard but if he wants to talk about the populous West African State, he is welcome. I knew it well and often worked there with Geelslang and Angelique in the old days. They are a classic example of capitalism run mad. They should be rich - they are the world's eighth biggest oil producer but they are not. Unlike other Middle East oil countries, the oil money doesn't give anything back to the common lad on the streets. This is causing a lot of anger and resentment. The rich are extremely rich; filthy is almost the word whilst the rest struggle for daily survival. Whatever their reputation as scammers, well deserved I assure you, they are physically attractive people. The men are tall and athletic; after all, that is where most American blacks or whatever they call themselves these days come from. They were excellent specimens for the plantations because they were such large handsome people. That is why they got caught and exported. Yes, I liked the Nigerians and always enjoyed working with them.

"What do you know of their military?" Sir John asked without explaining why.

He should know the answer; the UK lot has a large establishment of former soldiers in the oil industry and most of them report to MI6. These days they are also trying to help the Yanks with the Boko Haram problem in the north and failing miserably. As always, we on the side, the experts in counter-insurgency in Africa were not asked for our opinion and they went in and did everything wrong. It was becoming a pattern.

I answered truthfully. "They were decent enough when they were still under British officers, Sir John. The Nigerian Regiment, for example, fought well in the Second World War and before that." I shrugged. "And then came independence and they had the Biafra War. They are nothing special today as complete units and are underequipped. It is not their fault as it is the African way to keep the Armed Forces starved of equipment to prevent coup d'états. Individually they are good fighters and with the right leadership, a lot could be done. However, currently I rate them as a zero on a contract and their moral is very low. They will not win against a determined invasion or Western troops."

"Yes, the good part was proven with the Second Chindit campaign in Burma. That was back in 1944 was it not? Throughout history it is remarkable that colonial troops are always better at irregular warfare than professional soldiers. Why is that Foxtrot?"

He was now on a subject I liked and understood better than most. I was seconded from the police in the old days to attend a command & staff course with the brown jobs (Army). They were astonished at my military history knowledge and much less impressed about what I thought of them, the Staff wankers. They are of no use except to ensure that enough toilet paper is available. Actually, this was a misunderstanding which I failed to explain properly because I had a serious argument with one professor. He said that trenches were first used in warfare at the Battle of Magersfontein, 1899, by the Afrikaner, during the Second Anglo Boer War.

Of course, I get it that the Afrikaner would like to believe this but it was simply not true. Trench warfare took place centuries before this and more recently during the American Civil War. The only interesting thing of the Battle of Magersfontein was that the Scandinavian Corps (more a company of troops) fought with the Boers against the Pommy bastards. He did not like my answer. They still teach this nonsense at the Military Academy and there are even Egg Breakers who have faith in this story. I then offered to prove my point in a boxing match as was our way if a dispute arose. Being Geelslang's sparring partner I fancied the chance of knocking some sense into him.

Regrettably the professor, he was not much older than me but much fatter and a wanker by nature, refused my kind offer which led to the toilet paper comment. What I really meant was we, of Special Forces, always used Soviet weapons when behind the lines where we always were. Hence our supplies came via the Soviet Union in the form of captured arms. They, the Staff wankers, only supplied the toilet paper which is called in police slang, SAP 1000. Why I would not know. Anyway, he did not take kindly to this and I almost failed the subject which made me really mad. I got him in the end, Geelslang and I cornered him one evening in a pub and distributed justice.

The Chindit experiment which Sir John referred to is a bit of a puzzle to military historians with a lot of disagreement between them on the subject. Some men, like Brigadier Michael Calvert who served with the Chindits flatly stated it worked great. They tied down many thousands of Japanese soldiers, disrupted their supply lines and proved the concept. Others think it was a gallant but wasted effort. The answer is probably somewhere in the middle between the groups. It all started with one visionary as is often the case, Orde Charles Wingate, a British Army officer. The man was borderline insane, and it is not me saying this but none other than that arch liar and enemy of the Afrikaner, Winston Churchill's personal physician, Lord Moran. Crazy or not, Wingate was a good soldier and is rated as one of the fathers of modern guerrilla warfare tactics. An opinion I do not share and find plain stupid. I would have thought that the Imperial German officer, General Paul von Lettow-Vorbeck established that many a year before him in East Africa during the First World War. Wingate was then an obnoxious schoolboy in England. Von Lettow-Vorbeck could not be caught and used local black soldiers, known as "Askaris" to fight under white German officers. They only surrendered a month after the war stopped in Europe, the news being a bit slower in those days than today. It was this officer who is rated by the experts in counter-insurgency in Africa, the Afrikaner, as the father of modern guerrilla warfare. Before him there were many others, such as our own Boer General Christiaan de Wet. Before De Wet we think of the great cavalry commanders like JEB Stuart wearing a faded grey uniform. Despite this the British Historians have Orde Wingate and are clinging to him like a calf looking for milk on a warm day.

I am not surprised that Lord Moran thought and said that the man was borderline insane. You just have to look at his eccentricities and make your own conclusions. He wore an alarm clock instead of a decent watch on his wrist. The damn thing would often go off and wake the Staff wallahs from their sleep. I must ask, what if that alarm clock goes off and betrays your position? Or the large phosphorous dials are spotted at night by the enemy? And then he ate garlic and raw onions to ward off mosquitos in the middle of Scotland as well as everywhere else. He munched them as others would drink tea, the man had no manners or respect for decent people. I have strong feelings on this subject. Anyone eating garlic without reason or compulsion, like me, who is cruelly forced by Angelique and our twins to do so, is a scoundrel in my eyes. I remarked to Angelique when we were still niggling at each other that garlic is for lazy cooks. A real woman, never mind a decent Afrikaner girl like her, will know that it takes away all flavour and spoils the food.

That remark, innocent as it was turned out badly for me. She suddenly and always ordered garlic food for the next three years and since she had an expense account and was paying I could not really object. Good manners dictated I shut up and eat what I was given, it is the Afrikaner way. I tried in other ways to escape the garlic. I would cover my nose with a perfumed handkerchief until she wondered noisily if I had unnatural tendencies. According to her experience, only men with very unnatural tendencies even possessed a perfumed handkerchief. Perhaps Geelslang and I were more than good mates...she always sees us together now that she was thinking about it. Perhaps we had tendencies, not that she cared, it is just interesting to note our social behaviour down on our files at SASS headquarter for future reference. We have an unnatural weakness for men and across the colour bar too! Who would have believed that and ex-Special Forces officers besides? She even clicked her tongue in dismay showing her African heritage. Since that day I made Geelslang wear his wedding ring and show her pictures of his eldest child, the second was not born yet but came soon after. I also breathed through my mouth which is the recommended way of breathing when working with rotting corpses and garlic eating spymasters. Mind you that stopped as well. After a while she figured it out and gave me nose spray since my nose is obviously blocked which it was not. I still have nightmares of her coming at me with a gigantic nose spray device. Sigh, if any young fellow reads here...listen to good advice - shut up and eat and say it was delicious and you would love to have seconds. Then go and puke it out around the corner if you wish for none of that fancy advice you hear on eating parsley and mint tea and God knows what else works. It is a terrible thing so get used to it and Bob is your uncle (Foxtrot likes garlic these days, Angelique).

The one thing General Wingate (he died a Major General) is remembered for most is his extraordinary affection for Jews. Before the war he worked with Jewish groups, terrorists according to the Arab historians, to deal with Arab saboteurs who attacked the oil pipelines and Jewish settlements. He also raided, that is attacked, Arab border villages which the attackers had used as bases. No doubt fighting fire with fire - a very bad counter-insurgency tactic. He was not even Jewish but a deeply committed Christian who promoted Jewish interests far above that of the colonial masters, his own people, the London lot. He was so effective with his small unit hit and run tactics (also called Special Night Squads) that the famed one-eyed Israeli general, Moshe Dayan, later said: "Wingate taught us everything we know." That is very high praise indeed and probably has some elements of truth in it as by 1939 he was transferred away from Palestine to London. He had become too well-known and too radical to stay on but his name was made.

Then came the Second World War and his former Palestine commander, Archibald Wavell, 1st Earl Wavell, recruited him to Sudan where he promptly created something called the "Gideon Force" named after the Biblical character. This force used typical guerrilla tactics by mobilising locals against the occupying Italians in neighbouring Ethiopia. They attacked forts and supply lines and made a nuisance of themselves more than anything else. If you want to be nasty, you will say he became a legal terrorist in both Palestine and in Ethiopia. What is significant to us from a command viewpoint, is that he led the attacks himself. That is a big problem, an officer with his rank and experience, by now a lieutenant colonel, really should command and not lead attacks which is the privilege of a lieutenant. In my eyes that is bad leadership. It shows immaturity and schoolboy antics. He soon fell out with the leadership in the "normal" army - a trademark of a genuine Special Forces leader. They all have difficulties with those who do not quite understand their strange ways. Once again, he ended in the UK complaining that his men were betrayed. He was right, as with the Jews in Palestine depending on the 1917 Balfour Declaration, none of the promises made to get them to fight for the Crown were kept. He was getting wise to the way the Colonial Office in Whitehall operated and if he had bothered to ask us we would have told him that before he even started. The UK lot will promise anything to anyone as long as they don't have to fight alone. Even the so-called lonely stand they made between 1940 when France gave up and 1941 when the Americans came saving them is nonsense. The whole British Empire, about one hundred nations, were sending troops and helping them along. A place like India had to pay one million UK pounds a day on war loans. This almost broke India financially besides sending hundreds of thousands of well-trained soldiers to die. Sufficient to say that the Burma Theatre and to a lesser extent the North Africa and Italian Theatres would not have succeeded as they did without the tough lads of the Indian Army standing fast. They paid a terrible price for this loyalty. In Bengal, a state in India, starvation was taking place but still that arch liar, Winston Churchill, refused to stop food exports from Bengal. He showed his true colours by asking "if the famine was so horrible, why had Gandhi not yet died of starvation?" Leo Amery, the Indian Secretary of State bitterly replied he regarded that comment as "Hitler-like." A great insult but then the man was probably drunk, he often was during Cabinet meetings. What the Indians or Mr Gandhi said I don't know but we took note of it. It reminded us of the concentration camps on a much larger scale and showed what the Pommies will do to survive.

By this time, the end of 1941, Orde Wingate was yet again more trouble than he was worth and it is probably only the fact that Erwin Rommel's achievements chased Archibald Wavell to the Burma Theatre that saved him. He got drafted to go there by his old commanding officer and immediately wanted to form a long-range penetration group to work behind the Japanese lines. This was built on the ideas of SAS founder, Colonel David Stirling and the excellent work done by the Long Range Desert Group in the North African Theatre. No doubt that Popski's Army also played a role in his thinking; it was not original at all. His old mate Wavell agreed and so the Chindits were formed. They were a group of especially hardened men, trained to work in columns of more than a thousand plus behind the enemy lines in the jungles of Burma. They would be supplied by air which meant either cutting a rough landing strip or by parachute and sometimes by river. Pack donkeys were used to carry equipment. With the first mission they had some initial success and then crossed the Irrawaddy

River and into hell. Expecting jungles to hide in, they only found dry and inhospitable terrain, God knows how they planned the operation if they did not know what the terrain would be like. The Japanese threw them out by the seat of their pants. They had to scatter into small groups to escape, or in other words, they lost their ability to operate as a cohesive unit and with that became totally ineffective regarding their mission objective. They also suffered one third losses which is plainly ridiculously heavy for what they achieved. Later it came out that many of their officers were homosexuals and had very close, I am tempted to say "deep," relationships with their Gurkhas (true, you can read the autobiographies, Angelique).

Such a disaster could only be seen as a victory by the Pommies who had none at that stage and hence it was propagated as a brilliant attempt which it was most certainly not. All it did was to convince the Japanese that they too could then operate in such terrain leading to the offensive into India to capture the Imphal Plain and Kohima the next year. It was mostly units from the Indian Army that stopped them at Kohima, a battle largely forgotten today by the West. During that battle the words "Tennis Court" became synonymous with great bravery and sacrifice. Kohima saved India and was a turning point in the war. But back in London that great Special Forces wannabe - he created the commandoes - Winston Churchill, was awestruck with Wingate's ideas and stories of the first Chindit operation. He ordered operations to continue against the wishes of many experienced line officers.

Hence, late in 1944 the Second Chindit operation began. This time many men were dropped by glider and the rest walked or marched. The idea was not really guerrilla warfare anymore but more conventional. They would establish semi-permanent bases from which they would venture out and raid the Japanese. This alone destroyed whatever reputation Wingate had in our eyes as a guerrilla warfare specialist. Special Forces, guerrillas or irregulars

162

never operate like that and they never suffer such high casualties either. They are strategic troops, very valuable and designed to use the locals to do the fighting. I think Wingate got confused and a bit carried away. Field Marshal Bill Slim, reckoned by us as the best Pommy Commander ever, even better than the brilliant Montgomery, said later he thought that the Chindits had a negative impact on the war in general by taking away the best men from each Regiment. The Japanese commander admitted that both operations had some effect on them but not crucially so. Wingate did not live to defend himself. He died in an air crash on his way back from one of the bases. Perhaps it was a good thing as a man like that rarely does well in peacetime.

The Nigerian Regiment was part of this second operation, called "Operation Thursday" and conducted themselves very well. Sir John had a point about colonial troops and irregular warfare. The Australians for example are very good at this and achieved ten times the kill ratio than what American units did in Vietnam. Of course, they had been fighting everywhere shedding blood for the parasites of Buckingham Palace for the last hundred and twenty years. Why? Only they would know but that is their prerogative. We are very proud that the last South African who died for them, as a South African soldier, was back in 1945. We wizened up. It is proven in battle that African soldiers are as brave as any other nation but only if they have decent leadership. What went wrong in Nigeria, after independence, was tribalism. Only certain tribes, the Igbo, became officers and this caused serious resentment. The existing officer corps was also in no way capable of leading at high command. The UK lot made certain to train them only to company commander grade and never to general officer. Divide and rule was always the British Empire's best tactic to keep control. Yes, there were those who attended a few courses but you cannot really train a flag officer like that - he needs experience in every rank and every level to be effective. Jumping ranks and rushing through courses is not the way the British Army or any other army has ever trained generals successfully before. So why would the newly African Armies then be different? Obviously, they could never be and were not. It created armed mobs, not soldiers. But is that the fault of the black African? He is not a coward by any means of the imagination and physically fitter than most western soldiers. So where did it go wrong?

History will tell you that South Africa and Rhodesia when it still existed were the odd ones excluded from this lack of leadership. Both countries had a professional officer corps based on the British Army. Almost all of the Rhodesian Army cadets attending Sandhurst won the Sword of Honour. This happened so regularly that they sort of expected it and would wonder what went wrong if the cadet returned without it. There was no tribalism as such in these Armies. The white men, not part of any local black indigenous tribe fundamentally became the officers with a few black ones later on. The Afrikaner could perhaps be classified as a white African tribe; they have been in Africa for close to four hundred years and thought of themselves as such. The white Rhodesians were never Afrikaners and hence could not be classified as a tribe. They were more English than the Pommies anyway. As a rule, the white men commanded black men with great success. Put another way, traditionally, the white officers were the cement which held the tribes together and kept them apart. When the white officers left the Nigerian Regiments, tribalism came back as it did in every other African country you care to mention. That is except South Africa and Rhodesia until "freedom" arrived.

Interestingly for us in Special Forces is that the original lads who went for SAS Selection in the UK came back saying it was not nearly as hard as they thought it should have been. Some said, and that may have been beer

164

talking, that they came back less fit than when they left. They changed their own Selection to make it even harder than the UK one. Many a former SAS lad who came down south to fight communism would confirm this statement. The point being that the colonials are probably closer to the earth and hence hardier by nature. We saw this with the American Special Forces community also. Most of their men are from rural areas and the Deep South. In Vietnam, which we studied in great detail in order to see what we could learn; most snipers for instance were hunters. And they never worked alone behind enemy lines - that is Hollywood rumours which came long afterwards. We are not overly impressed with the Yanks either; they are way too reliant on air support and technical goodies and worse, are becoming entirely predictable. They would do well to go back to the basics and to take a step back and reconsider how their enemy has developed.

Counter-terrorism is not a static game. We see this with the techniques Al-Qaeda uses to counter the classic Special Forces tactics used against them. Someone, with specialist knowledge is advising them on counter strike techniques and it is a matter of time before their sleeper agents erupt in Europe and America. Years ago, Angelique mentioned that they are trying to infiltrate double agents into the West. They had done that from the beginning and quite a few Virginian Agents were killed in that way, by falling in traps and ambushes. If you think about it, it is very logical that they will play the great game. They know how to do so.

"Foxtrot, what does it mean to you and your fellow Egg Breakers? When you say that the Nigerian soldier, as an individual is an excellent fighter and warrior but without good leadership and equipment is rather third rate. Typical of Africans I suppose."

"Sir John, that last remark, it can be seen as racist and in certain quarters will cause you a lot of difficulties. Our conditions here are different than Europe. For instance, we don't need nor desire overly complicated equipment. It won't last. It has been proven time and time again that homemade purposely built equipment performed better than anything produced in Europe. Take for instance our Super Frelon helicopters which we bought for a vast cost from France - it was almost never used in combat in Angola because they could not fly properly in the heat or dust. On paper they were perfect as were our Mirage 3s which we bought because of their sterling reputation in the Middle East. But they had a serious problem with range; Africa is so much bigger than Israel where they made their name as superb fighters. Consequently, the Mirage F1 became the preferred weapon; it had a much longer range. But then we discovered that fast jets rarely play a significant role in counter insurgency. Yes, they keep air superiority which is important but it was the much slower Impalas (a copy of the Italian built Aermacchi MB-326) which did by far the most damage. It used guns, two 30mm cannons and free-falling fragmentation bombs to much greater effect. They are the ones who became renowned by shooting down enemy helicopters. There are many lesser examples. When we got the British Army SLR we changed it by adding a much better flash suppressor and removing the carry handle. My point is this, what may seem African or Third World to you is in many instances the only way and was learned from bitter experience."

"Yes, but we are talking of the calibre of man here. Equipment is something else entirely." He sounded defensive as he should be. We knew Africa better than any other military men.

"No, we are talking leadership. The calibre of the man is the same; he is born, goes to school and enlists. That is where the change comes in...

166

whether he goes to the police or army. If the African soldier is led properly, it is proven since time began, then he is as good as any other nation no matter what the skin colour involved. What bedevilled us was politics and bad leadership. I can answer your question - it makes no difference to the Egg Breakers because we never enter into battle with the brown jobs anyway. We are specialists, Sir John, we go in without any fuss, do what needs to be done and get out. Clashing with the Army, no matter how good or bad they are, is a failure with a capital F even if we get away with it."

I took another sip of tea; they really had nice tea on the HMS Astute. "Sir John, like almost every senior foreign military man I have ever met, you completely forget the most efficient counter-terrorism lads in Africa which are not the brown jobs. It is the Police Forces; you think of your own Scotland Yard or your Sheriff's Departments and apply that to Africa and dismiss the police. But do you know that in almost every country in Africa the police are the lads holding the line on parade? They are the senior service and the ones with the most experience."

"In our own Bush War, it was policemen, acting as highly mobile mechanised infantry in very small groups, platoon level mostly, who killed 90% of all terrorists. This was not by chance but by training and harsh experience. In Africa, it is not unusual to see a policeman with an assault rifle and he is used to killing for it is a violent place. He is harder than the average soldier because he is always exposed to what you see as a war zone. When he works on the mean streets he is almost certain to kill in the line of duty. Mostly, and this is fact, he is older and more experienced. He has seen more violent death than almost any soldier of any unit, including Special Forces, in the West. The tactics they use, in counter insurgency is Special Forces adaptions and it is not a matter of training all the time - the police actually apply this every day during the normal course of their work."

"What are Special Forces adaptions? I have never heard the term before. But carry on old chap, this is rather interesting." He sat back and smiled or tried to. I wondered what he wanted for he is not a man to ask unnecessary questions or even to be seen with me without reason.

"It means they use Special Forces tactics, small units, many times at section level of ten men or less, operating without body armour, helmets and most of the time without decent radio communications. They investigate and know their own area, do their own tracking and fancy themselves against any opposition no matter how well armed. They are aggressive, well trained and looking for trouble and will attack without hesitation. As far as they are concerned, they are the real elite and will only call and use the Army and Air Force as backup. The Army and Air Force will never, by law, be able to command them as they command the Army and Air Force units. They will, because they are under equipped, either steal what they need from the Army or adapt what they have to the best possible use. It is, Sir John, a mentality sadly lacking in armies which are more rigid and follow the rules more closely. The policemen follow their instincts which are sharpened to an unbelievable state of awareness because they work with criminals and the scum of society every day. Hence, they are more effective in finding terrorists and also, because of their daily work, more effective in killing them."

We did not like each other, Sir John and I, but I could see he was listening closely and leaning forward. "You have often said terrorism is a police problem only and not the military. Perhaps it is because you were a policeman yourself. The problem with this theory of yours is that the police are too small to handle terrorism. At some stage the problem becomes so large that the Army must get involved. We saw that in Northern Ireland and other places, Kenya for instance, Rhodesia too. When it reaches that stage the Army must be involved to protect innocent lives."

"I was a policeman yes, but that plays no role in my thinking. What you just said is indeed the conventional argument. My counter argument is what happens then? What does the Army do once it is involved? It goes back to what a terrorist is and the way he operates. When you plant a bomb or you behead a captive or use women as sex slaves you are committing a crime. No matter what your political or religious intentions, you are a criminal at heart. Hence all terrorism is a crime and crimes are dealt with by the police. The outlook and training are vastly different from that of a soldier though and this must be noted, an experienced policeman can easily be trained to act as light infantry and because of their small numbers and esprit de corps, crack infantry. The Army lads can never become policemen and don't want to either. The policemen are able to combine the skills of the two forces and that makes them so terribly effective in Africa. As an Egg Breaker, I fear the police more than the army, a lot more. I avoid the army but cannot always avoid the police and they are a suspicious people by nature. They would know if you lie to them, call it a sixth sense, Sir John, but it keeps them alive and they are finely tuned to it."

"And also open to bribery. It is a disgrace the way they carry on. Human rights abuses and lack of proper oversight." Sir John muttered.

"Yes, they have that reputation too and it depends where you are. In my own time, a lot of us went to jail and others were executed by hanging. No need to look so shocked Sir John; they broke the law, got caught, and were punished according to the law. In Apartheid South Africa the rule of law was always kept. You simply did not take liberties with it and expected the courts or the police to wash their hands."

He looked a bit dubiously at me and I continued explaining.

"My point is that almost none went to jail for taking bribes. They did other things which are wrong and against their training and salt but bribes were not a major problem. These days, the general impression is that all policemen are corrupt. I believe this is nonsense. There are still a majority, a vast majority which will arrest you for trying your luck. That is in South Africa where different standards apply...and remember most African Nations have one police force also, a national one. There are no such things as every town with a separate police department. We have what is called the traffic police. They work for the city council and are peace officers, not real policemen and not a member of the National Police. They are rightly looked down upon as a lesser force. Foreigners don't always understand the difference which is a pity. Sufficient to say no member of the police will ever stop you for a traffic violation, they don't do that. The despised traffic cops are on that beat. And they are the bribe takers giving everyone else a bad name."

"And what about Nigeria...they have a national police force also. How do you rate them? Let us forget about South Africa for the moment, that country is anyway rather weird and difficult to classify appropriately." He looked at me intently. I wondered again where he was heading to.

"I am afraid that the Nigerian Police are so corrupt that they can be bribed easily. It is something of a national institution to take bribes. Their senior officers are all in the pay of the Virginians or yourself probably. They have a tacit understanding that this will increase their income. It is a country where capitalism and dog eats dog went berserk. We know who the foreign sympathisers are. No normal policeman, no matter what his rank, can afford a child to study in the US or in the UK. They also seem to have no difficulty with visas at all. Another dead giveaway and sadly your people seem to think it is not noticed."

He ignored my jibe on their lack of security. "So all in all, you don't rate either the Nigerian Army or Police highly?"

He leaned even further forward and I wondered again what was going on in Nigeria that would concern us. They had a lot of Muslim problems there and there are Egg Breakers operating in that area because of it. He should not need my help. They are more than able to deal with the locals themselves.

"I don't but I have respect. If they are pushed, they will react. We try to work with them and certainly with the tacit approval of the local intelligence lads, the State Security Service or SSS as they are known. They are good people Sir John, we like each other and I have much respect for them."

"How good are these lads in the State Security Service?"

Ah, so he finally got to where he wanted to be or so I suspected as he asked it too flippantly. As if in an afterthought, something Sir John simply did not do. Now it was getting more to the point which could possibly concern me.

"They are a damn sight better than what the news reports. There is a strong Israeli influence on them. Take for instance their primary weapon. And that is how we picked it up first, is the Israeli made Tavor or TAR21. They invested heavily in explosives detectors, using Israeli technology. This happened after the 2009 'Underwear bomber' incident." Ironically, Angelique and I were inside Lagos International that day busy with other things and could have walked past the fellow. "They certainly uncovered a plot to assassinate Israelis and Americans in 2013. These days they are more concerned with Boko Haram in the north. Down south, where Biafra used to be in the Niger Delta, they have infiltrated MEND almost completely. As a terrorist movement MEND is a failure more concerned with forcing Oil Companies to pay them to be quiet than anything else. They are no threat to Nigeria as a country and they have reason to be angry."

"Well they are not winning against Boko Haram in the north. They could not even find the kidnapped girls yet."

He was talking about a much-publicised event where more than 200 school girls were kidnapped and sold as consorts and God knows what else. It happened only a few days before and created a worldwide "Bring back our girls" movement by mostly fat and ugly has-been American politicians whose husbands cheated on them. No doubt they jumped on the band wagon for publicity reasons and it too would disappear within a month as other news hit the headlines.

As a counter-terrorism expert in Africa, I can tell them that Boko Haram will not be shaken by their internet campaign no matter how well it is meant for future voters. They would laugh it off and welcome any American soldier to come within range of their guns. As they did in Vietnam, the Yanks would be blundering around waiting to be shot. Without intelligence you cannot fight a war. It is that simple and the Duke of Wellington said that back in 1814 already: "All the business of war… is to endeavour to find out what you don't know by what you do; that's what I called "guessing what was at the other side of the hill."

I answered flatly. "Neither could the American drones and the hundreds, probably thousands, of useless advisors the West sent in response. This is to be done by hard work on ground level by men who know the area. Do you know Sir John, I read a report the other day that these drones miss their targets an utterly astonishingly 97% of the time? The vaunted predator drone program has barely dented international terrorism in ten years." He looked

172

shocked and opened his mouth to say something but I did not wait. "This was from a report released by the US Senate Intelligence Committee and proves that you need Egg Breakers and Special Forces when you are in a terrorism war. Someone must be able to get the pinpoint accuracy needed for drones and you don't have it in Africa. The whole counter-terrorism approach is wrong and not intelligence based. It is not practically possible for so many women or teenagers to disappear without anyone knowing anything about it. That tells me two things, one the government lost all control through bad management and the insurgents are the de facto government already, in which case you lost the war and can go home. Secondly, they have no backup on ground level where it is needed. With this and it is absolutely crucial, comes the ability to strike fast and hard. It is no use to know something as SSS probably does and being unable to trust the brown jobs to do something about it. Did you know that every time that SSS pinpointed Western hostages the Nigerian Army involved themselves with the rescue attempt made by the SAS and other foreign Special Forces groups? And every time that happened the operation was betrayed and the hostages killed during the rescue. You have to wonder why."

He had the answer for that ready. "You know how the game is played with the Senate and Downing Street, Foxtrot. We always down play our abilities and successes. It bloody well suits us to be known as incompetent by the liberal press which is widely read by the enemy. However, I have to agree, the Predator strikes, when they miss, which is 97% of the time, is recruiting hundreds to the enemy's ranks. It is not the answer; I agree with you on that aspect. Terrorism is a police or rather an intelligence unit problem backed up by highly trained Special Forces. The usual infantry regiments and even armoured ones are useless at this type of warfare and they cost a tremendous amount of money to deploy."

It was obvious Sir John argued the above many times before. You have to admire the Pommies for going to war, conventional and counter terrorist with their nephews against their better judgement and solely out of misplaced loyalty. After all, the World Trade Centre is not in London but in New York and because of their loyalty they had the London Tube bombing and whatever else will happen in the future. The British Armed Forces, whilst still trained to superior levels, are not a factor today, too small, too outdated and without strategic reserves, a military joke under American command wherever they go, limiting what they are capable off. They paid the price of being exposed as a second-rate military power. Not so much because their men are any less devious bastards than always, that they stayed, no, they proved to the world how underfunded they are and it really affected their ability to conduct operations. They are the classic example of what happens when cheques are written that a military just cannot pay. In the Helmand Province of Afghanistan where they never wanted to be, they were reduced to 9 Chinook helicopters and a few Apache attack helicopters – albeit with more powerful British made engines than the US version and thus able to keep their masks making them vastly superior. These helicopters never flew or not often anyway, together, but in teams of two whilst the rest are serviced by ground crews or serving as standby air ambulances. Hence, they had only 4 Chinooks available at any given time. This was a fraction of what the Yanks had available in much smaller provinces and forced them to do the two things which they never did in Northern Ireland. They went against all counter insurgency doctrine by using the same old roads and hence became IED and ambush targets whilst driving totally unsuited vehicles, unprotected and without aircon in most. As in Iraq, fit men passed out from heat exhaustion with temperatures inside the vehicles reaching 55 degrees Celsius. There are only so many routes you can take before the pattern emerges and from then on it is a matter of time. In

174

Northern Ireland the helicopters flew them around reducing roadside bombs to almost nothing. Many men died unnecessarily because of this. Worse, they had to lock themselves in Beau Geste type forts waiting to be attacked because they simply did not have the manpower to do much else. And when they were attacked there were not enough helicopters to bring reinforcements breaking a classic counter insurgency rule. You want to be attacked but only if you can reinforce quickly enough to gain the upper hand. The French tried the same at a place called Dien Bien Phu in 1954 and we know how that ended. By creating these forts, they surrendered their mobility and concentration of forces. It could not work; it did not work before in Malaya, Indo-China with the De Lattre Line and failed equally badly in Iraq and in Afghanistan. It is a very bitter pill for they knew their history and advised against such tactics. Graeme, who fought in Northern Ireland, both Iraq Wars and Afghanistan told me how senior officers had to apologise to squaddies for their lack of equipment. That was where he decided to resign his commission and I have never seen the man that bitter before or since. It is a fact and a credit to their honour that many other senior commanders also resigned in disgust. This included a senior paratrooper commander well on his way to general officer rank. The world, or rather the Taliban and their mates, took good note. The old British Lion was humiliated and her soldiers betrayed by the Downing Street wankers.

As an Afrikaner I enjoyed that, obviously, as a Christian and military man, I felt their pain. What people forget is that the average Tommy is a popular fellow in Africa, the Afrikaner girls excluded; they don't like them since birth. But for the rest, they are easy to mix with, generous and kind enough if not provoked. Very much what Africans don't expect from soldiers who are seen as thugs, murderers and very unpleasant fellows. Especially those officers who were prefects at English public schools turned out to be very nasty people. It is traditionally one of the British Army's strengths - the ability of the lads to mix with the locals even if they are more interested in the women than anything else. As a group they are kind to children. They are also always willing to demonstrate their soccer playing skills which is a big deal in most places. According to Graeme, if allowed to mix with the Afghans instead of hiding in the forts all the time, they would have turned the tide. He may be right; they are devious bastards.

"So what is your problem in Naija" Sir John."

Nigeria is called "Naija" by the locals and those who like the place. It is unfortunate that in Afrikaans, the same word or parts of it anyway has an entirely different sexual meaning. Most Afrikaners when first exposed to Nigerian culture comment on this. An enigma is that the Afrikaner is closer to the average Nigerian than what the new lot is. Nigerians are proud people and though severely critical against their own they do think of themselves as better educated, better looking and certainly better people than the new lot in Pretoria. You can ask any one of them and they will tell you this.

I remember sitting with SSS officers in a coffee shop in Abuja. We had the local South African High Commission fellows with us. Why I would not know but I suppose Angelique, she was still my issued girlfriend, had to invite them with. A dispute broke out about Johannesburg versus Abuja, the capital of Nigeria. Both sides maintained that they had the best city which is plain madness - Johannesburg looks like New York in places like Sandton and Abuja had none of that though it is much better than Lagos. It cannot begin to compete.

We wanted SSS help and said that Abuja is the better place to live which is true. There is less traffic and much less danger, only a few car bombs now and then. I certainly felt safer and more welcome in Nigeria than in South

Africa where racial tensions are still high. You can really feel the hate towards the white man when you land and go through customs. In Nigeria...nah, there you are seen as someone to be scammed out of money in the nicest way possible. The High Commissioner lad described Sandton City. He talked of the largest shopping mall in Africa and what you can buy there. Anything from McDonald's to extremely expensive jewellery and clothing stores with genuine brands, not Nigerian fakes. What followed was a major embarrassment for us South Africans.

"Come now" says the senior SSS officer. "We know you. When you were still fighting your war of freedom" at this he rolled his eyes, the new lot were rather pathetic as terrorists "you ran away from the Boers all the time. You lived like baboons in the bush whilst your leaders got as fat as pigs in London. And then you inherited a modern country, developed and built under the leadership of these white men." He pointed his finger at me who kept quiet thinking that if I said such things at home, I would be accused of racism no matter how true. Whenever any type of criticism is raised it is racist and the liberal newspapers cannot wait to blacken your name. Most just keep quiet or leave the country to a place where they and their skills are welcomed. The brain drain was and is considerable and no country can afford it. Nevertheless, the SSS man was not finished yet. "Once you inherited that country you did nothing but f up. You are not even the biggest economy in Africa anymore or you won't be for long. We are overtaking you rapidly. Yes, we do not have a Sandton City yet. But we will and we will use these very same white men you chased to us to do so. Mark my words that in fifty years you will look like us and we will look how you are now. Don't you dare to come here and preach how great your shopping malls are at home! You did not build them or anything else except mud huts - the white people did. You are nothing and would forever be nothing without your white people who are now here, as our brothers and helping us."

His observations, though partly true, were really awkward for Angelique and me. At that stage we still wanted to believe that Mr Mandela's efforts would have a good ending. We smirked at the clever one's discomfort and started to talk about the weather as Africans do when they need common ground. The subject was not touched upon again and the cadre appointee had the common sense to shut up. Nigerians are devastatingly good debaters on any bloody subject but especially on their beloved Nigeria. Worse than that, they speak very decent Pommy when they want to but I noted with approval that their elite did their Master's Degrees in Europe or the USA. They don't like the Pommies much which made us natural friends.

"Terrorism is changing, Foxtrot. They are getting smarter and using more educated men than the lads running in the mountains or back streets of Syria. Yes, they have finally realised that explosives are a fifteenth century concept." Sir John looked at me as if wanting me to point out that explosives or black powder were used long before that but I got his meaning.

"I have long since believed that the next 9/11 will not be explosives Sir John. It is crude and ineffective as a weapon of mass destruction. Even nuclear explosions are old news; they are decades old and overrated. They would also demand an extra-ordinary retaliation. There are much better ways to create havoc in the West but I am listening."

"There is a Saudi National in Kano, Nigeria. He is experimenting with biological weapons to insert in London's water supply system. As an experiment only..." he paused and said. "The real target, we suspect, will be Washington. British trained I am afraid; a PhD graduate from the University of Manchester. I am sad to admit that student visa programs have proved to

178

be a terrorist loophole of note. In the US alone there were no less than thirty-six convicted terrorists using that method for gaining entry in the last ten years. In the UK, it would be more if the statistics are ever released."

"I read that report too, Sir John, it was released by those idiots in Homeland Security. God only knows what good they do as they cannot even close the Mexican border properly. A flat piece of semi-desert area which is the easiest terrain possible to defend but then, when only 3% of illegal immigrants are deported, what can you expect? The local agents and police are not even allowed to ask where the bastards came from. We would arrest anyone looking a bit too black for us."

"Even today...in the new South Arica, are you sure? The Police arrest people because they look too black?" Sir John looked positively shocked.

"Of course, it happens, Sir John. You understand it is tribalism in motion. The policemen don't like the illegal aliens and blame them for everything which is wrong in their own lives. They are rather easy targets. We deport tens of thousands every month and at times their papers are torn up by the police so they cannot prove who they are. And then it is bye-bye. To answer your insinuation, in my day we did not do that. We looked at their ability to speak decent Afrikaans. Any native, in those days, if slapped hard enough could speak the language and if not, he was deported. They also had different inoculation marks - if there wasn't a mark on their left shoulder, where it should be, we knew and it was bye-bye. Interestingly, the Security Police had another way to find out if a woman was black or white - it made a big difference in law. They checked her nipples and if not red or pink she was classified as non-white. That did not work well mind you, after birth some women do experience colour changes in that area or so we were told."

He just shook his head and muttered something. Sir John was never a fan of Apartheid and back in the early 1960s he had to run for his life after chatting up a coloured girl whilst on leave from his ship. He never forgot the incident as the police would not have helped him. Any kind of sexual relationship across the colour line was a serious crime, plenty went to jail for it.

"But to get back to the Department of Homeland Security, as always when it comes to empire building with federal money, they have their usual dependency on computers instead of on men on the ground. War is not an MBA operation, the 'McNamara Wiz Kids' proved that in Vietnam costing thousands of American lives. Computers are tools, not the ultimate weapon at this stage, maybe in the future. It is rather useless to show the money spent or blown instead of the positive results. Those results can only be achieved by using dedicated men and women to do what Is needed on ground level. That, I am convinced, will never happen in the US and hence, in the long run, they are doomed. Not because of the Muslims but because of their own liberals."

Sir John did not reply directly, his views on his nephews were his own business. "Anyway, this fellow was under surveillance for quite a while. He did not realise that many of the pro-Al-Qaeda websites are actually red flag operations designed to see who says what. We picked him up before 2005 already and tried to recruit him to our Neighbours without success."

I nodded appreciatively. MI6 refers to their colleagues; I would rather have said enemies in MI5, the counter-espionage lads, as "neighbours." The two groups don't like each other at all. Regarding the websites, it is a very well-known tactic first started by the Soviets back in the 1920s. They ran brilliant; there is no other way to describe it, operations against White Russian Émigrés in France. In fact, they controlled the "anti-Bolshevik opposition movements" and this tactic subsequently became known as a red flag operation. Naturally the intelligence world copied them immediately with varying degrees of success. The internet revolution made it much easier. I know that Angelique had more than fifty such fake websites under her control during her final years at SASS. All the right-wing whiners would reveal their identities on it (thinking their assumed names would hide them). They complained bitterly about things they simply don't get. Apartheid will never come back. We often chuckle about these brandy and keyboard warriors.

Bizarrely, most of them claim some sort of secret allegiance with us, the former Special Forces lads. It was really secret for we have never heard of them before. The Special Forces Association has a webpage where some of the wannabee's names are published. They are fighting a losing battle - the more famous SEALs stopped publishing names after forty thousand wannabees were discovered and it just kept on growing. Today there are more than three hundred thousand "SEAL" qualified fakers in the US alone. Most are so hefty that you have to wonder how they ever qualified for the famous Trident and the answer is obvious, they never did. No doubt some would read these books and call themselves "Egg Breakers." Be warned, we know each other by sight. It is a world where you don't want to be in unless invited and you ain't invited. Be gone I say before something ails you and your mummy is not there to comfort you.

I decided to get back to business and to the point. "You need him twepped? Surely the local lads can do that for you. It is not difficult with such academics. They live in their own world. Not security conscious at all."

"I want him snatched and in fact he is already snatched. The problem is getting him out of the country. Well, that will be your problem now. That is if you would accept instructions from me without clearing it with your wife first."

The way he said the word "wife" did not agree with me. It was with a sneer and unpleasant to my ears. She deserved more respect. She bled more for the cause than what this fellow did. He was certainly heading for trouble if he carried on in this fashion.

"Sir John, Angelique is not my wife when I accept instructions from her but my commanding officer or handler if you wish. There is a big difference between the two entities and we work hard never to mix it."

I said it softly but seriously. That part was true. When Angelique becomes what the French DGSE calls their "mon Colonel Cheri Angelique" she is not my loving wife but a tough hardnosed spymaster. Her way of indicating this was to put her aviator glasses on so you could not see her green eyes. It is a good tactic too. Once you stare in those eyes you stop concentrating and she starts kicking shins. On the other hand, as my wife, she would never dream of ordering me around. Our culture simply does not allow for such things. The man, the husband, is the head of his family and demands the respect naturally due to him. She may make suggestions but she cannot command. It is the Afrikaner way no matter what the women's liberal movement says about it and it is not abuse either. The system worked well for hundreds of years.

Mind you, a suggestion from Angelique is a command to me and we both know it but that was our secret and not his. We have long agreed she is always right most of the times. These days they, our twins and her, gang up using the democratic voting principle against me. I am outvoted most of the time. Not to worry, I am working on Lise who seems to be more willing to vote with me. I am at a disadvantage though. A tie means they win because

182

Angelique negotiated a double vote for herself to keep them in line or so she explained when I agreed to it. When it comes to serious matters she usually listens to reason.

The fact remained that I will never accept an instruction directly from him without Angelique acceding to it. It was simply too dangerous as she would react very predictably and would be within her rights to be angry. The lines of command were very clear.

I continued. "I beg of you not to ask me to override my commanding officer. It will have grave consequences for me and you when she finds out and she will. As you may know Sir John, a woman is a born lie detector and my wife is better at that than most. Why don't we run it via her first? How hard can it be? You have the best communication centre in the world less than a hundred feet away. It is a rather simple request."

"Ah well, you see Foxtrot, she is not in a place now where she can communicate freely with us. That bullet which shattered her forearm...it had some kind of a poison on it. She became very ill and nothing helped. She went into convulsions, paralysis and had respiratory failure. I am sorry old chap; she is now in an artificially induced coma to save the twins. We were not able to tell you before now."

With a start I recalled the exact words of Graeme's radio message to me before the fight with the fast attack craft. "Foxtrot this is Graeme, I have command and a message for you...all three of your family members reached hospital safely." So that is what he meant. They reached the hospital safely. Not that they are safe. It struck me that the wounded enemy soldier said the same thing to me. "Major, please convey my gratitude to Colonel Angelique and warn her that we will never stop as long as the TWEP order is valid. She's still not safe." Sadly, I missed the real meaning of his words. He must have known or suspected they used poisonous bullets and tried to warn me within the rules of his honour. But I missed it completely.

I jumped up and grabbed Sir John by the throat. Keeping such information from me was inexcusable no matter what the reasons were behind it. I would get Graeme later for playing along. Several men jumped on my back to get my hands off him but not before his eyes started bulging and he grew red in the face. I really wanted to kill the bastard. I roared with anger. "You of all people decided not to tell me? I will kill you, you Pommy bastard! Don't think I forgot about the concentration camps where you murdered our women and children! And now you are trying your luck with my wife and children? You will regret this."

I greatly increased the power in my fingers and his eyes rolled backwards as he started to lose consciousness. I began to enjoy myself but I knew I could not kill him outright without consequences. Three lads were already hanging on my arms shouting that "I should calm down. This was uncalled for and will not solve anything."

Under duress I let him go and he staggered back making delightful, I assure you, gasping sounds holding his throat. He still had some explaining to do and I promised myself he was going to regret this insult. But for now, it was time to play the game. "Let me go before I get violent with you too!" The last part was to the lads restraining me.

He rubbed his neck ruefully and stared at me lying on the deck where I landed after I let him go. There were three lads holding me down. "Now look Foxtrot, I get your concern about your family but stop this violent behaviour. It was Angelique who said we should not tell you until you are safe and sound. And to tell you the code word is 'Jeffrey,' with a J. Otherwise you would get obnoxious and overreact. That was just before she was induced. She is fine." His voice came out in a hoarse croak; it would take days for him to regain his normal voice. Not that I cared.

I got up slowly and sat down at the table reaching for another cup of tea which made them stand back watching me like a dangerous snake. I got the "Jeffrey" part - we have that code word to use if she ever needed to authenticate a message, she would use the word "Jeffrey" which sounds exactly like my own birth name, Geoffrey. No one but us would know the actual meaning behind it. This message was real. There was no way that bastard Sir John could have known our secret code. We had many others too.

"So how is she now? What about our twins? And where is she?"

It took a lot of willpower from me to ask this in an ordinary voice. Losing my temper like that and overreacting is not how I would normally do things. I would probably not react the same way if the news came from anyone else but Sir John. We did not like each other much at the best of times. They could and should have asked my Jamaican or Commodore Octavius to tell me in private. Them I like.

"First things first" he hurriedly jumped back as I stood up again but I was heading for the milk tray. I had to keep on moving to work off the stress and sudden anxiety. "She is fine and doing well, they are using the latest antibiotic medicines. So are the twins who are obviously also poisoned, they being part of her body, and to answer your final question, Bordeaux."

The medical officer approached me. He was standing in the corner observing and had seen everything. "Foxtrot, do you have any idea what kind of poison they would have used to shoot at Madame Foxtrot? We need to know."

I answered. "During the Bush War the terrorists used human excrement. They would dip their bullets in it and we dipped ours in Brasso - you know - to polish the bullets. It was not official policy and unnecessary anyway. The standard bullets did enough damage but because this enemy tactic was known, they learned it from their North Vietnamese instructors, all our wounded were given massive amounts of strong antibiotics on arrival. It was standard procedure and done via a drip if at all possible."

"Ok the ingredients for Brasso that would be what? I would say mostly isopropyl alcohol, ammonia, silica powder and oxalic acid?" He clearly understood what he just said because I did not.

"Yes, that is what it is made from and the effects of excrement are well known. However, I don't think this is what was used. The symptoms for Brasso are not ferocious enough to have to induce a coma...why didn't they just amputate her arm?"

I said it aloud as I was thinking about what had happened to my soul. I did not mind her having only one working hand. I am big and strong and could do whatever she would want me to do on her behalf. It would make no difference to me or our love. Angelique with one hand would still be Angelique.

"Eh Foxtrot, that was mentioned as a very real possibility. I understand she reacted a bit predictably and her Frog Minder had to intervene to save the surgeon. You know how she is. I also understand they will do so, if needs be, but not before they tried the induced coma for a few days. Look we really need to know what to treat which is why I was contacted in the first place, to ask you."

"You need to do two things here." I turned to Sir John. "You need to get Dr Thandiwe to her as soon as possible. She would know what symptoms to look for if they used African snake serum. Get Boris to fly her out to Bordeaux immediately. I suspect, and take note Doctor, I am speculating, that they used paraoxon. You will know the symptoms better than I do."

"Dr Thandiwe is Geelslang's wife? Lovely girl that. Ok that is already done; the French got her off to Angelique last night. And by paraoxon you mean Project Coast? Brigadier Dr Wouter Basson?"

Sir John obviously knew about Wouter Basson which was not strange. His criminal trial was widely published. What they said, it was never really proven and the good doctor denies it, is that the Apartheid Government poisoned the Reverend Frank Chikane with paraoxon in the late 1980s. He almost died and lost all his hair in the process. Basson, a cardiologist specialist was head of the Biological Warfare research which was done in the greatest secrecy at the time. Apparently, he supplied the poison to the security policemen who administered it. He denied it along with the allegation that two hundred prisoners of war were also experimented on by his department. Whatever was whispered, a competent court found him innocent of all charges. The Judge also made the remark that the State's case was based on hearsay and nothing else. That did not stop the liberal press from calling Basson "Dr Death" to sensationalize the affair. They often do such things for a few sales and did their very best to ruin him.

However, that was not the first time such tactics were used and if the liberal journalists were less lazy and knew more military history, they would have known that the Rhodesian Security Forces frequently left poisoned pairs of jeans in farm shops. The terrorists would raid it, meaning rob it and when they put the stolen jeans on, they died. They used paraoxon which works well as contact agent. That is what was done to Chikane and where the idea first came from. The security policemen involved were senior enough to have served with the police counter-insurgency units in Rhodesia in the late 1960s to middle 1970s. They would have known or heard the rumours and adapted it to their own use. It was typical of the dirty tricks section to do such things. Why they did not just shoot the man I would not know. Afrikaner tradition demands direct action, not procrastinating around with poisons. It was a queer affair to say the least.

"Yes, I mean Project Coast. It would not be Basson himself. He left the Army after being found not-guilty of all charges against him. He would not have had access to the poison and anyway he is a very honourable man."

Certainly, there is more to him than his wanker accusers. Unlike them he qualified as an Army Special Forces Operator but would only work as a medical doctor on operations. Such men don't murder pregnant women or shoot at marked ambulances.

"I doubt if the Brigadier is involved. Probably some of the poison was not destroyed as claimed and that is where they got it from. As you may know Sir John, Doctor, paraoxon is 70% as effective as the better-known Sarin nerve agent. It has the same symptoms too." I said it calmly; this was no time to get the wrong message across.

"Yes, I know...convulsions, paralysis, and respiratory failure possibly leading to death. Ok, I will forward this information immediately to my colleagues. I must say old fellow, if it is paraoxon it is not so serious. We know how to treat it and have anti-dotes for it. The same ones as for Sarin...I am surprised they did not pick it up already."

He left in a hurry to get the signal off and to their credit; the submarine immediately went to periscope depth to establish contact with the outside world. She would always be able to receive messages even under the water but sending is another story. I got a message back saying she is doing rather well and is stable. I insisted in reading the message myself for I did not trust Sir John not to make it up and lie to me. They are like that. When a Pommy believes he is serving Queen & Country he would lie, cheat, steal and break necks to get what he wants. It is called loyalty and patriotism.

I also sent a message to Angelique's Frog Minder to get an independent report and feedback. He basically confirmed everything including that Dr Thandiwe would join be joining them soon. I found out later that Angelique arranged for her to be in attendance before she was induced. What I did not know but suspected was that Angelique gave very clear instructions that our twins will come first in any decision made when she is unconscious. Even if it means she would not live to hold them. What bothered me was that Angelique did not figure the paraoxon out herself. She knew about it and that it was used before. Perhaps she thought she was throwing up from shock or our twins not having been pregnant before. As far as I knew she was also never shot before though there was an incident in Moscow once. The poison could not have been a large dose anyhow. If it was, she would be dead already.

Something was not quite making sense or perhaps they did not believe her. Which if so, meant a few medical men were going to understand the evilness of disbelieving Madame Foxtrot. Such an insult will not be taken lightly or lying down. Not by me anyway but to be fair I will ask her opinion first before acting. I smiled happily at this idea. Commodore Octavius later said it was the most frightening smirk he had ever seen on a living man's face. I did not even notice but sat quietly scheming away. I also intended to

189

subject whoever came up with this plan to use paraoxon on bullets to the same treatment. Perhaps even Sarin gas. An eye for an eye says our Lord. Fair enough, so be it. Biological Warfare and so it is written.

I became aware of Sir John staring at me. "Foxtrot? I am sorry old chap, but I must ask you about Nigeria. We need to get that fellow out and the local lads are otherwise engaged. It should be an easy mission. We land at a deserted airfield and pick both you and him up. If you wish Captain Geelslang can join you."

"I wish so and then?" I asked softly not bothering to even look at him. He should not see the hatred in my eyes.

"We talk to the bastard in private. What happens thereafter is not open for debate." He shrugged; the PhD was going to die. A brilliant mind wasted for the wrong reasons.

"Yeah I meant and then I go to see Angelique. In a coma or not, she stays my wife and mother of my twin daughters. I want to be at her side when she wakes up." I looked up.

"Agreed, once you have the target out of Nigeria and in our hands, I will do whatever is needed to re-unite you with your wife. You have my word and I call upon Commodore Octavius here as my witness." Sir John tried to sound convincing.

"I will hold you to that promise, Sir John. There will be hell to pay if you break it."

Commodore Octavius said it in a way which made me look at him in surprise. He meant every word and was not the usual happy go lucky pirate but a thoroughly dangerous man. Sir John noted it too and waved his hand as to dismiss any thoughts of him breaking his word.

We shook hands and that was that as far as I was concerned. Whoever this PhD fellow was he was going to come with me and thank me afterwards for the pleasure of being in my company. Still, I could not help to hear the nagging little voice in my head screaming that Sir John was lying. Why would he need me to do something which any Egg Breaker could do with his eyes closed?

*"If men make war in slavish obedience to rules, they will fail."* Ulysses S. Grant

## Chapter 5

### C130 Super Hercules, 2 March 2014

It was a rather long distance from HMS Astute to Kano, a small city in Kano State of Northern Nigeria. It is a city which is by tradition and since the ninth century dominated by Muslims. For those interested in historical sights it still has a wall 40 feet thick and in some places 50 feet high surrounding the old city. And that was about the only decent reason to visit it. In a way Kano is a typical forgotten African city in the middle of nowhere with dusty roads in a semi-desert area. It will never change or become anything other than that.

There has always been trouble there and it has an unfortunate recent history with riots and bombings. Because of the troubles there is a curfew in place since 2012 when four police stations and one SSS office was attacked by machete wielding youths. The Al-Qaeda linked Boko Haram fighters came later, armed with AK47 assault rifles. Many rumours were abounding that they "rented" the weapons from the local Nigerian Army Units. This was never proven but could have happened. Kano is not a place where a Western tourist should be and to be avoided if at all possible. You don't see many white people there but despite its sad history there are a lot of Lebanese. Why I would not know but they keep a low profile and are mostly traders. We have a few valuable contacts inside their community. Or rather, Angelique's people did, not me.

For me to get to Kano was another matter entirely. It is in Nigeria in West Africa. HMS Astute was off Mozambique in South East Africa cruising in the Indian Ocean. It could not possibly sail to Nigeria in the timespan we had. Besides that, I knew the submarine had other work to do for other Egg Breaker teams. So I had to leave and leave I did.

I do believe if the new lot down in Pretoria realised the awesome power of the Western Nations, they would have stopped their silly Truce right there and then. When you think about it, the Al-Qaeda movement and its allies are nothing more than a large bunch of armed thugs and terrorists running for cover and slaying their own people. They are not nearly as impressive or capable as the West and never will be. It is the liberal journalists and no doubt politicians with an eye for the White House & Downing Street who turned them into bogey men.

Criticism is part and parcel of a democracy but these people went totally overboard by inflating, sensationalising in fact, every single "victory" the terrorists had. It is borderline disloyalty and treason. Some British nationals, who did the same on behalf of Germany during the Second World War, were hung after the war. Someone like Jane Fonda would have been crucified during the Second World War but such are the times we live in. Since the 1960s the Military and Intelligence lads became the target of choice to be humiliated whenever possible. Angelique and I often wonder and giggle at the idea; of what would happen if those same "God-fearing & upright" citizens are confronted with a Muslim terrorist? Will their good intentions stand up to reality? I think we know the answer to this question and so do they. Why else would they stay safe at home whilst spouting their crap? Why not act out their beliefs and go to their Communist and Muslim paradise or sisters? For the reason that their dreamlike state of mind will be rudely shattered I suppose. Well, as Angelique always says, "this is life - get a helmet. Someone has to make us laugh."

The trouble with the Egg Breakers who snatched the PhD was that they could not get him away from Kano. Something I can well understand up to a point for a foreigner but not for Egg Breakers used to Nigeria. It should not involve me. Sir John was lying about something. Perhaps they were betrayed. I would soon find out what the bastard did or did not do.

On the other hand, the city is sort of isolated and in a semi desert area with no real roads and the one airport can be easily watched. It is not safe to travel by road and by train even worse - the fleas alone will get you. The original plan was to fly him out but it seems something went wrong with the execution of it - the pilot they hired crashed his light aircraft on the way there. Now the net was closing in on them for the Al-Qaeda lads knew he was snatched and were searching for him. Of course, if we did not get there in time, they would be justified to give him a last cigarette and a bullet in the back of head. They had orders to do so and then to go on the run. Alone, they would certainly be able to save themselves - that was not the problem. The problem was getting the bastard to a mother ship where he could reveal his nasty habits.

We decided to send a rescue team which I would lead primarily because of my link to the Egg Breakers and the Nigerian local intelligence lads, SSS. We would jump into Kano or rather a small drop zone chosen by the Egg Breakers. After assessing the situation on the ground, we would arrange a landing strip of suitable size for a large cargo plane. Once that was done the PhD would be flown out with us in attendance. Getting him through customs would involve more Nigerian involvement than what was needed and the same for us, therefore the covert insertion by parachute. It sounded all very simple and straightforward, run of the mill Special Forces stuff. On paper that is, on the ground I have learned that things often needed improvisation. Well, so be it.

194

As said before, getting to Kano was the biggest challenge and showed the extent to which the West was ganging up against the Muslim threat. First, we surfaced in the darkest hours of the night as no nuclear submarine is ever on the surface during daytime unless for the greatest emergency. HMS Astute did that once already on this tour; she surfaced next to the EBS Orlando to take off our seriously wounded and hence saved their lives. It was an act of supreme gallantry by her commander not to be repeated so we waited until the hours passed and when it was dark enough, we surfaced. Within a few minutes two French Navy helicopters arrived out of the dark night. There were four of us; I took the surviving three Sandrine men including my Jamaican with me. The helicopters hovered and picked us up from the heaving deck. Commodore Octavius was with us. He was supposed to go home, not to Nigeria. I would have preferred him to stay behind and ensure that Sir John did not do me in. However, it is strange how life works and if he was not with us at that time his life would have been very different. He would have missed out on his second youth. I often see that happening in life, that things come together when you least expect it. It is a matter of faith.

I thought of Angelique when the helicopters arrived and how upset she was that her French Minder forbade her to fast rope down to HMS Astute. We had to be winched down like wankers. She refused to talk to the fellow for a day or two. Not that he minded, he simply shrugged in his Gaulish way and ignored her. After a while they made up again. I believe, looking back, what pissed her off the most was that he confiscated or stole the thick manila ropes just before we boarded the helicopter. She could not fast rope down even if she wanted to which of course she wanted to. Her Minder had proved himself to be more devious than most which earned him great respect from her. They are the best of friends these days and she clicks her tongue at his romantic escapades when in France on leave. If he ain't careful she will hook him up with one of her friends yet. Thus far he has managed to run far and hard and I am not sure if that is wise. Every man needs a wife. She is an asset to him.

The helicopter flight was many hours long and we had to refuel from a US Navy airborne tanker. We were on our way to the French aircraft carrier Charles de Gaulle. She was a sight to behold when we landed on her busy flight deck. You don't understand how large such ships are unless you see them from above at range. She was a brave sight indeed with her escorts around her and a few helicopters doing anti-submarine work on the horizon. Their anti-collision lights were gaily flashing in the distance. The pilot gestured up and I saw the combat air patrol circling by the light of their glowing exhausts. You see a lot more stars and other things at night on the ocean. There are no man-made fog and smoke and lights to ruin the view. They were not taking any chances though I believed their biggest threat would be the remaining Type 209 submarines. We knew they had penetrated the escort screens and obtained locks on carriers before.

After we landed and were duly escorted off the flight deck, I made sure to search for the Rafale squadron commander. I wanted to shake his hand on behalf of the rest of the lads and convey our heartfelt thanks for the unmentionable Gripen incident a few days before. The Commodore, he certainly did not look like one, wearing jeans and an old wool coat, came with me. He tagged along to show his own appreciation on behalf of his crew. We found the man, a lieutenant-commander in one of the crew rooms cum wardroom. He was a stocky lad, full of life and looked like a real fighter ace. I was sure we found our man.

The naval aviator grinned like a Cheshire cat in heat after we explained who we were and why we want to see his pilots. He had a sense of humour that fellow for he motioned us to a petite officer standing in the corner of the wardroom arranging flowers in a vase. I am not sure where the flowers came from, there are none on the ocean, but she was attractive with her auburn hair in a tight pony tail and light blue green eyes. The Commodore gave her a long and very appreciative look. Female aviators are a special breed and this one saved our lives and was rather special but he stared so hard that I wondered if he expected a man or knew her or something. It was a bit odd and I was damn relieved when her commander introduced us before it became totally weird. I had never seen Commodore Octavius at a loss for words before.

"Lieutenant-Abeille, c'est Contre-Amiral Octavius. Il est le commandant de l'EBS Orlando. Commandant Foxtrot était là aussi, commandant les forces terrestres. Ils sont venus de vous dire merci pour votre, euh, de survol." (Lieutenant Abeille, this is Rear-Admiral Octavius. He is the commanding officer of the EBS Orlando. Major Foxtrot was also there, commanding the ground forces. They came to say thank you for your, ah, overflight.)

I noted that the Commodore became a rear-admiral which is typical French good manners. The commodore rank is somewhere between a rear-admiral and a senior captain. In order not to offend he automatically used the higher rank. It was not technically wrong of course but a nice gesture to the old fellow. If the Commodore noticed, he did not say anything; it would have been impolite to correct the lieutenant-commander in front of his officers. To be honest he was too busy staring at Lieutenant Abeille. The effects of his piercing blue eyes or stare or rank on the poor girl though was instantaneous. She snapped to attention. It took us by surprise. We have not had such an honour bestowed on us in many years. Yes, we got a salute from the HMS Astute captain but he was not snapping to attention like a recruit on the parade ground. Angelique, of course, outranked me anyway. I always have to stand next to her whilst others jump at attention to honour her (me beaming with delight, I assure you). Hence, I sort of forgot the feeling when done to me. It was rather strange to see this young woman showing such respect.

"Je suis heureux d'avoir servi la France, Amiral, le Commandant. Nous avons eu du plaisir cet après-midi." (I am glad to have served France, Admiral, Major. We had some fun that afternoon.)

She said it with the tone which all naval aviators have when they know they did something extraordinary, smiling slightly at the memory of her missiles destroying the Gripens. She had a very nice voice too, in a totally French way, pausing between the words.

"Oui, vous avez eu beaucoup de plaisir et nous en sommes très reconnaissants. Sans votre plaisir, nous n'aurions pas survécu à être ici ce soir. Merci." (Yes, you had a lot of fun and we are very grateful. Without your fun we would not have survived to be here tonight. Thank you.)

I meant every word and briefly shook her hand before the Commodore could say a word. The man was still staring at her. It was rather formal I am afraid. I had other things to think about. Not so for my companion, the man called Commodore Octavius. I could see now where Graeme got his debonair ways from. When he came out of his trance, he immediately asked to be called Octavius. He pointed out he is retired from the Royal Navy and only came back to assist the Egg Breakers. His flag rank should not be allowed to be of much importance in a wardroom now should it? He being retired and all...yes he felt that the brave lieutenant should relax and stop standing at attention. It makes him rather uncomfortable for he owes her his life for what it is worth. He should be saluting her and would have if wearing a uniform. He sounded so typical bloody English, slightly bewildered by the attention and letting the Frogs know that he is as tough as nails below that exterior. Yes, the man was as suave as his son and much to my surprise his charm actually worked on her. I am still shaking my head about that. Perhaps I should have told her about his bad language before her attack or his horrible son who is a real Pommy pirate.

I momentarily frowned at his blatant breaking of my cover and then shrugged it off. She would not know or care what an Egg Breaker was. She relaxed her pose and smiled at him. I am sure Commodore Octavius fell in love as it was the kind of smile a woman reserves for her soulmate. Whatever the case, the two started talking and soon had me and a very bemused squadron leader standing alone. They so obviously did not care about our company that we felt quite unneeded if not plain unwanted. Well, this was one for the books and if it worked out between her and the old Commodore I wanted to be invited to wedding. I made sure to tell him so when we said goodbye an hour or two later for my journey was just beginning. We had a long way to go yet.

The lieutenant-commander and I left them alone and talked about other things of interest...as to where I could find a bathroom, or heads, before the long flight which awaited me. From what I understood Lieutenant Abeille shot both Gripens down. Her wingman, a much younger sub-lieutenant's Matra missiles malfunctioned. He still looked furious but gave a brave smile when we thanked him too. I had no doubt, studying them, that they would have closed in with cannons if it had been necessary. And they would have won. There was an air of competence around those aviators which defied logic but then they are all like that. There is no such thing as a humble fighter pilot.

Washing my face at the heads, I mentally reminded myself to ask Angelique if a woman that young, she was in her late thirties at the most, could really love an old Pommy goat like Commodore Octavius. It was uncanny, beauty and the beast I am sure but Angelique was delighted and demanded much more information than what I had available. In the end she called the Commodore directly saying to me over her shoulder that I may be an excellent Egg Breaker (I bloody well am) but rather useless when it comes to observing the important things in life. And so, two years later, we stood and attentively watched their wedding ceremony praying that our twins behaved (see Code Name Devorah). This was before we got used to the fact that toddlers never behave as angels when they could help it. I hope God would one day bless them both with twins so we can enjoy their discomfort for a change. Angelique's Minder saved the ceremony by taking our twins for ice-cream around the corner and away from the chapel. He looked quite dapper, the bridegroom that is, in full uniform wearing very high decorations for bravery and Fleet Air Arm wings which took me by surprise. Apparently, he flew Phantom IIs from the old Ark Royal as a younger man which probably explains what she saw in him. The bride was in a long dress which was off white with flowers in her hair. I am sure Angelique would be able to describe exactly what colour and what material and how many pearls were in the dress but I am a man, an Afrikaner man and would not have a clue where to begin. It was a very nice wedding though. Even Sir John and his mom attended although we gave each other the usual evil eyes.

My lads and I were leaving. We had a mission to complete so I could get to my wife who was still in a coma in Bordeaux. First, we had to fly to the island of Madagascar, change planes and then continue on to Nigeria. Since there was no time to waste, we left in the same two helicopters we arrived in but with different crews and flew off into the cool morning air. Dawn was breaking in the east bathing us in golden rays. The last view I had of the massive carrier was Commodore Octavius waving goodbye from the observation deck. He looked very debonair and saluted. We would meet again in the future as the war was by far not over and his skills still needed. Lieutenant Abeille was also standing there; her hair blowing in the wind for it is always windy on a carrier. Even where there is no natural wind the ship moves at such a speed that you have to hold on and look where you are going afore a jet kills you. Mind you, it is not nearly the most dangerous place to work in the world. I can think of many other places that can claim that title above a carrier flight deck. I waved back and tried to sleep but it was impossible because of the noise. They were really pushing the helicopters and we were obviously in a great hurry. The airframe shook violently at times as they came to the limit of their designed speed.

Just more than three hours later we landed at a deserted military airfield the French built years ago when they still had some control over Madagascar. A platoon of Legionnaires stood around making sure we were left in peace. It was a beautiful place. Whilst the helicopters were refuelling for their flight back we walked to the side of the runway to stretch our legs. The flower-scented air was very welcome after the fumes of the carrier. I even heard birds singing and decided the sea was not for me. I want to wake up next to Angelique, hear our twins fighting and smell the fresh earth. Birds singing too, there are many of them at the Ukuthula Ranch.

Looking around I wondered if I could take one of the Bougainvillea with me to plant in Angelique's garden next to her studio. They grow wild on Madagascar and are something to experience. However, we noticed an even more beautiful sight at the end of the runway...a newish C130 Hercules transport plane. We guessed our transport awaited and walked over carrying our rifles and almost nothing else. We lost all our gear on the Orlando when she went down. According to Sir John everything else would be supplied and he would not lie about such things. If he had I would cancel the mission and walk out.

There is a certain amount of magic about the C130 Hercules. When you hear the four Rolls-Royce AE 2100D3 turboprops you know you are back in the airborne world. The aircraft was used, since the 1960s, as the preferred heavy lift and para drop aeroplane of the West. Every paratrooper and many other troops would have heard those engines growling and would know they were either heading towards trouble (for the other side) or home. It is a very sweet sound and very reassuring to me. I first started parachuting from the old Dakota which is called the DC3 in America and then transgressed to the Hercules and its smaller French nephew, the C160 Transall. Of all of them the Hercules gave me the fondest memories. The worst was the helicopters; you don't tumble out in the airstream but fall straight down with your guts around your ears. A very uncomfortable few seconds that is too.

I noted from the tail insignia as we walked closer that it was our old friends, the British front company called Acklington Air. They were last seen by Geelslang and me at Bisho Airport near East London in South Africa when they delivered a hazardous parcel for us. Where they got that Hercules, I would not even begin to speculate on for it was the new J-model, the Super Hercules. It was painted in grey US Marine Corps colours but had no other markings of national identity which I could see. Just the Acklington Air logo on the tail and even that was faded on purpose. They really did not want to be seen without reason.

Acklington Air was a British MI6 front company employing only ex-RAF and ex-Fleet Air Arm members. They flew the world doing things and transporting things, including men, which could not be done by normal means. At times they would develop "engine trouble" and land where they were not supposed to land. You can bet your last penny they would then either load someone or something or offload someone or something which could not or would not be dropped by parachute. As an outfit they were very professional, dedicated and totally insane in the risks they took. I have heard of operations which had to be true as no fiction writer would be able to come up with such outlandish ideas. Nonetheless, I was glad to see them again.

As could be expected the crew gave us the hard look to see if we knew what not to do on their aeroplane. They are all like that and get obnoxious when the talking passengers arrive. Is a matter of superiority I suppose...air crew fancy themselves. These were specially chosen men who had thousands of hours of military flight time behind them. Well, we were also specially chosen men and much more dangerous if not better looking. We too fancied ourselves and gave them the look of "Do you actually understand all those bloody levers and knobs mate? You look like a wanker and Air Force puke to me with your stupid Ray-Ban glasses and pressed flight suit."

"Oi, you bastards, and what you doing here then...decided to help us win the war? Have you got my tea ready, my man? You know I want mine with three sugars now."

That was my Jamaican, the former colour sergeant of the Royal Marine Special Boat Squadron when Graeme was a snot-nosed lieutenant. He recognised the cargo master and one pilot as old friends. It is often that way, the Special Forces men fly so often with the specialist crews that they know each other. They promptly replied with a sense of hurt that "They came to save him, again, and would gladly kick him out in mid-flight being a smelly bastard to begin with. And he can make his own tea too."

It was obvious that a lot of respect existed between the two groups and I relaxed a bit. The biggest problem with Special Forces pilots is simply that they always seem to drop you miles away from where you wanted to be, asked to be and were bloody well told you are. Then you walk or run, depending on the conditions and time constraints all the way to your target thinking you are going to push those very same Ray-Ban sunglasses up in places where they were not designed to fit. Somehow the next time you meet you forgot about your threat and am anyway thinking of the mission and how they really, actually, genuinely will drop you right on target this time. Clearly it was the wind which blew you so many miles away from the actual drop zone. Ask my navigator, he lies just like me. Yeah, you are, of course, trained to be positive about life in general and try to look as if you believe them.

After that friendly greeting and some banter, we went aboard to check our equipment. It was the usual HALO stuff we have used for many years. They were like old friends and best of all there was Geelslang grinning from the inside where he slept until I kicked him in the ribs. He jumped up and shook our hands. Apparently, Boris dropped him off the night before and he waited patiently for us and the Hercules who arrived an hour before us. He decided to get some sleep - an old soldier's trick. You sleep whenever you can for you never know when you will sleep again. It is not laziness.

He gave me my Glock pistol and Heckler & Koch MP7 which he brought with. I did not think we would need long rifles for this mission though the rest had their L85 Individual Weapons. The last time I held that MP7 was when I was eighteen feet under the water trying to escape the SAS Amatola. I checked the optical site. It worked as well as always. I would have preferred the others to have AK47s so they could blend in a bit more. Especially the Jamaican as he looked like he could be a small Nigerian as long as he kept his mouth shut. I was worried about the lack of 5.56mm NATO ammunition in Nigeria. They use the AK47 or the old British SLR rifles which had different calibres. However, that was what was available and perhaps also a good thing, you need confidence in your rifle and you get that confidence by shooting with it at targets which you always hit. We had no time for such things on this mission. We simply used what we had. Perhaps, I mused, that should be the Egg Breaker slogan, "adapt or die."

Going by air from Madagascar to Kano is 3,365 miles or almost nine hours of flight if you don't encounter headwinds or other problems. It was impossible to do so with one load of fuel. The Hercules, even the latest Super J model which had an increased flight range of 40% longer than the older ones could not do so. It would not land but fly on to a military airport at Abuja another 300 miles away and wait for our signal to fetch us. Hence, we would have to refuel in flight. I was glad I did not have to work the logistics out for this. Just taking off from Madagascar meant we flew over the Mozambican Channel, Tanzania, Malawi, Congo, the Central African Republic and Cameroon. Some of these countries, the Congo especially, is war-torn and the last place you want to be without a good reason. Half of the time the government in place, not the elected ones because they have more often than not, not seen fair and free elections for generations, lost control. It is what is known contemptuously as the real Africa, where nothing works, with no real hope for change and each bastard for himself.

There are airports to refuel, of course. The commercial airliners do fly there but not a Hercules on a covert infiltration mission. Back in the day the Belgians built wonderful landing strips, all paved for strategic bombers, in the Congo. The Soviets were only too glad to use it and today it is ruined because of neglect. The airports are famous in military flight circles though.

Those old enough to remember the early 1960s will know what Operation "Safari" and Operation "New Tape" stand for. It was the largest airlift since the 1948 Berlin blockade and one of the United State Air Force's greatest peacetime accomplishments. They airlifted UN troops to the Congo after it fell into disorder when the Belgium administrators left. A few years later they returned to airlift them and the fleeing white Congolese out never to return again. After that the Congo and the shortly lived Republic of Katanga, a Western orientated state, turned to South Africa and white mercenaries. The mercenary outfit called the 5th Commando under Colonel Mike Hoar, a former armour officer, became famous at a place called Stanleyville. You can read about it in the books written afterwards on why they did. Such chaos, misery and a lack of respect for human rights is always an eye opener for those liberals who condemned the colonial rule as pure evil. Yeah, we saw first-hand in Africa what happened when the colonial masters left. We are still seeing it in the Congo and many other places famous for barbarism.

Historically, the poorly trained UN troops of the early 1960s turned out to be as useless then as they are today. Many of the UN soldiers were so backward that they did not even know how to use onboard toilet facilities when flown around by the USAF Transport Command. Most of the UN soldiers were never on an aircraft before and had no idea what to do when nature called. The poor pilots, no doubt wearing their trademark Ray-Ban sunglasses, had to disinfect the aircraft after every flight. They took severe chances in the air. Many pilots reportedly completed the entire flight without once having radio contact with the outside world. Some were given up as missing, presumed dead when they finally surfaced. The navigation beacons, supposed to help them navigate were off the air so they flew under visual flight rules, always a problem in Africa where there is nothing much to see to begin with and in the Congo, nothing but rain forests. (The newly freed Congolese Government completely forgot they needed to keep the generators on to charge the batteries so that the navigation beacons signals could be streamed continuously, hence guiding the aeroplanes. One such beacon could only be reached by donkey and that was after a 9-day ride but they forgot to bring the fuel with for the generator. Therefore, they had to go back and so it went on. Chaos was the name of the game, Angelique.) The post-independence leaders made Africa the laughingstock of the world and proved beyond doubt that a populist leader or community organiser hardly every turned into a good commander-in-chief. He simply doesn't have it in him to do what his mouth promises as his only talent in life is talking crap. They are not "doers."

Ironically, some of the USAF transport pilots got their asses kicked as a reward for flying in donated medicine and food. Not understanding Africa, they foolishly allowed a mob of Congolese soldiers aboard whilst the aircraft was being offloaded. The soldiers promptly ordered them off at gunpoint. When they left the safety of their cockpits, the soldiers and civilians kicked seven sorts of shit out of them. There was no reason for this brutal attack except, and this was obviously denied, they were white men. A few were then thrown in jail which almost was their end before their time; an African jail is not a place where you want to be. In the end, they were released and flown out; their wounds treated and awarded the Air Force Commendation Medal whilst three received Purple Hearts. They should have sued the United Nations and let the Congolese die. Sometimes people must learn that there are consequences for uncivilised behaviour. Since then trillions of dollars of aid money were given to be stolen by the begging African politicians. Nothing was done with it which could possibly be of any assistance to the starving Joes on the street. It is a big swindle which will probably never end. During the next crisis, some UN flight crews were captured and most brutally tortured to death, not by the Katangese, but by the Congolese who thought they were Belgian... (See Code Name Dawn, GMJ 37, on a history of the Congolese / Katanga problem, Angelique.)

"How are the HALO rigs?" I asked Geelslang. The rest were already investigating it, checking the air supply and inspection dates.

"Oi Mon, everything is where it should be. It is the standard NATO rigs. I don't foresee any problems. We even have a few spare sets. This is good stuff."

The Jamaican spoke with great authority. He had done more HALO drops than the rest of us combined. I would ensure he took us through the steps just in case. When you have an expert, he becomes the leader on that subject. It would be very foolish not to use the strengths of the expert for the benefit of the rest.

HALO drops; it means "high altitude - low opening," started operationally in the early 1960s and is a method of entry into an area used by Special Forces worldwide. There is not much to it, the aircraft flies at thirty thousand plus feet and opens the doors. You, breathing oxygen from a small scuba like bottle, jump out, fall for twenty-five thousand feet and then open your parachute. The nice thing about it is that you land unobserved by the naked eye. The aircraft is so high that the engines are not even heard at ground level. This made it very popular for that era.

With the advances of radar, it is now virtually impossible to do this covertly and not be noticed. Even the men, as they leave the aircraft, can be counted on the radar screens. It is still used in less well defended areas such as Africa where radar coverage is sporadic. It will never work down south closer to South Africa where every inch of airspace is covered and monitored. A SEAL team HALO'd into Somalia a while ago to rescue a few missionaries who really should have known better than to be there in the first place. The missionaries often get themselves into trouble and then have to be rescued at great cost and risk to the soldiers.

I'm not sure what good missionaries do in Africa. It was the missionary soldiers who started the Great Mutiny of 1857 in India and I have noted in Africa that they do the War on Terror no favour either. Why they constantly have a need to come to our shores and not look first at the considerable log in their own eyes as set out in Mathews 7 is strange to us. Geelslang and I often discuss religious issues - he being our pastor at the Ukuthula Ranch. A place like America for instance, it's sad but true, has no tangible difference in life style between the non-believers and the so-called believers. In fact, the atheists give on average more to charity than the believers. This cannot be right. There should be a huge difference between the groups. So, it is our opinion that missionaries should go home and work on themselves first. Hypocrisy never goes over well and at least the Muslims are anything but that. They may be wrong and misguided but they act on what they believe. We respect such things.

It was learned the hard way in the Second World War that slow moving transports (they have to slow down considerably) dropping paratroopers are excellent targets. Before the HALO concept you just had to live with it and many were shot down by opposing ground forces. Flying high made the aircraft invulnerable to all anti-aircraft guns but not missiles. Though not perfect it is better than the static line method where paratroopers jump from a low level to get down to the drop zone in one group (hopefully because it seldom happens that way in real life). The greatest advantage of HALO jumps is that it is pinpoint accurate. With enough training you are able to focus on your target, sometimes lit up with beacons and then land right on top of it. There is no other way. Once you leave the aircraft you are going to land somewhere, you cannot fly away or climb back in. You are fully committed. It is not dangerous but because of repeated equipment failure, mostly due to the oxygen bottles, all rigs now have an automatic baric pressure device fitted. Even if you pass out because of a lack of oxygen your parachute will open automatically when you reach a certain, programmable altitude. Many experienced operators scoff at this idea (they should know better) that they may become unconscious, but it has saved countless lives. I would not jump without one and would not allow any man under my command to do so either. I always check and make sure it is adjusted to open at five thousand feet myself. I don't trust anyone else to do so.

The rest was the usual helmet - the same type as is used by ice hockey players but without the frontal cover. It is really only there to protect your head against a rock whilst landing for it will not stop a bullet. There are no helmets in service able to stop a high-powered rifle bullet. Shrapnel and splinters yes, but not a well-aimed shot. It is also the in-thing these days to use steerable parachutes which are able to flare just before you hit the ground slowing you down so much that you should be able to stay on your feet. If you flare too soon your parachute may collapse. You too will collapse a short while later when you hit the ground with tremendous force. It is a matter of experience and good hand and eye co-ordination.

You cannot talk nonsense to your mates whilst free falling. If you open your mouth - all recruits are told to try and say something - the wind will blow your cheeks askew and the lesson is learned. Shut up until the canopy is open. Under my command, if you then start yelling high fives and God knows what else, I will shoot you for compromising the mission. The idea is to enter the area without being seen or heard. You would be extremely

210

surprised how far sound travels at night and even a poor African knows there ain't no angels coming down from heaven shouting high fives. Praying and singing hymns perhaps but not making the ghastly sounds originating from the Deep South of the US of A. In fact, all I want to hear is the oomph sound you make when you land on an ant hill. Anything other than that is unacceptable and would be dealt with rather severely. I would even want the parachute to crack open in a less spectacular way to reduce noise. It too can betray you especially if there are many of them cracking open. We don't want that. Africa is not empty; there is always someone around to report what was seen.

The senior pilot came to greet us. We formed a semi-circle around him. He was grey haired and trim, speaking with a soft Cockney drawl. We started speaking about the upcoming HALO jump so it became an impromptu briefing.

"Lads, we are going to drop you over the landing zone but only if Major Foxtrot give us the go ahead. That depends on him being satisfied that we don't drop you into enemy arms. Is that not so Major?"

"Yes, that is so. Once we are in radio range, I will establish contact and if satisfied with the answers we will drop. Otherwise we will call the operation off. This is my decision to make and I will make it."

I answered with the easy confidence of a man who knows what he is doing. Making decisions has never been hard for me and this one was easy. No decent codes, no drop.

The pilot went on. "As you see, we have here the latest model Hercules, the Super Hercules and since we have only you lot onboard, we are able to go as high as forty thousand feet. Hence, we suggest dropping you at forty thousand feet. Is that fine with you Major Foxtrot?"

I looked at the Jamaican who nodded in agreement. It was higher than what we dropped before but that just meant free falling longer. I was beginning to look forward to this. It would be fun.

"It is fine with us. We will just fall a bit longer before opening our parachutes. Mind you, it will be extremely cold at that altitude, minus 67 degrees Fahrenheit. We are not dressed for that, though we would have thermal undies to protect the essentials. Fortunately, we are dropping to a place where the ground temperature is plus 100 degrees so it will become warmer the lower we get. I suggest we don't waste time. Once we have established contact and decompressed...we will jump and fall at terminal velocity down to safer temperatures where we can breathe." I explained my ideas and they agreed. It made sense to dive down as fast as we could.

"You just give us the green light and we will leave you." One of the lads said from behind me. Everyone smiled, we had not come this far to be afraid of jumping into the night. We would jump all right.

"Will you give us a thirty-minute warning as well? We need to rehearse mentally and to breath pure oxygen, of course"

What my Jamaican said made a lot of sense. You have to close your eyes and mentally rehearse the jump. What will you do when x happens, ok do so. Ok, now what? And so it goes on until you hit the ground. Everyone does it. The pure oxygen is breathed in to clear your bloodstream from nasties so you don't get the reverse of the better-known bends. The oxygen comes from internal tanks on the aircraft as you only switch to your own right before the jump commences. The bottles are limited and won't last long.

Our friendly pilot had the oxygen aspect under control. "Yes, we will give you pure oxygen 35 minutes before the jump. You can then rehearse. Remember to hook to your oxygen bottle when the two-minute sign comes on. At that time, we will open the rear cargo door since it will be too cold to do it earlier. Check your mates constantly to ensure they breathe and remember nice normal breaths now, not too fast and most certainly not too shallow either. When the green light goes on, jump for we will be at the right spot."

He did try to look sincere and ignored our polite smirks. This was standard stuff. If you breathe differently from normal the carbon dioxide will slowly increase and kill you. You have to breathe and luckily it is easy enough. The air is forced into your lungs. Just to be sure you should not smoke for a few hours before the jump either. That would not bother us; as no one amongst us smoked.

I made my rules clear; besides Geelslang I have never jumped with them before and neither had they with me. "Lads, the Egg Breakers on the ground will have a white / blue flashing beacon pointed skywards. Try to land around it and not on top of me. No talking or yelling during flight please. We are landing in an area where non-combatants are and they may be working with the Muslims. Most people you see there are Muslims and hence not to be trusted. We really don't want to be found before our time. Keep quiet and Bob is your uncle."

They said they will be quiet and I believed them. I knew what they could do and saw them in action. I also knew the former colour sergeant would kick the shit out of anyone not obeying. He was a wiry man and not one to be crossed without consequences, civilian or not. Amongst the men he was held with great respect.

"Our mission is very simple. We will assess the situation on the ground. Get the snatched one to a place where the Hercules is able to land. Prepare the landing strip and fly out with the target. The Egg Breakers will probably not leave with us but that decision is theirs."

I looked at each man. "Now let us talk about escape and evasion. We are operating in a country which is not our enemy. In fact, we have the local intelligence lads unofficial support but they cannot show their hand too much. Hence, we are not counting on them. If we have to go on the run...get to Abuja and your High Commission. They will smuggle you out of the country. You have the numbers to call but try not to embarrass them. Ditch your weapons for it is a dead giveaway and do not drink the water without purifying it first. You have food, concentrated food with you, use it wisely but you can eat local food if it is fresh, washed and fully cooked."

I saw Geelslang smile. One of our instructors was a former Selous Scout, a highly secretive and effective Rhodesian Army Special Forces Unit. One of their and subsequently our milder tests was to be given a long-departed rotting baboon cadaver to eat. By that time, you are so hungry you will eat anything. However, you do remember to cook it very thoroughly, because if you don't, you will die. And you will also die if you eat it once it's cooled down again, no matter how hungry, you will not eat it. And the maggots and smell will not bother you either for it contains the calories your body needs to survive Selection.

They had all sorts of tricks with food to play mind games on us. You would be given food, delicious to be sure but dipped in gasoline and inedible. Showing umbrage would be noted and from then on they would needle you to see what would happen. There is no time or place for acting at Selection. You are totally exposed to what you really are and it better be what they consider Special Forces material. Your water would also sometimes be poisoned with gasoline and you learned the hard way, which is the only way, to never take food or water for granted and to use what you did have wisely. Of course, you have heard these stories before you went on Selection but when desperately tired, abused and cold and praying to hang on for just another hour it is very hard mentally to keep smiling. You have to reach into reserves you never knew you had and switch off. Pain becomes something which can be ignored and when the whistles blow you better be there, ready, alert and take leadership. It is not for everyone.

"Your legend, if asked, is that you work for an oil company, let us say BP and you got lost prospecting for new oil reserves. They will probably not believe you and you cannot hide that you are not Muslim. I believe that most of you are not circumcised. They will check and they will ask questions about the Holy Koran if caught. If at all possible, don't get caught. Any questions thus far?"

"How reliable are your contacts on the ground, Foxtrot?" They did not believe they would be caught and neither did I. Nonetheless the briefing was necessary.

"The Egg Breakers are as reliable as me. The SSS or Nigerian State Security Service lads are first and foremost Nigerians. They will not deliberately do you in but they have other loyalties towards their own country which must be respected at all times. They are not as far as I know penetrated by radical Muslims. What they have, their outlook towards us I mean, is probably one of positive neutrality. They agree in principle on what we are doing but their hands are officially tied. We really don't need more than that to operate in their country."

"What do we do with our parachutes on the ground?"

"We destroy them, bury them, and get rid of them. The Egg Breakers would have probably arranged for that already. We will wear normal civilian clothes during the jump and the operation. The special undies, protection against the cold, will soon be old news once you feel the heat. Mind you, we all were in Iraq in the summer. It is much cooler in Nigeria than Iraq so we will be good. Just drink enough water. You cannot drink too much; your body will get rid of any excess water."

"What about the Rules of Engagement?"

That was a good question. They have never worked with me on a clandestine Egg Breaker type operation. The sinking of the SAS Amatola and the rest were reasonably easy. You just shoot and keep on shooting. Here it would be much harder to make such decisions.

"We are operating in a semi-friendly country. You are not cleared to fire on the police or army or civilians without very good reason. I would be grateful to get through without a shot being fired but with the Al-Qaeda lads different rules apply. There are no rules with them and if you need to kill, do so with the normal double tap method. Follow Geelslang and my own lead as well as the Egg Breakers on the ground. We don't want international incidents but if you see us shooting or running...just come with."

The double tap method was first used by the SAS Regiment in the UK when they became interested in counter-terrorism. Up to then they stuck to normal sabotage and behind enemy lines work like reconnaissance. They proudly called their newly developed techniques "Close Quarters Battle" which

216

comes down to what the police have been doing for decades. That is to storm a house and free the hostages. It is not a big deal to do so and happens all the time. However, they turned it into an art which everyone copied. At the time they used the Browning Hi Power pistol, one of my own favourites even if it is an old design going back decades. Rather awkwardly the standard military full metal jacket 9mm Parabellum bullet did not do very well on terrorists. In hostage situations you really needed him to die so quickly that he cannot hurt innocents. So they combined the well-known Weaver stance with firing twice in very rapid succession. This was the double tap method and is so fast it almost sounds like one shot. We adapted it in our Bush War for our assault rifles and spent hundreds of hours practising it until it became second nature. I would go so far as to say it is the mark of professionalism to shoot like that. It is very accurate and deadly. Just hearing it will give you a fair indication of who is coming after you. We are not impressed with anything else like the short bursts the Virginians are famous for. It is wasted ammunition and holds your attention too long on one target.

"Lads, you have to understand something about Egg Breaker Operations. We are always on our own and never count on hot extractions. There are hardly ever such luxuries in our world and we are completely deniable and will be denied. We are not bound by the normal rules of war and you can use any type of ammunition, hollow points too, if it will do the job and is reliable enough. Remember they used to cause stoppages but that is largely sorted out now. Besides that, we generally keep a low profile and never attract attention. We just go in and get the job done."

Geelslang took his extra magazines out. He preferred the Heckler & Koch MP5 far above the newer MP7 which has a smaller but vastly more powerful cartridge than the 9mm Parabellum of the MP5. He loaded the magazines with mostly hollow points and every fifth round a tracer as would be the last four. We always counted our shots; God knows it becomes second nature but we would also know when only the tracer leaves the barrel that a magazine change is at hand. This could be relayed, meaning roared to your buddy so he keeps firing for the second it takes to drop the empty magazine and load a new one. Changing the magazines was also second nature to us. We practised that ad infinitum and glued weights to the bottom of the magazine so it would drop faster. We were really slick with all types of weapons and that was not by chance. It is hard work and then harder work to maintain the level. We know weapons and ballistics better than most.

As a back-up, besides our Glocks, we carried Spyderco knifes which could be used from cutting out an eye - I did so with one of Angelique's former thugs who assisted in her torture - and or cutting webbing away. We knew how to use those knifes against humans or animals to ensure a quick if not quite painless death. Such things are standard to Special Forces men. We don't even think about it but just act. It is the way we are trained and the way we are. I don't think we could ever go back to the wide-eyed innocents we once were and why would we? To pass Selection is not for everyone and only for a very few who manage to break through pain barriers at will. The worst part, however, was not the Selection itself but the final part where you are "captured" and subjected to interrogations which could be anything from a few beatings, nothing serious and expected, to being buried alive for a few minutes.

We call it the "Dark Phase" and there is nothing in this world, except to save Angelique, that would make me volunteer to go through that again. It is said that even the medical doctors, who are kept close to ensure that no one dies, are at times traumatized by what happens there but hear my words, it is

218

necessary. This is Africa; if you go back in history and see what was done to the German mercenary Colonel Rolf Steiner in Khartoum in the seventies and Wynand du Toit, a serving South African Special Forces Operator captured in the mid-eighties in Angola you would be utterly shocked. And it will never change. If caught by the enemy, you will suffer brutalities unheard of in the West or the East. Ask Simon Mann, a former SAS officer and Nick du Toit (no family of Wynand), also a former South African Army Special Forces Major what happened to them in Equatorial Guinea in 2004. They got caught planning a coup d'état and suffered the logical consequences. Barbarians will act like barbarians, there is no such thing as reasoning with them when they have you in their claws.

The second pilot took over and his words shocked me for I did not expect the level of protection afforded to us. Normally we are told to piss off and get out when the job is done. Not this time though. The West was starting to flex their muscles.

"You know that we have had some problems over the Congo before. No, I am not saying exactly what but that place is dangerous. We intend to fly over it at forty-two thousand feet which is as high as we can get. Don't worry; you will be comfortable as we will be fully pressurized at that stage."

"There is quite a large South African Army contingent there under the auspices of the Africa Nations. They are mostly men from the 6th Infantry Battalion and three companies of the elite Paratroopers. They are not our threat but the Intelligence lads say they have three Rooivalk attack helicopters in support. As you may know the Rooivalk have a limited anti-air ability when their Mistral Missiles are in range. They cannot fly high enough to bother us but their Gripens can. True, we are not aware of any

Gripens around but will take no chances as we have no way to escape them if they find us."

After a pause the senior pilot continued. "We have a few friendly fighters taking care of us. We are told that four French Navy Rafales will be going that way; by chance I am sure, and up to the border of Nigeria. Therefore, I doubt if we will have any trouble along the way but if we do, they will handle it. What exactly the Rafales have lost in Cameroon, a small country and former German Colony and then a French Mandate, I don't know, but I understand that is what their flight plan says. If anyone asks, so be it. Personally, I believe they will divert to Mali and not land in Cameroon."

We laughed at this. The Rafales were not going to Cameroon or Mali to see the view. They were escorting us all the way and it was something new to me. Egg Breakers are never taken care of like this. I wondered what caused it but decided not to look a gifted horse in the mouth. I had a feeling that one senior Lieutenant Abeille may be leading the flight in which case we would be safe enough.

"Ok men, we will leave just after 15h00 so we arrive during the night, that will be at 23h45 hours. Is that good Foxtrot? I am afraid I cannot change it much as the scheduled inflight refuelling is taking place at 21h00. The tanker is only available at that spot at that time. It too has F18 Super Hornet escorts as the refuelling will take place somewhere over the Congo. I don't need to tell you, by then we would be long past the point of no return. If that tanker is not there we will have to land or jump. If so, I will advise you on what we do then."

He said the last part with a smile because the tanker will be there. They are utterly reliable but you then have to refuel for them to be of any practical use. A lot depends on the skill of the pilots. They needed to get that probe connected and it is known that a few aircraft went down when they failed to. Such pilots are usually then asked to leave the service and fly for civilian pukes. They are obviously boring people and somehow got through the system by cheating.

"The F18s have just more than one third of the combat range of the Rafale. They have short legs and will be refuelling a lot more than us. However, they can fight just as well and we are glad they are around. I will make sure..." at this he smiled ruefully "that our IFF transponder is on. We expect that the Rafales will refuel before us and we will have to hang around a bit to wait for them to finish. I am hoping it will not affect our expected time of arrival, it is obviously, factored in."

The IFF part is an electronic signal sent from the Hercules to indicate she is friendly afore the Hornets get ideas and attack us. They will protect their tanker, of that I have no doubt.

I vaguely wondered what the tanker crew would say when a civilian Hercules wants to take on fuel. I shrugged; it was not my concern and it would be dark anyway. Very dark for it was what is called a "waning crescent" and the moon would not be seen until just before dawn. I checked on the Charles de Gaulle to make sure. We don't like jumping at full moon, too many crazies running around.

I took over again. "Ok then, all clear? Let us check our equipment again and ensure our weapons work as they should. Each man will draw a Glock 19 pistol with four magazines. I am sure Geelslang brought enough hollow points for each of you. Lads, also check your night vision and ensure it is fully charged as well as your two-way radios."

If they were lesser men, they may have opted to pull faces at this piece of unnecessary advice but they were not lesser men. They knew that our equipment would be the only thing between us and certain death. Each man including me checked his equipment without any complaints or what Field Marshal Montgomery called "belly aching." As with the famous Pommy Commander I had zero time for such things. It is expected that each man keeps clean and not shaven on operations to break your silhouette, depending on what you do. We were not recruits that needed to be checked if our weapons were cleaned and lightly oiled. If they weren't and it had a stoppage I would know and you would be returned to your unit. It is that simple and only if you survive your mates who will take a very dim view on such things.

At 15h00 exactly we took off and started the long flight. I always found the Hercules a bit like a fat boy at school for its length is less than its wingspan. It looks a bit odd, like a flying whale. With only us five lads and the jump master in the bay it was rather large and we could sleep in comfort. The two ex-SAS Sandrine men produced small hammocks and looked as if they belonged on the beach. The Jamaican showed his Royal Marine background by frowning at their contraptions and made a very passable bed. Even his jeans were neatly pressed. Geelslang and I simply threw sleeping bags over the fold down canvas chairs and curled up like dogs against the walls.

After a few hours I went up to the crew cockpit. I have never been inside the new ones and looked at wonder at the glass screens. The older models I was used to had more dials than most and would keep any real man happy. This here was almost devoid of anything mechanical and looked complicated but also a bit spiritless to me. It was as if the soul of the Hercules changed when the dials disappeared. Of course, the pilots were not impressed with that comment. They had "George" on to fly whilst they monitored the cockpit screens' instruments with well-practised eye movements. For once their Ray-Ban sunglasses were in their pockets. We were far above the few clouds with engines roaring steadily in the background. It is a wonderful sound, in my opinion, better than jets.

They had every reason to be proud of their new aeroplane. It even had a heads-up display which I had never seen before except in Geelslang's Mercedes S-Class. He was a bit of a Mercedes fan and I called him to come and have a look at this one. Geelslang was impressed and being the smarter of the two of us started asking questions of a technical nature. This led to a discussion which rapidly became boring so I left to make coffee for everyone. As with all large aircraft they had an excellent small galley for this very purpose. Strangely enough, the bastards, they stayed Pommies, had no decent Earl Grey tea onboard. I made a mental note to remind Geelslang to bring ours with next time. He surprised me by throwing two bags my way. Trust Geelslang to remember what is important in life.

We sat drinking tea and coffee and talked about what had happened on the way back to the Ukuthula Ranch. In fact, his story was rather boring unlike ours which I briefly explained. The convoy went across the border and simply kept driving, only stopping to refuel at Ponto do Oro. Thereafter they made a dash; they were not stopping for anyone or anything, to the military airfield next to Maputo where a very concerned Senhor Feradi waited. He had heard that his liaison officer, she is a distant relative, came under fire and that Angelique was dead.

Though glad that Angelique was not dead he was not pleased with the ambush on Mozambican soil and promised to increase Army patrols in the area. Geelslang shrugged. In theory that is fine but the Mozambican Army had no chance whatsoever against the professional South Africans. It would

223

not help much and was more of a gesture than anything else. Oh, and Graeme was a great help when not mooching with his liaison officer. He obviously liked the woman and she him. It reminded him of something now. Yeah, Foxtrot and the "Bitch of SASS" and is it not strange how history repeats? And he, Geelslang Peter Ndebele always has to be the one who has to watch? Couples staring like goats at each other instead of mating and getting done.

I replied I often thought of that scenario too. Why, I remember a certain Geelslang and Thandiwe staring at each other for two years whilst he saved for her lobola payment. They looked like goats in love. Irritating that was too to us who had to endure it. We decided to call it even and move on to important stuff.

"Foxtrot, how is Angelique?" I wondered when he would ask. I was wondering about that myself. Worrying in fact but what can you do. As always, the mission comes first and she would agree to that.

"I don't really know..." I told him what I was told by Sir John and her Minder. It did not take long. I was frowning.

Geelslang confirmed that his wife, Dr Thandiwe was flown to France before he even arrived at the Ukuthula Ranch. The timing was something else and almost good enough to make us suspicious. Boris was at the Maputo airfield and loaded all the vehicles and guns for the flight to the Ranch. Most of the lads stayed behind to be flown out later. Graeme excluded, he and his liaison officer went with to the Ukuthula Ranch for her rifle training lessons and for him to speak to Angelique's Analysts if they would speak to him which was not at all guaranteed. He promised to have the ZU 23-2s set up in the positions prepared before we left as was our agreement with Senhor Feradi.

We did not trust SASS not to try a sneak attack as they did a few months ago.

However, Geelslang never even left the Antonov. There was no time. The call from me to come to Madagascar came through as they were still in the air. He guessed it would be normal Egg Breaker work and arranged that our Head Mozambican brought the Heckler & Kochs to the airfield with enough ammunition. That fellow told him that Thandiwe left for Europe the day before. He was even more puzzled when told his wife left in a small aircraft, a two-seat fighter jet with French Air Force markings. Apparently, the thing landed, picked her up and off they went. She did not take anything with and was in a great hurry saying she will contact him, Geelslang, later.

"Rafale B, it is the only modern fighter jet France has with two seats. I cannot think of anything else which could have picked her up." I whistled thinking that Thandiwe was really not built to fit into the small cockpit. She was what I would call broad beamed and always on a diet. It was a bit of an in-house joke amongst us as she has a heart of gold. As a doctor she is excellent. British trained, and South African in experience with trauma and other diseases. Both Geelslang and I, and sometimes Angelique when female patients are involved, help out in her clinic. We are all highly experienced medics.

He chose to understand my whistle as astonishment which it was, in a way. "Well whatever it was, it left with a terrible bang by which I suppose the man meant it went through the sound barrier...which means afterburner which means inflight refuelling. Foxtrot, this is way bigger than what we thought. It takes time to get a Rafale B from France to Mozambique. And then the tanker aircraft on the way too."

I agreed. We were using every asset the West had to offer and it was a lot. We had to be careful not to start thinking like the Virginians. It is nice to have such backups but you really should never depend on it. In a way I missed our traditional ways which were so much simpler and hence worked better in practise.

Geelslang continued. "Regarding Angelique, I have a message for you."

I looked up sharply. He paused to make sure that we had eye contact. "I quote to you, Foxtrot, from the book of Psalm 30 verses 2 and 3 'O Lord my God, I cried to you for help, and you have healed me. O Lord, you have brought up my soul from Sheol (the grave). Weeping may tarry for the night, but joy comes with the morning.' She is tough Foxtrot, more so than you. All will be good."

I stared at the floor to hide my emotions. Even if she *was* as tough as he said I wanted to be next to her. She should not be alone and neither should I. Through the years Geelslang developed a knack to cheer me up when I needed it most. This was one of those times. I was grateful for his prayer and felt better already. She would be good.

"Amen, Geelslang. So be it. We praise the Lord, no matter what. "

We continued talking until the jump master asked if we wanted to experience the joys of inflight refuelling. Never being someone who says no to something you can learn from we watched, fascinated as the tanker came into view. It looked like a Boeing 707 with USAF markings on it to me. The pilot pointed and I saw the fighter jets above it which placed them at about fifty thousand feet. Suddenly one of them, it was a Rafale, came down and hooked up on the tail boom trailing from the tanker. It was I have to admit, a very impressive sight. Call me biased but who can blame me after the Gripen incident. Those Rafales really saved our lives.

After the fighters refuelled and buzzed off, we lumbered in. The pilots, for once, kept quiet. They were concentrating rather hard. There was a sigh of relief when the boom slammed home. It is a much noisier sound than what I expected. After taking on about half a tank of fuel and the glass screens showed us to be filled to that position - they cross checked with a stopwatch too - we broke off and waved the tanker goodbye. At my raised eyebrow they explained that is all what was needed with a large safety margin. They wanted to be as light as possible to get back up to forty thousand feet. Filling to the brim would have prevented that. I was impressed but for them it was normal everyday stuff.

For a while we flew in formation with the tanker and the fighters. They were at almost idle speed, a dead giveaway on any radar screen that we were military but I suppose it did not matter. We were so high and well-armed that nothing in that part of Africa could get to us.

Their tactics were interesting to me though. Two Rafales flew ahead, according to the pilot at about a hundred and twenty miles to scan for anything and anyone. They were probably glad to be back at decent fighter pilot speeds. Back in Vietnam and before that in the Second World War fighter pilots realised they needed freedom to manoeuvre. They could not stay tied to the bombers and do their job properly. So they stacked themselves in layers around the bomber formations and buzzed around. The same was happening now. The remaining Rafales flew two miles to our left and about a mile from each other like the fingers of your ring and middle finger, one slightly in front of the other. It was a loose formation but one proven by the Virginians over North Vietnam.

The tanker was to our right at the same level as us. The F18s never left the tanker and stayed quite close to it during the time we observed them. They could not scout around with their miserable 460-mile combat range as they had to refuel all the time. I wondered aloud if they could not have used something with a better range. We started discussing this.

The youngest pilot, he was a former Typhoon fighter pilot before Acklington grabbed him shocked us by saying that the much vaunted F14 Tomcat was even worse and never rated highly as a fighter. It was too big and heavy and ran out of energy at the worst possible times. We, who watched Top Gun in the mid-eighties with open mouths felt a bit betrayed by this revelation. Mind you it was true. I asked Boris, a former Sukhoi Su 27 Flanker pilot and he said the same thing. They did not rate the F14 but had high respects for the F18 when it came to dog fighting. The F18s were lacking in range he said, because they did not need more than that. They operated reasonably close to their carriers and could refuel when they liked with their armadas of tankers across the world. They deployed other longer-range strike aircraft like the A6 Intruder with the F18s at that time so the lack of range was no great factor. This made the tankers valuable and why the primary Soviet targets were not the F18s but the tankers. It was so crucial in their plans that they would gladly use Spetsnaz troops to attack the tanker Air Force bases before anything else. Even if the Spetsnaz lads were destroyed afterwards it would be worth it. Getting the tankers became a Soviet Aviation slogan.

I also seem to remember our Mirage lads, the F1 fighter jocks saying they don't fear the F14 at all. It is too heavy and cannot turn fast enough. Not to worry, they will always get them first if they can get close enough for missile lock or guns. We dismissed that as usual fighter talk. Nevertheless, they then point out that their colleagues in the Israeli Air Force agree. Why else did they fly the F16 which they preferred above the F15 and F14 which they never wanted?

Yes, it was interesting and I suppose we will never really know. What we do know is that the East German Air Force MIG29s outflew the West German F15s in trials held just after the Berlin Wall fell. That shocked everyone except us. They had the stolen South African Kukri helmet aiming device linked to a good airframe. It gave them such an edge that the now German Air Force MIG29s did the same at Red Flag and Top Gun schools. They won every dog fight against the Yanks. It was plainly embarrassing. The USAF did not deploy a helmet aiming device until 2003 and only because of the lessons learned from the MIG29s. This made us believe they would have seriously struggled against the Soviets no matter what Hollywood says.

Our deliberations were interrupted by a radio message from the escorting Rafales. It came through the speaker in the roof. "Abeille à Hercule, Godspeed Major Foxtrot. Nous reverrons." (Abeille to Hercules, Godspeed Major Foxtrot. We will meet again.)

The pilots frowned at her soft female voice and gave me a questioning look. I smirked and grabbed the microphone. No way did they need to know why she called me or even knew me. "Godspeed Madame Octave. Nous reverrons. Merci." (Godspeed Madame Octavius. We will meet again. Thank you.)

Her answering laugh came over the speaker; she rocked her wings and went flashing past giving us a lazy wave of her hand. Geelslang, who understood a little French wanted to know why I called her Madame Octavius. He asked in Zulu which the pilots could certainly not follow and looked at us in consternation. They hate anything on their flight deck which they don't understand.

I explained to Geelslang the goat eye incident and he grinned happily. At least he left it at that unlike my wife; bless her soul, who did the third and fourth degrees on me later on. If I had known, I would be grilled like that I would have shamelessly eavesdropped more than I did.

We were approaching our drop zone and the Rafales left us. It was time to jump and we greeted the pilots to get dressed and kitted up. I made very sure that the straps between the legs would not cause the old "nutcracker" when it opens. Through the years I have seen tough lads red in the face landing in a crumpled heap and staying down for a while. Yeah, that happens only once to you. We also started to breathe the pure oxygen. As we sat with the red cargo lights softly glowing we went through the motions of free falling. Not much is said at such times and every man sits in his own world. You work it out, every eventuality.

About twenty minutes before the jump I got the message that we were inside radio range to contact the Egg Breakers. The jump master patched me through and handed me the microphone. I raised the microphone; it was set to a pre-determined frequency, to my mouth.

"This is Foxtrot to Stone Belly." I said and waited. Stone Belly was the code name for the senior Egg Breaker on the ground.

I am not too sure where he got the nickname from. Such things are a bit strange. I once heard myself being referred to as "Oros," a well-known South African orange squash drink. Why? I have no idea for I hate the stuff. You cannot really get away from your nickname either whether you appreciated it or not. Providentially most started calling me "Foxtrot" soon after and the "Oros" part disappeared. Foxtrot is a name I got used to and answer to. I don't really know where it came from. There was a Foxtrot base on the Maleoskop Counter-Insurgency training ground where I did my initial training in counter insurgency as a young constable just out of the Police College. Somebody called me "Foxtrot" at Selection and so I became "Foxtrot." Shrug. Even Angelique calls me that ninety percent of the time though she knows my real name. She is called Madame Foxtrot at times but that is not our real surname either.

"Stone Belly to Foxtrot, I receive you fives."

So the radios were working, I was not surprised. I was using the Hercules's which could speak to the moon if needed. The added height also helped with distance.

"Foxtrot to Stone Belly, we are less than twenty minutes out. Are we ready for reception?"

"Stone Belly to Foxtrot, yes, our mates are also waiting."

I supposed he meant the SSS Nigerian lads. That would make sense; the Egg Breaker program was designed for them to have excellent local contacts. Many of the Egg Breakers consider themselves "honorary citizens" of their adopted countries. That is one of major reasons for their success, they fitted in and were humble enough to give credit where due.

"Foxtrot to Stone Belly, roger that. Do you have any other news of importance?" This was the code and a lot would depend on what he had to say. It was a very loaded question.

"Stone Belly to Foxtrot. Yes, wind is negligible and clouds scattered at nine thousand feet. We will activate the usual strobe for visual in ten minutes. Copied?"

The drop was on and the strobe would be flashing in the normal range of eye sight. We would not need infrared goggles and would see it miles away. It flashes in very bright white / blue every ten seconds and is designed to be seen from the top and a few degrees left or right of it but never horizontally. If he had troubles below, he would have said "No, all clear, you can jump" which is what his capturers would expect. We would then have flown on and called the operation off. With that out of the way I slapped the Jamaican on the shoulder. He looked up as did the rest. I made the thumbs up sign to indicate the jump is on. They gave me the sign back and the jump master left to tell the pilots to decompress as fast as possible.

"Foxtrot to Stone Belly, see you later then. It is copied."

The Egg Breaker went off the air. There really was nothing more to say. When we speak again it would be face to face on the ground.

The red light came on and we did a final check on each other's equipment. This was done before every jump and never in a hurry. You have only one chance to scan each man carefully. We looked bulky. Each had a large digital altimeter fastened on the right wrist but that was personal choice. It does not really matter on which wrist as long as you can see it clearly. The automatic parachute activation device was dialled to five thousand feet and the parachute on my back. Tied down to my left side was the MP7 and the Glock 19 pistol on my right hip where I preferred it. My Spyderco knife was tied to my webbing with Parra cord where I could easily reach it.

The rigs were all standard and the rest comes with experience and personal preference. Some like their rifles tied down on the right. Geelslang and I were trained to have it on our left and so it was for us. As long as you could achieve stable flight whilst falling - you need to be stable when the parachute opens - it did not really matter and also depends on the type of weapon. Some are longer than others and it is never loaded. The story of shooting at the enemy whilst in the air is not entirely nonsense but could only have happened very rarely. It would be highly inaccurate and would have to be from a pistol, not a strapped down rifle. It simply cannot be reached and wouldn't always work anyway. You almost always land hard with non-steerable parachutes. It is known that rifle barrels are bent at landing and then you need to beg your mates to shoot a terrorist so you could use his rifle.

The rear ramp doors were now lowering away and the cold air struck me with incredible force. It became shivering cold within in seconds. The wind howled in the cargo space. You could not possible hear anything but no words were necessary. We stood poised on the ramp glancing down into the black night and then only to the red light to our left mounted against the side. When it turned green, we jumped or rather stepped out and began to fall.

*"The history of a battle is not unlike the history of a ball. Some individuals may recollect all the little events of which the great result is the battle won or lost, but no individual can recollect the order in which, or the exact moment at which, they occurred, which makes all the difference as to their value or importance."* Duke of Wellington 1815

## Chapter 6

### Drop Zone close to the Challawa Gorge Dam, Nigeria, 3 March 2014

The first thousand feet is always to get stabilised and into the free fall position. With warmer clothing that might have worked. Here we simply went head first down to get away from the death zone for it was terribly cold. Terminal velocity means nothing in the dark - you cannot really see how fast you are falling. You can only see the altitude meter spinning like crazy as it compensates. When I was at a more decent height, I got into the free fall position and looked down for the first time searching for the flashing strobe.

What would you know? It was actually just to my left and I homed in on it. I did not know where everyone else was. We had no strobes on ourselves and the night was reasonably dark but I knew they could not be far away. Terminal speed is the same for everyone and we should be at the same height. At five thousand four hundred feet I pulled the ripcord and the parachute opened with a sharp and very satisfying crack. I heard the others opening too and spotted them around me. The rigging and everything worked as designed and I grabbed the steering toggles firmly.

Some of the lads wanted to fall down to three thousand or even two thousand feet before opening but I overruled them. Firstly, you need space between you and the ground if something goes wrong with your main canopy. At five thousand four hundred feet that is not a problem. The closer you are to the ground the less time you have and it becomes a matter of seconds. Your reserve chute comes into play only after you cut loose from your main canopy. You need time to do that. If not, the reserve will tangle with the main chute and that is it for you. If you are brave enough, you will keep your eyes open until you slam into the ground. It is unnecessary in the extreme.

Secondly the crack of the canopy opening is a bit fainter to the fellows on the ground than at lower altitudes and lastly, we may have to steer to the strobe if we got dropped on the wrong spot and the higher you open the closer you can be before landing. It is a matter of physics how far you can drift or glide from different heights. Five thousand feet was the perfect height according to my experience and so it was.

I looked down to the strobe which was now rapidly approaching. It never ceased to amaze me how quickly a parachute jump ends. You hang in the air quite relieved and pleased with the world and suddenly the trees become larger and then the ground approaches with a terrifying speed. It really jumps at you. There is not even time to worry. You just react and get your knees and feet together or as my old sergeant said, "into the virgin position lads." We chuckled dutifully but never heard anyone else ever use that description again. He put the fear of God into us that bastard.

At the last possible moment, I pulled down hard on the toggles to flare and made a spectacular landing or one which I thought was spectacular. No one applauded but at least I avoided the others, the short trees and the Egg Breakers who stood below, one watching us with night vision goggles. The rest of the team landed without incident and started to haul the parachutes in for disposal. We were on the ground...now for the hard part.

I shook hands with the Egg Breakers and their mate from SSS. "How are you doing Stone Belly? Man, I am glad to see you got us a nice thornless drop zone for once."

I was referring to an incident many years ago when he selected a drop zone next to a cactus field and some lads drifted into it. He was damn lucky to retain his Stone Belly name. The lads promptly made up some other less than complimentary names for him. Truth to be told the word "cactus" played a major role and included entertaining references to his body which is unmentionable in decent company.

"Good evening Foxtrot, Geelslang." I could see him grinning. He shook hands with the others and introduced us to his mates.

That is an Afrikaner tradition and not to be taken for granted. When an Afrikaner doesn't offer his hand to you, he is either intending to kill you or has decided you are not worthy of a firm handshake. In both instances I will advise you to sort it out before it becomes a blood feud. Just apologise and say you are sorry. He is bound by tradition and the Bible to forgive you and let it go. Otherwise, see the hatred between us and the Pommies. As an individual the Afrikaner is capable of great violence and is known to be unreasonable. His mate from SSS was a typical Nigerian of the Igbo tribe. Way over six foot and athletic with a clean-shaven skull. He too was smiling for we knew each other. He was last seen discussing Sandton City with our idiot from the High Commission.

"Foxtrot!" Nigerians, like the Pommy bastards usually used your last or surname first when talking to you. "I heard you and Mrs Dawson got married? And you did not invite me to the wedding? How is she and the twins?"

"Adewale you bastard...I knew you would be here. I am glad to see you my friend." We shook hands for we went back a long way. "Yes, you heard correctly. Mrs Dawson (Angelique's SASS name - one of many) and I got married last year. We are expecting twin daughters. Sorry about the wedding invitation, one day when all this is finished we will have a formal ceremony."

I thought back on the marriage ceremony. It was inside the French nuclear attack submarine Casabianca just after we made a static line jump into the Indian Ocean for the rendezvous. This was after she was rescued and on the run and Boris flew us out in his Antonov-124. The skipper was first flabbergasted and then delighted with the idea of the first marriage on a French submarine since, well since never, it hadn't happened before. One of the officers attending cried and all the other men (they were French you know) lined up to kiss the bride with me giving them the old evil eye. It was a very big deal for Angelique and me.

"Not even I was invited" growls Geelslang standing to my left.

He tried his best to sound aggrieved but at least he was on the beach when Angelique and I first realised we were in love and souls. He said to me later when he saw me holding her hand and lived, that is, she did not become as violent as he expected, he knew. He was pleased for us, we both lost souls before, Angelique and me.

Obviously, no one was invited to the wedding. At that stage we were not planning a wedding though we knew from the first moment it would happen. At that time, it was more about survival with her being on the run and out from the cold. However, when the time came to get married, I grabbed it with both hands. Then she was taken away to be debriefed and when I saw her again, months later, the Egg Breaker vs. SASS war had broken out. She took strategic command and the rest is history. There simply hasn't been any time for a formal wedding ceremony yet.

"And how is she and the twins?" Adewale asked again. He was a sharp fellow and like most African spies held a law degree. He noticed I did not reply directly to his question. He was still shaking hands with Geelslang and the rest and talking over his shoulder to me.

"She was wounded a few days ago (it felt so much longer) and is now in hospital. The bastards used a bullet dipped in what we think may be paraoxon so she is now in an induced coma to save our twins." I shrugged. Whoever ordered that was going to die a really horrible death but first things first. We needed to get the PhD away.

"Paraoxon you say? That is biological warfare...the bastards. Well, let us go to our safe house and take it from there." Stone Belly walked away and we all got into the waiting Land Cruisers.

There were three of them, the last a light truck used for cargo and in Africa, humans. The parachutes were thrown into this one for later disposal. I am sure that the Nigerian SEALs would score them in the end. Well, the parachutes did their jobs and it was on Sir John's account. Still I came from an era where we tried to recover parachutes for further use. Even after combat jumps we tried to get them out. We simply did not have enough to be able to waste.

In Nigeria you drive on the right hand side of the road as you would in the USA. The roads are mostly bad and where not bad plainly terrible. Because of that there is only one vehicle of choice which is the Toyota Land Cruiser. I have never seen so many together in one country before. You almost never see a German made car but there must be tens of thousands old Series 2 and

3 Land Rovers. Most of them are ex-military. They lost their paint decades ago and are full of dents but they are still working hard. Any British Revenge fan would either cry or be proud or both. They are odd people, Land Rover owners. They take themselves and their silly vehicles way too seriously. Since we have yet to see one which does not leak oil, we banned all Land Rovers on the Ukuthula Ranch. If we want oil in our soil, we will dig for it.

The safe house was hidden on a small holding on the shores of the Challawa Gorge Dam. It was built back in the early 1990s and it was impressive enough with four hundred feet high containing walls. The water stretches back almost seven miles, which for that semi-desert area, was a lot. The dam itself is seventy miles southeast of the small city of Kano. We had landed about eight miles to the west and took the Tarau Gwarzo road to reach it.

I still could not understand the problem of getting the PhD out of Nigeria. If he was still in Kano where they snatched him, it would be a problem but out here something could surely be arranged. I wondered what Sir John did not tell me. Well, it was all revealed when we drove into a roadblock and were surrounded by Nigerian Army personnel pointing their rifles at us. The soldiers were nervous as they had reason to be for the Boko Haram fighters were known to be around. For a moment I suspected we had been betrayed and they had decided to shoot the Egg Breakers first, however, they were nonchalant about it. Adewale leaned out of the window and shouted like a real Nigerian Oga. We were soon on our way again.

There are many languages in Nigeria, more than five hundred, and hence everyone speaks English. The word "Oga" is from the Igbo tribe, the closest translation would be "man in charge." It is a title bestowed on wealthy or powerful men (almost always both). Just below that you may be called "chairman" meaning to chair the board which is seen as a high honour.

The problem for a foreigner is that they speak fast and sometimes in Nigerian which is a peculiar slang of English. Then it may happen that you hear the word "Okada" and think it is maybe "Oga" which it is not. The Okada refers to 125cc motorbikes, imported from India and China. There are literally millions of them and you would be amazed by what they do with the bikes out of necessity. Seeing a family with a mom, dad (driving) and two kids on one bike is common. In my time I saw one with a fridge on the back tied to the driver's (he was a strong lad) back. It is amazing what you can do out of necessity, these people have no other way of travelling and so they do what needs to be done. They frequently crash and are banned in the capital, Abuja where it is a real pleasure to drive. In other places like Lagos and even Kano, not so much and not recommended for the faint of heart.

At the safe house I wasted no time and asked what was going on. We were sitting in the lounge whilst the rest of the lads sorted our kit out and looked around. They were quiet and had not said much since we landed.

Stone Belly answered first "Foxtrot, the problem is to get the Nigerians to allow the prisoner to leave Nigeria. The target is not in Kano as we were told by Sir John but here, with us. We can smuggle him out but that would be the end of Egg Breaker operations here."

His sidekick continued. "The Nigerians want him as bad as you do for he planned to poison the Challawa Gorge Dam. As you may know it supplies all Kano's water. We suspect it was going to be a trial run for the Washington and London attacks. The thing is, we don't know if he already did it or if was caught before he could. He is not talking. So it is

240

complicated and this is why we called you here so you can negotiate his release."

"We are a close to the Nigerians and not that sympathetic to Sir John" continues Stone Belly. You could see he was upset about the way things turned out.

"Do you think this is about money?" I knew how the Nigerian system works...somewhere a senior officer heard of the snatch and set in motion the wheels to grease his palms. I asked the logical question first.

"No, it is not Foxtrot. We want shared access to the prisoner." My mate Adewale had come into the room and sat down across me.

"We understood your preventative action in Kano and agreed to it. But now we found out he may have already started the motions to poison hundreds of thousands of Nigerians. That is why we cannot allow you to take him out and leave us, forgive the pun, in the dark here."

"Adewale, what is the problem in sharing him? Who denied you?" This did not make any sense. No wonder they got the Nigerian Army to surround the Egg Breakers and were demanding the prisoner. How did it ever get to this? I scratched my head in frustration for I knew the answer before he even said it.

"Sir John did it. When we approached him via our man in London, we got a message back saying we can wait." Adewale sounded angry as he well should be. It was not the most diplomatic of answers.

"We cannot wait, Foxtrot, we want shared access of the intelligence for the reasons given. And we will get it, one way or another. Through the years we always dealt fairly with you lot and we expect the same in return. This is not acceptable to us. If needs be, we will take the prisoner by force and kick your lads out. That is how serious my Ogas are feeling about this."

I understood his anger and marvelled, not for the first time at Sir John's foolishness. Angelique would not have made such a comment as it shows a lack of respect towards the citizens of Nigeria. Though the entire world thinks of them as shysters and scammers they do like each other at times. And they are fiercely patriotic. They don't trust the Pommies and blame them for the Biafra War which may even be true. It may not be the biggest deal for Sir John if hundreds of thousands of innocent Nigerians die but for them it was a big enough deal to ask the Egg Breakers to intervene.

"Adewale, calm down, no one is denying you anything." I looked at Stone Belly who watched me like a hawk. "Did you contact Mrs Dawson? She has overall command on strategic level."

Stone Belly answered flatly not attempting to hide his annoyance. "We sent a flash message to Mrs Dawson to intercede and make the final decision. We got no answer. We now know she is unable to make such decisions because of her wounds. Since we could not wait, the message was relayed to Sir John and he sent one back stating Mrs Dawson works for him and what he says goes. The Nigerians can wait. Is that true Foxtrot? We need to know and I need your word of honour. You know how we feel about the Pommies and this is not what was decided at our meeting in Addis Ababa."

Stone Belly was looking at me hard for he was a senior Egg Breaker and the one that supported me first to be elected as their leader for the SASS War. I silently cursed the silliness of Sir John. This was unnecessary. Intelligence is frequently shared between Agencies. He probably decided that SSS was penetrated and unreliable. Even if they were, it was the wrong strategic decision. What Adewale was asking for was not unfair, this was their country and we were guests. I was thinking fast for they were suspicious as hell. Who could blame them and I wondered where else Sir John had caused unnecessary trouble with his offhand remarks. No wonder he did not want to properly explain what had happened. The bastard knew he was wrong but was too proud to admit it.

"Do you mind if I call Geelslang to testify to something for you. It may be better if he confirms independently what I have to say. I know you will probably ask him behind my back anyway" their guilty looks confirmed that "so let us not waste any further time. He will not answer your questions without me present anyway. Let us sort this out as soon as possible."

I sat down with a glass of cold water and waited for Geelslang to arrive. He walked in and picked up the mood immediately. I noticed he placed himself to look squarely at the men in front of us. And his back was securely against the wall. I knew he had his Glock 19 with him but so did the other Egg Breakers. I also noted the MP5 hanging over his shoulders and the earplug in his left ear. That meant he had opened the radio channels and the other lads would be listening to our conversation. If the Egg Breakers noticed, and they said afterwards they did, they did not betray their knowledge.

"Geelslang, I need to ask you a few questions which may sound bizarre but will become clear as we speak. Would you mind?"

"Of course not, now what did that Pommy bastard do?" He asked with a slight smile. It was always good to have a common enemy. It created unity of command. We all laughed at that and the mood became a bit better. No one amongst us liked the Pommies much but we respected them. We knew from bitter experience how dangerous and sneaky they could be. We were all colonials in that room and all Africans.

"Yesterday your wife, a medical doctor, was flown out from the Ukuthula Ranch to an unknown destination. We suspect this was done to help treat my wife. Is that so?"

"Yes on both accounts and we believe she has gone to France."

I saw the Egg Breakers and Adewale glance at each other. No one outside our circle knew that Angelique worked for France. We kept it very quiet and just said it was a major country in Western Europe. Not for the UK lot, obviously, she is an Afrikaner girl with ethical standards. We never mentioned France before.

"You did not see her flying out from our airport at the Ukuthula Ranch but you were told she was in what type of aircraft when she left?"

"She was, according to our Head Mozambican, flown out in a two-seat fighter jet with French Air Force markings. We suspect it was a Rafale B model and the pilot went on full afterburner breaking the sound barrier just after take-off. They were obviously in a hurry."

"This Mozambican, is he what we can say fairly reliable?" I asked softly.

Angelique taught me years ago that if you want someone to listen to you, you need to talk softer and then they have to listen then really carefully to hear you. I asked why she then kicked me on the shins all the time but only got a glare in reply. You can be sure I stood a few yards away before asking.

"Yes, utterly so, he was an officer in the Portuguese Paratroopers before independence and since then one in RENAMO, the anti-Marxist movement created by Rhodesia and taken over by us. He knows aeroplanes and national markings. If he says it was a French Air Force fighter jet, I believe him."

244

"How was my wife wounded? Would you care to explain to these gentlemen?"

"We were attacked by a rogue SASS patrol just north of Ponto do Oro. She was driving, and may I say escaping with our Casspir ambulance when she noted one of her bodyguards, in an unarmoured Unimog, was wounded and passed out. The said Unimog was burning so she stopped and jumped out to save this fellow. It was an act of superb bravery if you remember she left the safety of the armoured walls and stopped driving away from the ambush to do so. During this process she was shot in the left forearm, the bone was shattered. We found out later that she was also poisoned with paraoxon. The bullet was dipped in it."

The others shook their heads in wonder. They admire bravery but she should have stayed in the Casspir which is armoured and left him. On the other hand, they all had to deal with her in the past and knew nothing in this world would have stopped her from doing what she thought was best. As much as I was admired for being her husband I was, I am sure, also at times wondered at. Mind you, they don't get Angelique the way I do. I like her strange ways. It is cute and endearing to me.

"Two more things and then we are done with this unless the rest of you have questions. Where is Mrs Dawson now and do you know where we got married...Mrs Dawson and me?"

"I don't know where she is right now but I believe she is in France. Otherwise my wife would not have gone to France." He smirked faintly. "The doctor follows the patient you know, so it is a very logical deduction. Regarding the second question...you got married on the French nuclear submarine Casabianca. You jumped into the ocean by static line and waited to be picked up as part of her escape route out of South Africa. The submarine's captain performed the ceremony. I was not there but that is what you and she say. It was also independently confirmed by her French Minder whose brother is the Navigation Officer on that submarine. Apparently, he started crying because it was so romantic."

The last part was news to me. I knew the Minder had grown up in an orphanage and did not know he had any family. Nor could I quite remember who was crying as I was staring at Angelique's green eyes. They have a terrible effect on men you know. You stop noticing everyone else and fall in love. I also had to give each bastard the evil eye with their kissing of the bride idea and then get her away from them to our cabin - the first officer was thrown out - to do what souls do when in love.

I considered Stone Belly and his men. "Gentlemen, I think we have established that Mrs Dawson has very close ties to the French Republic. When she fled South Africa, she was rescued by a French nuclear submarine. She got married in a French submarine. Her Minder is French and she is a French citizen now. When she was wounded a French military jet flew her personal doctor out to her."

"She speaks French too. I frequently heard her make such noises in the old days" says Stone Belly. "What is your point Foxtrot?"

"I will admit to you, under duress to cover myself from her wrath..." They all started laughing at this "that she works for the French DGSE or have some arrangement with them. Sir John is nothing more than a liaison officer for MI6 and probably getting funds from his nephews in Virginia to pay the Egg Breakers. I hope this information will never leave this room?"

They nodded. They will not betray me to her tender mercies. They knew from experience she is "otherwise." Actually, when I told her she shrugged and said it had to be done. What did it matter? Our enemies figured it out too and so it is.

I continued to make my point and to sort this out. "Now let us look at the command lines here. She is the commanding officer for these operations and directs them on a strategic level. She reports to DGSE who also give her analysts and a lot of other important assistance. Her bodyguards, by the way, are all French. Whatever instructions she gives is with the consent of her people at DGSE. Sir John plays no role in her decision making. Hence, he cannot be her boss, not even indirectly."

"Yes, we get that now. And you were elected as our leader for now. Who do you report to, Foxtrot?"

"Mrs Dawson only, when she was indisposed off, I report to no one though I keep her French Minder informed. He is now our link to DGSE but he is not in strategic command. Major Graeme, whom you have met, has temporary command and liaison with DGSE on behalf of Sir John. But he does not give orders to me, only suggestions and all that is subjected to DGSE control. As far as the Egg Breakers are concerned, I have full command and I am acting under the last orders I received - that is to destroy the SASS teams and drive the Muslims down south into South Africa."

"Therefore, Sir John acted totally out of line refusing us permission to share the intelligence? We don't work for the Pommy bastard. Not even indirectly as you said."

They confirmed what they knew to be the truth. I would not lie about such things. Besides, Geelslang confirmed it.

"I believe it is established the Egg Breakers are not working for MI6 though the bastards are involved in this war. Sir John is a liaison officer only and deals directly with Mrs Dawson, the rest of us tolerate him. As far as we work for anyone it would be France and higher than that, God. The Pommies are providing the money which they begged from the Virginians. The Sandrine lads are also paid by the Virginians or so I suspect. The point is Sir John is just stirring and is out of line. He is even spreading rumours that the Egg Breaker Program was an MI6 initiative and he may well be right. No one really knows who created us. But we morphed into something else and crossed the Vaal River, again."

When our ancestors left the Cape Colony and the British Empire in 1834, they wanted to and did cross the Vaal River to get away from the Pommies. I used the word as describing our break with MI6. We don't like them and so it is. Once we crossed that river, we were free of them.

"Why would he do that?" Adewale sounded pissed off. They had their run-ins before. "Does he not understand what damage such action causes in the field? We almost started a war with the Egg Breakers!"

I shrugged. "He is a hard man to follow at the best of times. What he most probably meant was that they want to interrogate the prisoner first themselves and that you will have to wait your turn. This can easily be solved. I will authorise one of you SSS lads to attend his debriefings and the proper sharing of the information. Would that suit you?"

"Yes, I am authorised to shake your hand on that." Adewale and I stood up and shook hands. This crisis was over and the real one, caused by Sir John, beginning.

"Ok we need to get this fellow away where he can be dealt with properly. What do you suggest? I have one Super J Hercules 300 miles away in Abuja to pick us up. I am open for any ideas on this."

I asked Stone Belly as the senior local Egg Breaker. It was his sphere of interest and for him to assist tactically. He would know the local conditions better than what Geelslang and I could. This was his place as Mozambique was ours.

"We have the prisoner right here at the house." He gave a lopsided grin. "This is our fishing hideaway where we come once or twice a year to entertain those who don't want to be seen with us. Not that there is much fish in the water but we try." He carried on. "There is a landing strip not too far away, about fifteen miles towards Chad, or north from here. It is an old RAF one used for emergencies. It is overgrown but it can be used. As far as I know the new Hercules uses a shorter runway than the old ones. Do you two perhaps know how short?"

"I know the answer to that" answers Geelslang, our local statistics man. "I believe, when almost empty, the distance needed is 3127 feet or 954 meters."

"What about rough landing capacity?" Adewale asked.

"Yes, same as the old model, as long as the ground is reasonably hard and there are no tree trunks she will be good." I recalled that Geelslang was asking exactly this from the pilots when I left to make the coffee. He was like that, always planning ahead.

"What about taking the Cruisers and simply driving to Abuja with the prisoner? Wouldn't that be easier?" I asked not so much because I wanted to, but because we needed to go through all the options. That was our way of doing things and how you a the right decisions.

"I doubt if that is possible, Foxtrot. It is unfortunate but Boko Haram controls the urban areas more than we do and they are looking for him. If he is found with us or even his body, I am sure you would TWEP him on the spot to prevent rescue, we would be in deep trouble. They are known to have roadblocks. I really would not recommend that strategy."

I knew how much that took from Adewale to admit. He was a proud man, a Nigerian and did not like to admit they lost control over Kano State. However, this was no time for him to be glib about things. We needed to know the truth or we could make the wrong tactical decisions. Adewale was too good a man to mislead us but he did sound fed up.

"Well we could have done so and did plan to do so just after we snatched the prisoner. The light aircraft was always only a backup plan so it did not bother us when it crashed. Of course, then we would have reached safety before they knew the target was gone. They don't have much influence the further south you go - they are very much a regional force." Stone Belly's frustration was clear to all of us. Sir John scuppered that plan and now we were forced to improvise.

"This landing strip...is it suitable? Perhaps we should scout it out tomorrow and then call the Hercules in tomorrow night? Do you have any other ideas?" I had made up my mind. This was the best way of proceeding.

"Yes, the landing strip is fine but I must tell you, Foxtrot. You lads may have jumped into the fire. Not that you would have changed your minds but we have reason to believe we may not have that much time. We may have to make alternative arrangements before tomorrow night."

Stone Belly frowned angrily and then continued. "We, meaning Adewale also, have people inside Boko-Harm. They are really limited in how fast they can communicate with us. It is the age-old problem which is as hard to solve now as it was a hundred years ago. Mobiles are the obvious answer almost anywhere except here. They don't agree with anything Western. Like Al-Qaeda they have a rather strange radical version of Islam. We use means other than electronic devices, like mobiles, to communicate and that takes time. Nevertheless, we have, as is expected, emergency plans for such eventualities."

He looked at me and the lads. "Foxtrot, that warning was activated just before you arrived. An attack is imminent according to the message."

"Do you feel this information can be believed?" I had to ask though I knew the answer. No Egg Breaker is given to dramatics. He would never have become an Egg Breaker if he did and this one was a known warrior who had done amazing things in Angola during the war.

"We will be attacked before the night is over. Boko-Harm knows we are here and they know the prisoner is here. I expect the attack just before or after dawn as that is what they traditionally do. They probably don't know you and your lads are here and that will make a crucial difference." He said it in a voice which left no scope for argument. As far as we were concerned, we had a fight on and so it was.

"Adewale, do we have any chance of back-up from the Nigerian Army?" Geelslang and I asked simultaneously. We had very little confidence in them anyway.

"I am afraid not. These days they seem to run the other way. We don't like each other at the best of times. I would not count on it but I did send a flash message to our headquarters asking for help."

He did not look particularly worried but he would not be. Adewale was another Graeme in a black skin. The Igbos, his tribe, was well-known as warriors and looked down on almost everyone else because of it. The flash message would probably not have any effect or nothing quick enough to be of use. We were on our own.

"Stone Belly, I do not wish to interfere with your arrangements but I need to know where to place my men. We are under your command. Would you mind if they attend this briefing? It would really save time."

This was the standard Egg Breaker way. The local lads always have tactical command because they knew their area so much better. You cannot just walk in, or drop in as we did, and take over. Such things are unheard of.

He nodded in accepting formal command. "Please invite them to come."

Geelslang left and a few minutes later the lads were standing around us. It was obvious to me, who knew them well, that they listened to the whole conversation and were not the least scared of what was coming. They all had their weapons with them as expected and looked mean. Looking at them I felt proud. They were men amongst men. The British Army had come a long way since the old Duke said they frighten him more than the French did.

Stone Belly stood up to show us a scale model of the house and surrounding area. We were on the northern shores of the Challawa Gorge Dam. Around us we had a clean three hundred yards field of fire in all directions. The house was most probably built at that spot because of it and well protected with high walls around it...that we noted when we got through the steel gates. We were also able to withdraw to Niger, Chad or Cameroon where we would not necessarily be safer, but would be able to make contact with other Egg Breakers. Somehow I did not believe that was in the cards.

"We had the time needed to take proper precautions and are able to withstand a normal siege against a mob like them. Anyone with tanks and artillery will get through but not them. Though they have captured armoured vehicles they do not know how to maintain or use them effectively. We have fifteen men here including you five for which we are very grateful. On each corner..." he indicated with his finger "we have a covered bunker with an RPD light machine gun. Each man also has his AK47 and ours have optic sights on them."

"What about ammunition?" Geelslang asked immediately.

"Tens of thousands of rounds are distributed amongst the bunkers. That will not be a problem. Loaded with our usual one in seven tracer round and standard ball in between. We even have two cases, about five thousand rounds of 5.56mm NATO rounds which your L85 Individual Weapons use. Foxtrot, I am afraid you will have to be careful with your MP7, we don't have extra ammunition but can offer you an AK47?"

I said I will be glad to have an AK47 and he produced one on the spot. It was, I was glad to see, a Russian made one and not a cheap and nasty copy. Though old it would work perfectly and was lightly oiled. There are few weapons which give me more confidence than an AK47. Battle tested, perfectly balanced (much more important than you may think) and accurate enough up to two hundred yards. It was to be honest my weapon of choice and even the lack of optical sights did not bother me. The standard iron sights were good enough.

"My lads are well trained and will not close their eyes when shooting. I expect great accuracy from them or will know the reason why." Stone Belly sounded proud as he should have been. He spent years training them and it was show time.

We smirked at his comment though. Most African soldiers when they first shoot a rifle will close their eyes but then, white ones do this too. They are afraid of the noise, the rifle and the recoil. We had a sure-fire method of preventing such things. A match stuck between his shooting eyelid made sure he kept it open. Of course, it would become teary eyed if kept open too long but he should have listened when we said keep it open. That was no excuse to remove the match and none would have tried to do so twice. Many a soldier who had gone through our basic training will testify they got kicked in the ribs, jumped upon and hit fairly hard on the head with sticks if they kept on tempting fate (us) on the firing range. I am not saying they are liars, it happened and they learned our way was the only way and Bob is your bloody uncle mate. Those who survived became decent shots in record time only if to stop the beatings and kicks. Our methods worked very well with untrained and unsophisticated troops.

"We also have claymores and trip flares all around. Each bunker has the control wires and will use them when I give the order." He smiled proudly and pointed at a few heaps on the scale model. "What we have here is napalm...nicely buried in konkas (Afrikaans, drums) with a small C4 plastic explosive charge to be detonated on command."

Napalm is a mixture of a gelling agent and petroleum. It was first developed in 1942 at Harvard University of all places. Today, you would not believe that liberals could do such things, but those were different days, when liberals were Yanks first and liberals second. They immediately used it against Nazi Germany and much more extensively against Imperial Japan. That is where it became a tactical weapon against bunkers and trenches. In Europe it was more often than not used as a strategic weapon to firebomb cities though of course, tactically you had the British Crocodile tank spewing it out. As a weapon it is very effective if only for a short while, it burns out too fast.

I found that white phosphorous or "Willie Pete" worked better in practice. It comes in smaller packages like grenades and mortars. It is quite effective. Those who survived the initial dousing would die later as the wounds turned into gangrene infections. It is beautiful to see when it goes off at night looking a bit like a waterfall of lights. Oddly, it makes almost no sound; there is no explosion like a normal hand grenade but a soft pop noise and then all hell breaks loose. The only way to get the phosphorous off your body was to dig it out of your flesh with a knife. Water won't help and if left alone it will burn right through you. It is nasty stuff but effective and not against the rules of war. Not that we cared about the rules of war anyway.

"Opposition forces, Stone Belly?" I asked because I had to brief my men on what was facing us. They have never operated in Nigeria as did Geelslang and I. We knew who and what the wankers of Boko-Haram are.

"The Boko-Haram Movement is not rated highly by us. They are not soldiers, not well-trained and unable to execute any attack which is not a drive-by shooting or involving mobs. Performing flanking movements or anything higher than platoon level is beyond them. Mostly they rely on plain brutality and frontal attacks. Their tactical skill level is way below what is acceptable."

"Then why are they winning?" I asked before I could help myself.

"The usual factors, like bad leadership amongst the Nigerian Army officer corps. Woefully inadequate equipment including basics like ammunition and afraid to be honest.... the Boko-Haram fighters are as cruel as their mates in the Middle-East and elsewhere. However, as soldiers, they are not good and will die against a well-trained Western Army."

"The thing is they know a lot about psychological warfare. Almost intuitively I would say." Stone Belly waved his hand in the air in disgust. "The Congo Syndrome again after all these years."

He did not mean a disease, though I supposed it could be called a disease in a way. We found back in the 1960s, all the mercenaries under Mike Hoare were interrogated when they came home, that the Congolese had a problem with witchcraft. Something that may be so crazy to a Westerner that it is dismissed however, for African soldiers it can be a big deal...they found that a mere look from an enemy soldier was enough to make them run away. Hence, they won many "battles" by just showing up. It did not work against the white mercenaries who simply exterminated them on the spot.

We saw the same thing in Apartheid. Some of the rioters, now departed, believed if washed with muti (Zulu, a witchcraft concoction) they would be immune against police bullets. It did not work like that in real life. As in the Congo and everywhere else, witchcraft doesn't work against whites or even blacks if white officers are around. However, this witchcraft is widely believed and we saw it again, very recently at a place called Marikana in South Africa. The rioting miners underwent the same muti ceremonies - there are pictures of them standing naked taken from a police helicopter. This happened just before they stormed the police and 44 died. For once Apartheid could not be blamed but of course was. Everything in South Africa is and will be for the foreseeable future. You have to wonder when the Muslim Truce will also be blamed on Apartheid.

I had no doubt that whatever Boko-Harm tried would not succeed against us. We were highly trained and skilled with weapons and entrenched. We had water, food and ammunition. The only thing which bothered me was that this was unnecessary and keeping me away from my wife. Surely Sir John was going to regret interfering with Angelique's command. The idea of her finding out gave me lots of pleasure. I could well imagine how she would react.

"Ok, gentlemen we don't want to split our forces so that unacquainted men are fighting together. Foxtrot, would you lads mind defending the southern wall for us? We expect some sharp action there and will leave you two RPDs. I need one lad to command our 82mm mortar section."

I liked this idea. It would be better to keep the men together though in theory you are allowed to add Special Forces lads with others to reinforce them. They are after all experienced soldiers who held command in their own regiments before being reduced in rank when they passed Selection. It seemed that Stone Belly had so much confidence in his own men that the beefing up was not needed. Well, that suited us fine and we walked out to check our new positions. Of course, we barely had enough men to man the machine guns and load them. Still, it could have been worse.

*"The friend in my adversity I shall always cherish most. I can better trust those who helped to relieve the gloom of my dark hours than those who are so ready to enjoy with me the sunshine of my prosperity."* Ulysses S. Grant

## Chapter 7

### Egg Breaker Safe House, Challawa Gorge Dam, 4 March 2014

Our Jamaican became the new mortar commander and spent the next twenty minutes observing the Stone Belly lads going through their paces. He suggested a few things regarding the fuses but seemed happy with the proceedings and very happy when given the firing table showing the exact ranges all around him. With that he would be able to lob mortars with pinpoint accuracy.

They certainly had an impressive load of mortar bombs available. From illumination rounds to Willie Pete and the usual High Explosive lying neatly stacked around them. For the duration of the coming fire fight we christened them as "Mike" for mortar. We had an extra short-range squad radio with us which I gave to Stone Belly. He could now communicate directly with us and the Jamaican. What he did with his own men I am not too sure but I heard him roar now and then. It was rather impressive. The man, to put it mildly, had a powerful voice. I recalled he was a much-feared sergeant major before taking his commission. Such men in general have an amplifier where their stomachs should be. I avoided them wherever I could even when I outranked them.

The Soviet made 82mm medium mortar is a good weapon system. First manufactured back in 1941 they saw service all over the world and in every combat zone where the capitalists and the communists clashed. It throws a six-pound shell just less than two miles at maximum range. When it lands it explodes with a satisfying crump sound killing everything close to it. That was nice to know but our problem here was not long-distance range but short distance. If the attackers closed in on us the mortar would have to fire almost vertically to drop right in front of us. I knew the Jamaican would do this if needs be. Rather him than me as a shell falling short is always an embarrassment. Mind you, we were under cover in bunkers and it should not bother us that much. The 82mm mortar rate of fire is with a good crew, and this crew was good enough, on average twenty to twenty-five rounds per minute. That is for a short time only. Thereafter you have to slow down otherwise the barrel could overheat. Once it overheats you have a real chance of the bomb cooking off and exploding in the barrel. In such cases the crew rarely survive.

My Jamaican had a plan for this. I saw a few fire buckets standing around filled to the brim; he obviously planned to douse the barrel or tube when the time comes. In the movies and in real life, to be honest, the mortar men urinate on it. From experience I know you can not always count on nature working for you at such times. Quite a few lads almost busted an artery trying to get the liquid aimed properly, load the mortar while ducking the incoming bullets. A man is not a circus animal able to perform on command. The other problem is if you miss the barrel and hit your mate - a fisticuff is bound to take place right there and then. Such an insult will not be taken lightly.

Both Geelslang and I did the police mortar course at Maleoskop, in Eastern Transvaal. We used what was called a "Patmor" which is of 60mm calibre. Our instructors told us it was a South African invention but it was not. It was based on an earlier British Commando mortar as our ex-Rhodesian Instructors subsequently confirmed. As a mortar it was different, I suppose. Normally all mortars have the same three basic ingredients. A barrel or tube which comes in different sizes, a foot pod on which it rests to prevent it from sinking into the sand when fired and two legs holding it in position. The Patmor had no such legs. You simply aimed it by pointing it approximately at the right angle towards the enemy. A mate fired the Patmore by pulling on a lanyard. It does not have a fixed firing pin as normal mortars do. Today it is called a "Commando Mortar" but despite the fancy name it stays a Patmor at heart.

As silly as this sounds it actually worked very well. You soon learned to shoot it instinctively and accurately. We carried it loaded, like a rifle, which made it rather unique and fast to get the first bomb away. As a weapon system the police counter-insurgency units discarded it quickly. We used armoured vehicles with heavy machine guns on them to chase the terrorists down. We seldom had time to be bothered with mortars. This one could not be used in the sustained firing role either and as always, carrying the bombs added much unwanted weight to your equipment. I pitied the Army infantry patrols walking miles and miles carrying all prescribed equipment as the book said they must. Their effectiveness rate, that is to kill the enemy, was almost zero. They could have stayed at home as far as we were concerned.

We would have no such problems with the 82mm. It was designed for static defence and would fire all day and night if needed. It was the fact that it could not fire to positions less than one hundred and twenty yards away which bothered me. Nevertheless, that was not my concern and I made sure to concentrate on our own task at hand. My Jamaican said he will deliver covering fire with the mortar and so it would be.

The bunker was neither big nor luxurious. It was however damn well built with the old and tested way of sandbags. I noticed we had at least four feet head cover above us. It would do the job for what it was designed for. In front of us were clear fire zones. It would take a company of trained infantry to take us out without heavy weapons.

There were five of us in our sector. Geelslang and I manning one RPD light machine gun and the two remaining Sandrine lads on another. Stone Belly left one of his men, a large Nigerian, to detonate the claymores and napalm on his command. We could not since we did not know exactly where it was planted. This fellow looked competent enough and grinned evilly at the idea of frying his enemies. We took the precaution of understanding the general layout of the claymores and napalm so that we could replace him if needs be. It was not personal; we did not know him and thus watched him.

"Geelslang, do you want to be the shooter mate?" I asked whilst taking deep gulps of water. It was still, even in the middle of the night close to a hundred degrees Fahrenheit.

"Not really, Foxtrot. I will load for you and take a few shots with my rifle now and then."

I saw he got an Individual Weapon with him besides his MP5. It belonged to the shooter or gunner on the next door RPD. He would not need it as long as his RPD was shooting. However, we all knew Geelslang was a crack shot - the best sniper between us and able to pick off leaders or anyone showing leadership faster than what we could do. Therefore, it made sense for him to have a long rifle with him. The Heckler & Koch MP5 is a sub-machine gun and had a short range. It was not suitable for the longer ranges we intended shooting at. That is the problem with sub machine guns; anything above thirty yards is a wasted effort.

The RPD, although an excellent weapon in its own right, was not as good as the FN MAG we loved and rated far above the Yankee's M60 machine gun.

The RPD was different from both the MAG and M60. Firstly, it rather weirdly loads from the wrong side, the right instead of the left as Western machine guns do. That takes some getting used to. It uses the same AK47 round so the recoil is less than a MAG and M60 but also has less penetration power. At short distances that would not be an issue, it will still kill. Geelslang and I have linked the ammunition belts together to form a continuous 250-round belt. Firing short bursts, such belts should keep us happy and the enemy very unhappy for a while. There were many spare belts lying next to us ready to be used. I began to wonder how many fighters Stone Belly expected and asked him when he arrived to check our positions.

"Och, I don't really know. Say between 140 and 200. They are like vultures Foxtrot. Always arriving with mobs and trying to scare the opposition. If less, well that is also good, we will deal with them."

That made the odds about 13 to 1 which was fine. We fancy ourselves and I had an ace card to use in dire emergency. Thus far it was not nearly an emergency and we looked forward to the fun. I suspected that Boko-Haram is going to get a nasty lesson in combat. Well, that is their bad luck. I could not care less.

The sun rises early in Africa during the summer. Of course, by now this was early autumn. Nigeria doesn't really have seasons - it is either wet or dry and always hot. For now, it was dry, the rains would come in a few months. By five AM we heard the first indication that the enemy was on their way. The guard dogs, highly trained Alsatians, began to growl softly whilst staring into the dark. Well it was dark for them, not for us with our expensive night vision goggles. They were the same goggles that the SEALs used when they killed Bin Laden and much better than the normal infantry issued stuff. We could see as clear as daytime though in green, the colour which the experts say is best because the human eye can separate many more different shades in green than any other. Geelslang and Angelique disputed this wisdom. They say grey is the better of the two. Geelslang said so because his Mercedes S-Class had a grey night vision system and Angelique because she is Angelique and "otherwise." For me, who cares? I was happy as long as I could see clearly in the dark. I could see the attackers about three hundred yards away. We reported it and waited.

They were standing around as if not too sure of what to do and it seemed were waiting for orders or daylight. They wore the now expected Arab turban looking like the typical ragheads we saw in Iraq too. It must be said though it was not all show; in that part of the world such headgear is essential against the dust and sun. However, I also noted they were trying to hide their faces which showed me they were nothing but a mob, scared of being recognised. Why else would they hide their faces? I began to wonder how popular they really were for it seemed to be a bit of a paradox.

Like most Nigerians I know, except the rich ones, they were well muscled with no spare fat on them. They wore a greenish camouflage uniform, probably stolen or bought from the Nigerian and other West African Armies. As with most such mobs we have seen before, boots were not indispensable. They wore sandals. From a purely military viewpoint they were not the least impressive. None had body armour on. None had individual radios and only a few had chest webbing with extra magazines. Their weapons varied between the AK47 - almost silver with age and use and the old Belgian FN rifles known by the Pommies as the SLR. We also used it as the R1 rifle. The latter must have come from the Nigerian Army and Police - they had lost many weapons during the years. This was an insurgency in its infancy without many skills which would impress the professionals.

Boko-Harm is reasonably well funded by bank robberies, kidnapping and overseas donations. I expected better equipment but probably the leaders stole the money for their own entertainment. We saw that often in our wars. The leaders lived in luxury with a great love for fancy cars and good food, the rest, well they suffered in the bush with a lack of medical care. Weapons they had abundantly, the Soviet Union and the rest of the communists supplied them free of charge. As always history would repeat itself. Back in Sierra Leone in 2000 a mob of Sierra Leone rebels ran into a British Army Paratrooper Company. The consequences were entirely predictable. The few surviving rebels lost rather badly and ran as fast as they could. Some say they are still running fourteen years later. This lot too would soon be running.

"Stone Belly, if I may make a suggestion?" I asked politely as not to give offence. I was his guest as were my lads.

"Of course, Foxtrot. You know our rules. All suggestions are welcome but I decide." He looked at me inquiringly.

"Keep the mortar lads quiet and when the mob runs away, as they will, we drop the bombs behind them so they run into the death zone. You know, we push them that way with rifle fire and the bombs keep them coming this way."

"Excellent, we will do so. Good luck." He left to have a word with the mortar men.

The Boko-Haram fighters attacked at dawn. There was nothing impressive about it. They simply gave blood curdling yells to make them feel tough and stormed the place. We waited until they were quite close, about forty yards before we got the command to shoot. Stone Belly was kind enough to give all orders in English and not Afrikaans. It was the common language between us.

All hell broke loose at that point. We had long since aimed and tracked the mob. Geelslang had his L85 Individual Weapon aimed at the leaders and when the order came, he double tapped the first one straight through the head. Death must have been instantaneous.

I opened up the RPD feeding it with my right hand. It worked as designed and streams of deadly tracer and ball ripped into them. The Sandrine lads were not far behind and between us we cleaned the area within a few minutes firing short bursts. It took Boko-Haram less than five minutes to break and run away leaving more than a dozen corpses and many more wounded crying for their mommies and Allah, the Merciful.

They were lying so close to us that I let the RPD go and shoot each wounded man in the head with Geelslang's MP5. There was not one survivor able to leave the battlefield. Well, they wanted to go to paradise and we aim to please. It was a massacre for them and the same happened on all fronts. Listening to the gunfire you could tell how much training Stone Belly did with his men. It never slackened as the gun teams relieved each other and they never fired out of place. At the first command to cease fire or for us, a lack of targets, the silence descended again.

For a while things were quiet and then they tried again with the same results but this time the mortar lads got into the action. I heard Stone Belly calling the fire mission and it took me back to the days when he did the same in Angola...calling one airstrike after the other onto a MIG airfield. Later on our Mirages ran out of fuel and he switched to long-range artillery which caused terrible damage to the enemy. Nothing has changed; he was still Mr Cool himself.

"Mike, this is Stone Belly. Fire mission, acknowledge."

"Mike, acknowledged."

The Jamaican answered immediately which made me proud. He may be a semi-Pommy but he was one of my men and whatever he did reflected on me. I need not have worried. Once he had the co-ordinates the mortar fired one round for effect. It did not take them long at all.

Mike, shot out!"

What he meant was to warn he started shooting. So that all would know the mortar bomb will explode somewhere. It was spot on, exploding above the bastards. He was using airburst which is the best tactic when destroying a mob.

"Stone Belly to Mike...very good on your last shot. Fire for effect, fire for effect."

"Mike, we are firing for effect. Out." The mortar now fired a bomb every three seconds and then slacked to one every two seconds. I could imagine the men dropping it down the tube and ducking away to get another. With two men loading like that you have a near constant stream of explosions going off. It is really impressive to watch.

I noted with great approval, I assure you, that they were firing four high explosive bombs for every Willie Pete. The effects of this were dozens of casualties and for a while the mob simply did not know what to do. They were caught between hell and us. After a bit they outran the mortar which is frankly amazing but not unexpected. We have seen that before. Calm descended again except where the wounded were loudly crying in pain. Geelslang took a few men with him and minutes later all was quiet again. It was obvious that they would not be back anytime soon. As always with such things their sandals were lying around as they ran.

I approached Stone Belly for permission to leave. "Stone Belly. We need to get a move on here. They won't be back soon. What about that airfield?"

"Foxtrot, go ahead. I assure you the landing strip is suitable. I suggest you and your lads take the prisoner and one vehicle. Get to the landing strip and do what you need to do. We will police the area and get going too. That is unless the Nigerian Army arrives but as you know, we prefer to avoid contact."

"I am going with you." That was Adewale grinning on the side. He long said that Boko-Haram would one-day stumble into professional soldiers. Now that it had happened, he was thoroughly enjoying himself. I saw he got his own FN rifle which was typical of the man. He was trained by the Brits long ago and hence would go back to what he knew best.

"You are welcome mate." I turned to Stone Belly. "May I have your prisoner?"

He called a few men by name and they soon had the prisoner on display in front of Geelslang and I. We noticed straightaway that the said prisoner was another lie told by Sir John. The "he" turned out to be an athletic "she" wearing a full-face hijab around her head. I looked a bit dubious at her for I did not know if this was the right prisoner. For the rest she was neatly enough dressed in a black full-length dress or abaya as my late wife, Marwa, called it. That was before Angelique and she still married to her husband. He died of cancer long before we got involved. Mind you, Marwa hardly ever wore an abaya; she was a jeans girl and what is known as a "modern Muslim." She told me it was too restricting. Angelique said the same thing when she visited Saudi Arabia a few years ago and made me act as her bodyguard. She was still my issued girlfriend then.

Geelslang removed the prisoner's hijab and revealed two pairs of deep brown eyes underneath raven black hair. They glowed with hatred and she tried to smack him. Geelslang is not a violent man unless provoked. He swiftly ducked and grabbed her wrists. It was entirely a reflex movement to throw her down on the floor. A few seconds later her hands were cuffed securely behind her back. She then made a few nasty comparisons with his ancestors which we ignored. She was lucky he did not floor her. I am sure if she were a man she would have regretted that attempted violence very much.

"Was she searched, Stone Belly?"

Geelslang asked from the floor where he had his knee in her back. We needed to know and would search her if needs be. In fact, she was now running the risk of being stripped naked. With terrorists you have to throw decorum to the wind. Not that we were interested in her body, I supposed such cases are for us like a doctor seeing a patient; we don't see flesh but organs. It is not about pleasure at all but safety. The golden rule is that the moment a female prisoner becomes attractive, as a girl, she should be executed for her own good and your sanity. You cannot have conflicting emotions about a prisoner.

"Yes, the prisoner is unarmed and unharmed. She is not under any medications and able to understand and speak Pommy as you heard. I am keeping her DNA sample we took to ensure we are returned the right person. Do you agree with this statement?" He showed me the DNA sample.

I studied the DNA sample in his hand; it was a small vile of blood. We had long since agreed that whoever is snatched will be given back for proper disposal to the Egg Breaker snatch team. Sometimes when a person is waterboarded or given truth drugs of just beaten, his face may not be as recognizable in death as in life. He may also be unconscious and unable to answer questions on whom he is. To prevent misunderstandings all Egg Breakers take DNA samples to match with the body afterwards. You cannot believe them anyway, they lie when they open their mouths. DNA samples are standard procedures.

I noted he said "person" and not "body" and wondered if her gender had anything to do with it. Generally, we make it clear that it is a one-way trip and that a quick death would be the reward for information. Anything else would prolong your arrival in paradise and why would you want to do that now? It is a very fair system I would say.

"I agree."

With that she became my responsibility. The handing over was complete.

"I also have her mobile phone and computer hard disk drive and memory for you." He motioned to his men and they returned with a large microwave oven, the plug still trailing behind them.

Geelslang promptly cut the cord and gave the plug back to them. We did not want mishaps with it being turned on and frying the electronics inside. This too was standard Egg Breaker policies. Once the electronic devices are inside the oven it is shielded against remote wiping. Someday, I am sure; a smart lad would make a fortune selling a bag to Special Forces able to prevent remote access. Carrying a large microwave around was a bit cumbersome at the best of times but it had to be done. There is also software which operates only in memory and never on hard disk, hence we remove the memory too when confiscating a computer or laptop. At times the motherboard is requested and then we comply.

"Thank you. I acknowledge one prisoner in good shape and the microwave and its contents. Anything else you wish to hand over?"

"No." He turned to the prisoner. "It was a pleasure holding you Doctor. I pray for your soul. These men will now take you further on your journey to Allah, the Merciful. I would advise you to obey them at all times." With that he walked away and never spoke to her again.

She just glared at him but kept quiet. It was obvious she could understand English. After all, she studied at an English University and cursed Geelslang and his ancestors in the same language. We were left alone in the room with her now sitting on a chair where we deposited her.

"Doctor..." She looked at me. I tried to read her soul, I have a talent for that, but she revealed nothing but hate and anger. Yes, she was getting madder by the minute. Typical female I would say.

"Doctor, I am Foxtrot and I am in command of you until we hand you over to the correct Authority. As long as you follow my instructions you will not be harmed. If not, I guess you are a small girl under that abaya. No more than a hundred and thirty pounds. If you wish to be difficult, we will knock you out and carry you. It is your choice and I hope you make the right one. Believe me, escape is impossible and we will kill you and even if not, you will still regret your attempt."

"My people will take revenge on you for this...you bloody kaffirs. I hope you die." Her voice took me by surprise though it should not have. It was feminine, well-modulated and under controlled fury.

In South Africa the word "kaffir" has the same meaning as "nigger" in America but in the Arab world it means a non-believer. A non-Muslim or a Christian, which is where the word comes from and what she meant. We did not take offence. She was right, none of us were Muslims. We did not believe and could not care less. The revenge part of her sentence was not much of a threat. We aim to please.

It did show me though that she recognised our accents for South African and tried to needle us. Prisoners do that at times. The smarter ones would try to provoke you into killing them before they could be made to talk. Everyone has a limit when it comes to interrogation. You can delay in many ways, even play along, but in the end, you will talk. Hence it is better to die as soon as possible and needling is the best way to obtain that quick death.

The liberals will tell you that the waterboarding done by the Virginians had no real effect on the War on Terror. It was a wasted exercise and did more harm than good. I have news for them. No Egg Breaker or other lad on the ground thinks so. We know it revealed valuable information and the reaction from the Muslims proves it. If it really was unimportant, they would not bribe liberal journalists to sprout the human rights abuse claims. They would ignore it as no threat and take the credos for the new recruits who flock to them because of it. But strangely enough, they are not doing that. Why not? Sometimes in my world you look at the shadows to find the answers. It is not a new concept. Back in the 1960s when the SR71 Blackbird spy plane was developed the Soviet spy satellites noticed the shadow where the super-secret aeroplane used to stand on the runway. With infrared they could clearly see the outline against the warm desert air. That gave them the first clue what to look for. This came out decades later after the fall of communism.

The only mistake the Virginians made with their waterboarding programme was to keep them alive afterwards. Why only they would know. You cannot fight terrorism with a Bible under the arm - it is either all the way or it is not. They should have been TWEPPED after revealing what they knew. This was the first agreement we reached with Sir John, whoever is snatched will be returned to us to be properly dispatched. It also meant that the good doctor will be dead soon. She knew or suspected it as she should, our methods are well-known.

"Threats will not help you Doctor. Note we will not kill you without reason but if needs be, you will die first. And no, we are not interested in your reasons or your beliefs. It may surprise you but we respect that enough not to even argue the matter. Nevertheless, the fact that you are a woman will not help you."

Her dirty look said all she wanted to say and it was not nice. Well, you cannot please everyone. It is a mathematical impossibility. I shrugged and left to find Stone Belly outside talking with his lads.

"Stone Belly, I have to leave. I am sorry about Sir John and will sort it out via my wife as per the proper channels. Please contact me anytime if you have such complications again. Thank you for your hospitality."

With that we shook hands, loaded the prisoner and Adewale and left. The microwave was placed at the back where she could not reach it. Not that she could have anyway; her hands were tied behind her back. The hijab replaced, rather roughly, by Geelslang. In a Muslim dominated society, it is expected that she would be wearing one. We did not bother to tape her mouth shut. I am sure she understood that a vicious jab in the midriff would take all ideas of talking away. Yeah, I think she got the point.

*"Hold fast to the Bible. To the influence of this Book we are indebted for all the progress made in true civilization and to this we must look as our guide in the future." Ulysses S. Grant*

## Chapter 8

### Bordeaux, France, 9 March 2014

I walked into Angelique's room just after four in the afternoon. It was a Sunday and it took me five days to get here. After we left Stone Belly with our prisoner, we drove to the landing strip to check it out for ourselves. It was not an airfield by any sense of the imagination. In Africa, any building left alone for two weeks is stripped of its roof, windows and door sills. Hence nothing was left of the old RAF control tower which admittedly was not much to begin with. After more than fifty years it was hard to even see the foundations. Despite this the landing strip was everything we wanted...about two miles long and one hundred and forty yards broad. The thing is we were not alone there. We drove into an ambush or almost did. Geelslang spotted them first.

"Stop the car mate. I see something." He jumped on the roof and looked at the far side of the landing strip through his optic sight. I handed him compact binoculars and he cursed. "Yeah, tanks, Foxtrot. Our old friends, T55s, I can see two of them standing under a tree and some men around them. Hmmm, they are manning them. We better be going mate."

We had met the Soviet made T55 tanks before in Angola and other places (Code Name Green 41 comes to mind, Angelique). They are brutes and in the right hands very effective. Their 100mm rifled main gun would shoot us to pieces and more importantly, also the Hercules. Most have a .50 calibre machine gun also. There was nothing we could do against them with the weapons we had at our disposal. We retreated and I made the decision to head towards Niger where we would find another landing strip away from any tanks. This was getting complicated as I knew the Hercules was about forty minutes away. Whilst driving away I got the radio out.

"Foxtrot to Mel Three Eight." I called the Hercules on the name we agreed upon.

"Mel Three Eight, go." They were not people to clutter the airwaves and I went on.

"Foxtrot, we have company on the ground. Two old Soviet made T55 tanks with damn evil intentions. We are diverting to position..." I glanced at the GPS coordinates which Geelslang held in front of me "do you copy?"

"Mel Three Eight, roger that. Just stand by on this frequency for a few minutes. You can take evasive action, by all means. We suggest that hill to your north."

"What does that mean? Take evasive action?" I asked Geelslang who was driving for we were leaving to get away from the tanks.

I was in the back with the prisoner and the other three lads whilst Adewale played passenger. It was his job to get us through roadblocks if needed. It looked better to have black men up front, it is the Nigerian way.

"I think it will become clear in a few minutes. We are not far from Mali or Cameroon and we have assets in place there." Geelslang answered as he drove towards the nearby hill to hide behind it.

I hoped he was right because the first tank had started its engine and had huge clouds of black diesel smoke pouring out of it. I wondered when was the last time the filters and diesel injectors were cleaned. Probably at the factory if you ask me.

I replied formally to the Hercules. "Foxtrot to Mel Three Eight, roger that."

This better be good for we really needed to get away from the tanks. They were poking their long noses out of the trees and scanning for us. Soon the shells would be coming our way. Well, we were almost behind the kopje (Dutch, hill) and out of view. Now it was up to them or we would have to leave in a great hurry.

"Just look at that..." shouted my Jamaican and I turned my head to see a Rafale coming in low and fast over the scattered trees.

The shape was unmistakable and she was moving at a fair pace. It was a delightful sight for us and I suppose a very evil one for the tanks.

"Lieutenant Abeille" I said to no one in particular.

Geelslang stopped and we got out, including the prisoner to take cover behind a large rock formation. We knew what was coming and a few seconds later the first tank exploded when an AS30L missile hit it on the turret. It was originally designed to destroy bridges and had a massive five hundred-pound semi-armour-piercing high-explosive warhead. This is almost twenty-six times more than the better-known American made Hellfire anti-tank missile. Of course, the French Navy did not regularly encounter tanks on the water. This was all that they had available and it worked just fine. It blew the whole tank apart. The shock waves reached us a good few seconds after. We all applauded except our prisoner who tried to escape. She did not get far before my Jamaican dragged her back by the scruff of her neck. In the meantime, the second tank also exploded. We stared in awe at the remains. Usually when a tank is shot out it still looks like a tank. It may have a few extra holes and scorched paint because it burned but these two were just not there anymore. They were blown apart with nothing left which could be recognized as a tank. Five hundred pounds of high grade explosives are really awesome. I heard the howling of the Rafales engines, her wingman now came into view and got up to wave at her. She rocked her wings and zoomed off to the clouds and away to where Chad was.

"Foxtrot to Mel Three Eight. Thank you and you can land now. The wind direction is north and not strong at all. Confirm your approach please."

What I was asking was where we should wait...the north side or the south side? There was no time to waste for we did not know if any other tanks or terrorists were around. Not that I worried, with Lieutenant Abeille and her Rafale around I knew we could deal with them too. However, we are mission focussed and needed to get the Hercules on the ground and then away again with us safely inside.

"Mel Three Eight, we will pick you up at the northern side if you don't mind. Confirm."

The voice came back immediately. This sounded like music to our ears and we drove off to park about a hundred yards away from the northern side of the landing strip. The Hercules came roaring in from the south and made a perfect landing leaving huge clouds of dust in her wake. The rear ramp was already half lowered before she even came to a stop. They were also in a hurry to get us loaded.

We drove up to them. The pilot, on the right side stuck his head out of the window and gesticulated to the rear. Geelslang got the meaning and drove around. We jumped out and helped the loadmaster adjusting the ramp. This took a minute and then Geelslang drove into the Hercules's hold and acknowledged, with a cut-throat motion, that the Land Cruiser was switched off when he reached the indicated spot. You could not hear the Cruiser's engine and it is an old military technique to indicate the engine is off. Of course, these days with rev counters in them you can check like that as well. The fact is, it needed to be switched off because it is a fire risk. Immediately the Hercules engines started to increase power and the aircraft turned around for the take-off. The two Sandrine lads were lying next to the vehicle attaching snatch chains to it and to the floor. There was no way the vehicle would move anywhere which was important. If it were to come loose during the flight it could cause a serious loss of flight control. My Jamaican was watching the prisoner and had her sitting against the side on the folded down seats. She was not going anywhere.

The second pilot stuck his head out of the cabin and indicated to Adewale who was standing in the rear with the loadmaster. It was clear they did not expect him. I walked over and shouted above the roar of the engines he is coming with and no arguments about it either. We could have thrown him off at gunpoint, even in mid-flight, but why? The Egg Breakers function with the local lads. They often had the same objectives. I gave my word to him and that was sacred to me. In this world, you cannot afford to lie without reason.

They only lifted the ramp to the halfway position and then we took off. The engines were roaring in full power and the aircraft began to shudder down the landing strip until we were airborne. I looked at Geelslang and the rest who gave me the thumbs up. The prisoner sat next to Adewale. Two tears were running down her cheeks. For her it was the end of the road. The Nigerian landscape was rapidly growing smaller as we closed the rear ramp to start pressurizing the hold. I now walked to the pilots and greeted them. It

277

had been an eventful few hours since we jumped the night before. I realised I was tired and had to sit down but first there was work that needed to be done. I took the microphone from the chief pilot.

"Foxtrot à Mme Octave. Encore une fois, vous nous avez sauvés. Je n'ai pas des mots. Merci et que Dieu bénisse!" (Foxtrot to Mrs Octavius. Once again you saved us. I have no words. Thank you and God Bless!)

"Tu m'as donné mon âme Foxtrot. Je dois vous saluer. Jusqu'à ce que nous reverrons." (You gave me my soul Foxtrot. I should salute you. Until we meet again.)

"Au revoir." (Goodbye.) I replied to this wisdom. It seemed to me like the old goat actually won her heart. What do you know? Well, so it was.

"Au revoir Adieu Foxtrot. Saluez Colonel Angelique." (Goodbye Foxtrot. Give my regards to Colonel Angelique.)

The senior pilot, Mel Three Eight, looked around and grinned. Obviously, the bastard could understand French or enough to understand. He waved me to sit down on the jump seat.

"I hear we have an extra passenger?"

"Yes. He is a senior Nigerian SSS officer." I rapidly explained why he was there and that I take full responsibility for him.

He nodded, that was fine with him. I asked where we were going. I have an appointment with my wife.

"The USS George H.W. Bush is waiting for us in the Western Atlantic, Foxtrot. That is where we are heading." He smiled at my frown. This was not what I expected.

"No, you are not jumping again. We will land on the aircraft carrier or try to."

He shrugged and so did the other pilot. They even looked at each other and made the sign of the cross. I am sure the bastards planned and practised that move before just to impress me. To be honest, it did. To be sure, it was done before. Back in 1963 a US Marine Corps Hercules made about twenty-one landings on the USS Forrestal as a test to see if it could be done. Still, I was taken aback by this and walked back again and down into the cargo bay to tell the rest. They just shook their heads in disbelief but what can you do? If we need to land on a carrier, then so be it. If not, we will jump. We had a few parachutes left and as luck would have it, we took the same Land Cruiser where we deposited our parachutes on when we landed. The Jamaican immediately started to pack them again. At this the loadmaster just shook his head but said nothing. Our obvious lack of confidence hurt his feelings. Mind you, he asked if he could have the spare one.

The rest of the flight to the carrier was uneventful. We were met halfway, just as we left Nigerian airspace by two F18 Super Hornets. I had no illusions that it was our prisoner who rated the attention and not so much us. I sat down next to her to ask if she needs anything. Perhaps some water? What about the toilet? We did not need to be uncivilised. She ignored the last bit but asked for some water. I gave her a bottle with a straw in and held it to her mouth. Her hands were still behind her back and must have started to hurt but she said nothing. She took some deep sips before asking.

"Do you know what they will do to me, Major Foxtrot?"

Her voice was soft and I could hardly hear her. I put the water down and gave her an extra set of earphones and plugged it in. Now we could speak easily. I wondered if she knew it would be recorded. Not that it mattered;

she would never have privacy again in her life. Whatever she says or does will be monitored.

"Yes, I have a fairly good idea."

I answered honestly. Out of the corner of my eye I noted Geelslang looking at me. He could hear every word in his own earphones but ignored us beyond that warning look. Between the two of us Geelslang as always was the more dangerous one or perhaps more professional - in our police days he never listened to any justifications as I would. He simply arrested the culprit and left it for the courts to decide.

"Will it be quick? When I am executed? She asked without real interest but I sensed it was important to her.

"Yes, it usually is. No need to be unpleasant about such things...a needle prick and blackness. There will be no pain and no further suffering."

She wanted to know as does all Muslims we ever executed. "And my body disposed of according to Islam?"

"Yes, according to the will of Allah, the Merciful."

I remembered the one fellow we fed to the sharks off the coast of Mozambique. That part was not guaranteed at all (Code Name VFO565). It depends on circumstances. She was so important that she would probably be cremated to destroy all evidence.

"You are a good man Major Foxtrot. I know you are lying to me. But thank you anyway." She shook her head in disagreement.

We sat in silence for a few minutes. I must be getting soft. In the old days, no prisoner would know I was lying but women are like that. They know.

What the West forgets is that they are also constantly bombarded with horror stories on what would happen to them. Some are trained by experienced Intelligence Officers to resist interrogation. They were evolving fast.

"You know; it does not need to be like this." I said it softly but earnestly.

As expected, she did not fall for that. "I will not betray my faith. Not for you or anyone else. This is my fate and so it is. Insha'Allah. I am ready to die." She chuckled which was startling under the circumstances. "Don't you understand, Major Foxtrot? I don't want to live like my Western Sisters as they call themselves? It is not me. It is not my culture or my beliefs. They have nothing I want or could ever desire."

The "Western Sisters" part was said mockingly. I knew she had lived at least four years in the UK and would know how the other side lived. She had made a conscious decision to reject whatever the West could offer (see Code Name Wednesday 7 where Muslim fanatics are discussed in detail, Angelique). Many do and go back to the old ways. In that they are not much different from any other tribe. As an African I get that reasoning better than most.

"What if it is not?" I said.

It was obvious that she misunderstood my question. Probably deliberately to bring over her own point, she was smart and wanted me to get where she was coming from.

"What do you mean? I don't want men to look me up and down with lust in their eyes. Or be saddled with a husband who is constantly exposed to half naked women. Or to live in a place where alcohol is abused until it becomes a problem to everyone. Or crime is not punished."

She was genuinely angry with spittle coming out of the side of her mouth. I wondered what happened to her in Manchester. Since her hands were still tied, I took my sleeve and wiped the spittle away. I tried again to read her dark eyes. They were full of emotion now. The most difficult part of interrogation is to know when to shut up. Once the words come, they are hard to stop. I kept quiet so she could continue which she did.

"Do you know when I arrived in Manchester, I was a virgin. I waited for the right man which Allah, the Merciful, would send to me. A man I could be a good wife to.... a man who would have loved and honoured me and be welcome in my father's house. And now I cannot be because I was defiled by drunken louts. They deserve to be flogged to death but your police would not even arrest them! They said it was just a drunken incident and I should not have been there at that place at that time! That is when I decided I have knowledge to use against the West."

Her voice became emotionless again, as if already dead. She stared into the distance reliving the sad event as she would for the rest of her life.

"I agree with you. Rapists must be flogged to death. We did that in Sierra Leone and other places I served (Code Name One Alpha). They are not men...I agree. No real man has the need to use force and never on someone he loves more than himself. It is unthinkable."

She looked at me again. "I wonder if you know Major Foxtrot that you are known amongst us? You and that fellow Geelslang, that you are feared? That we even know why you became our hunters? We know about Marwa and we know about your current wife. You were not our enemy until Marwa died."

I said. "And you were not our enemy until that night in Manchester. What happened is not right and they will be punished one day, even after death. But to answer your question...I was not and still am not your enemy. I am the enemy of those who hate Allah, the Merciful." I lifted my hand to stop her from replying that she did not hate Allah, the Merciful. Geelslang frowned, you should never stop a prisoner from talking but I did not care. "I can bring you hundreds or thousands of Imams who will tell you that Allah, the Merciful, never wanted this war. That the teachings of the radicals are not the true faith and that they are on the wrong road...it was not the West that attacked Islam but Islam who attacked the World Trade Centre in 2001. How many have died since then and how many will still die? From a military view, it was plain stupid. You are an educated woman; you know it will take a million such events to even hurt America enough for them to be bothered. The result was that Islam is hated and feared and that is not what Allah, the Merciful ever wanted. It is not a hateful message which I got from my late wife, Marwa, who was a true believer but one of love and dignity and yes, mercy. America is not going to change and you will not either. The best solution is to leave each other alone as we did for centuries."

She kept silent and I continued. "I want to tell you something, Doctor. Soon we are going to hand you over to men and women who you have every reason to fear. But hear my words for it is meant well. When you are questioned, at some stage, an offer will be made for you to live. It will depend very much, utterly in fact, in how far you are willing to explain what you did and intended doing. Death is not always the logical end result for people like you." I looked in her eyes and read something there. Enough said for me. "When that time comes, promise me you will consider it carefully for it will not be repeated. You will get one chance only."

"I promise Major Foxtrot; I will consider your words when the time comes. If not, I will give your love and regards to Marwa. It is written."

An hour later, it was just before dark, we landed on the big US Navy carrier. It was not as simple as that. We first overflew it and I noted that they got rid of every aircraft on the deck which they could have. I have never seen an aircraft carrier on patrol with so little aircraft around. They also turned into the wind and dramatically increased speed. Geelslang and I were standing behind the pilots to watch death in the face. We made a long approach with the radios constantly giving corrections and at the last moment the big Hercules slammed down and started to brake. It had no arrestor gear but it came to a full stop halfway down. A horde of sailors immediately stormed it to ensure it did not fall off. I asked the pilot what now. He shrugged and said we are delivered and what do I want to do with the Land Cruiser?

I completely forgot about the Land Cruiser. Geelslang immediately claimed it for the Ukuthula Ranch where Thandiwe now uses it. Sir John, the bastard, had to pay Stone Belly a fair price as compensation. The Hercules lads dropped it in the UK where Boris picked it up and delivered it with other stuff including Geelslang in his Antonov-124. He said it was much more comfortable than the Hercules but he missed the old bird. I get that. Soon after this I said goodbye to the lads and the pilots. They would take off again and fly to the UK, stopping at Cape Verde and other places for fuel. By that time, I was already on my way to France by fast jet. Sir John had kept his word.

The prisoner, Adewale and I got off on the George H.W Bush. They were escorted by a few marines, one of them carrying the microwave oven with a bemused look on his face. What happened further to her I would not know and never asked but I do know I have yet to read of Washington or any other place of importance suffering from biological warfare in their water supply. Perhaps she is still alive and made enough reparations to be left in peace. Adewale is alive and kicking as we say. He resurfaced, was promoted, and often comes to the Ukuthula Ranch to see Angelique on business as they call their world of intrigue. It takes two roubles to get out of the Great Game and four for someone like Angelique. For many years we would be invited for tea somewhere or they would come to us to ask her about certain things which had happened in her past. It was always done via DGSE or she would not talk to them. I get that too and the fact that I am politely expected to piss off when they speak. I take a walk to Geelslang's for a beer to hide my irritation. As far as I am concerned, we paid for her freedom from the Great Game many times over and we deserve to be left alone, in peace. I don't need to worry about her safety regarding them though, the new arrivals are very thoroughly vetted and given the evil eye by her security team long before they are allowed close to her. She is better protected than a US President because she has to be, her knowledge is that important (I was a senior spymaster, I like what I can contribute, Angelique).

I sat next to her bed holding her hand and thinking about the last time I saw her when she got into the Casspir ambulance to drive to Boris and the Antonov. I was leading my men down south to attack the fast attack craft. That was eleven days ago...a lifetime. Apparently, she suspected paraoxon poisoning but they didn't immediately believe it. It took my message and Thandiwe to get them to listen. I listened to this with growing anger but said nothing at the time. It was neither the time nor the place but I made a few promises to myself.

Dr Thandiwe told me that Angelique was holding on. After I identified the paraoxon, they treated her for it and she responded very well. In fact, I arrived just in time for they had just decided to bring her out of the coma. It was a slow process, I don't really know why and don't care but assumed they knew what they were doing. It would take three days according to them to get her talking again. I don't think I left her side once for more than three minutes and that was only when nature called. The rest of the time I sat there planning our future once the Egg Breaker vs. SASS War was won. We had the initiative now and would go on the attack whenever possible. On the second day, her pulse rate increased dramatically, something which did not surprise us. She later said she knew I was there and could feel my hand holding hers. The medical staff shook their heads at this - it was impossible they said. They obviously don't understand soulmate love at all. Moreover, calling my wife a liar is guaranteed to endanger your existence. I gave them the evil eye and smile which would have frightened Satan. Their list of mistakes was growing rapidly to a scale which they could not possibly get. At this her Frog Minder hurriedly intervened and said he is sure they mean they never heard of such things before. They agreed to that.

I told her unconscious body about the mission and what happened since she left. We were alone in the room with her Frog Minder and his lads standing outside and keeping a close eye on everyone so it was safe to talk shop. That she remembered too when she finally woke up. I did not even ask the doctor if that is impossible too. I then started talking about our twins and she opened her eyes a day before the medics said it was humanely possible. They don't get Angelique at all. She is tough and resilient and "otherwise" to begin with. It was a wonderful sight though, to see her green eyes staring at me. She softly said something I could not hear so I leaned closer to her.

"Angelique? Can you hear me, my love?"

"C'est Angelique" she whispered. (This is Angelique.)

"Parlez-moi Angelique. Je t'aime ma femme." (Talk to me Angelique. I love you my wife.)

"Our twins are good. I can feel them kicking my husband. I love you too."

"Yes, they are good and so is your arm. And we are one again."

We hugged and much later, when we were back on the Ukuthula Ranch, I asked her what bothered me for a long time. "Angelique, when they wanted to amputate your arm...why didn't you just allow them so you could live for us? Our family and me, I would have been your hand. You know that I would have."

"But Foxtrot, it was my left hand...where would I wear our wedding ring? You ask such silly questions Geoffrey. Besides, I was right and they were wrong and so it is."

She chuckled and gave me a hug.

**The End**

**About the Author**

George M James is a pseudo name for the author and used for security reasons and the safety of his family. He is an expert on counter-terrorism and counterinsurgency operations in sub-Saharan Africa, a military historian and published author of more than 50 books. In the GMJ Series, you will learn about Covert Operations, Special Forces techniques, current political analyses and military history not known outside the select few. Every GMJ

Book is based on historical fact and often what is revealed in a GMJ Book is published by the mainstream media a short while later. Many of the GMJ Books are used as training material by Police Forces (SWAT) across the world. Each GMJ Book has a large element of the truth inside it, they are well researched. The GMJ Books may very well change the way you look at counter-terrorism and espionage. George M James's books, both under his real name and as GMJ, are widely read among military veterans of many nations. Note please that GMJ does not claim to have served in South African Army or Police Special Forces. Regarding my books - "I make up my opinions from facts and reasoning, and not to suit any body but myself. If people don't like my opinions, it makes little difference as I don't solicit their opinions or votes." William Tecumseh Sherman. I don't write PC books, however, for what I have to say in my books, it was Martin Luther that stated: "I cannot and will not recant anything, for to go against conscience is neither right nor safe. Here I stand, I can do no other, so help me God. Amen." And so it will be, GMJ

**Connect with Author online**

Contact me at georgemjames48@gmail.com

Facebook: https://www.facebook.com/georgemjamesbooks

Website: http://www.georgemjames.com

YouTube: https://www.youtube.com/channel/UC89xiDq-jbHsIDVsgvUtfAQ

**The GMJ Books are available in eBook and print**

Print: http://www.georgemjames.com/paper-versions.html

eBooks: http://www.georgemjames.com/gmj-books.html

43052937R00161

Made in the USA
Middletown, DE
19 April 2019